Understanding Groupware in the Enterprise

JoAnne Woodcock

Understanding Groupware in the Enterprise

Published by **Microsoft Press**
A Division of Microsoft Corporation
One Microsoft Way
Redmond, Washington 98052-6399

Library of Congress Cataloging-in-Publication Data
Woodcock, JoAnne.
    Understanding groupware in the enterprise / JoAnne Woodcock.
       p.   cm.
    Includes index.
    ISBN 1-57231-561-X
      1. Groupware (Computer software)   I. Title.
  HD66.2.W66   1997
  658'.0546--dc21   97-12282
                                             CIP

Printed and bound in the United States of America.

1 2 3 4 5 6 7 8 9 QMQM 2 1 0 9 8 7

Distributed to the book trade in Canada by Macmillan of Canada, a division of Canada
Publishing Corporation.

A CIP catalogue record for this book is available from the British Library.

Microsoft Press books are available through booksellers and distributors worldwide. For further
information about international editions, contact your local Microsoft Corporation office. Or
contact Microsoft Press International directly at fax (206) 936-7329.

Macintosh is a registered trademark of Apple Computer, Inc. Microsoft, Microsoft Press,
MS-DOS, Visual Basic, WebBot, Win32, Windows, and Windows NT are registered trade-
marks and ActiveX, BackOffice, FrontPage, MSN, NetMeeting, NetShow, Outlook, and Visual
InterDev are trademarks of Microsoft Corporation. Java is a trademark of Sun Microsystems, Inc.

Other products and company names mentioned herein may be the trademarks of their respective owners.

Acquisitions Editor: **Eric Stroo**
Project Editor: **Ina Chang**

Table of Contents

Acknowledgments

Books benefit from the work of many people whose names do not appear on the cover, and this book is no exception in owing a debt to some exceptional and very nice people. First and foremost, special thanks to Thomas Rizzo, Product Manager, Microsoft Exchange Server, for his valuable review and comments on the manuscript. Errors of fact are not his responsibility; nor do interpretive or speculative statements represent either his or Microsoft's stance.

At Microsoft Press, thanks to the following people, in order of appearance: Sally Brunsman, who suggested the topic; Eric Stroo, acquisitions editor, who patiently saw the manuscript into being; Ina Chang, editor, whose talents made it so much better; David Holter, graphic artist, and Travis Beaven, illustrator, who brought the pages alive with their usual flair; Katherine Erickson, compositor, who turned word-processed copy into the book you see; and Teri Kieffer, proofreader, who managed to read both for sense and for errors. Finally, thanks to Kate and Mark from a lifelong fan.

Introduction

This book, as the title indicates, is about groupware in the enterprise. But what about it? Is the book about how to use e-mail, how to use conferencing, or how to use other types of collaborative or group computing software? Is it about how to implement groupware in the enterprise? No, those are subjects for other books. The series to which this book belongs is titled Strategic Technologies, and the objective of the series is to explain, in everyday language, the technologies that underlie present-day computing. And so this book describes the technologies that create the computing environment that makes groupware happen.

This book is about the groupware environment

Because groupware means collaboration—working and communicating as part of a group—the topics you will find here include networks and protocols and operating systems and databases. The book is about e-mail and conferencing, too, of course, as well as about the technologies that make the Internet popular and viable and make it the foundation of a new way of sharing known as the intranet. But ultimately this book is about *understanding* high-tech rather than about *applying* high-tech.

It covers networks, operating systems, databases, the Internet, and more

If the book is about high-tech, does that mean it's for high-tech people? Not at all. It's for intelligent, curious nontechnical people who want or need to know how things in the cyberworld work. If you have ever wondered about how

But it is not for technical professionals

your network functions or about what enables your desktop computer to talk to a machine on the other side of the world, this book should help you. Along the way, the book and its glossary should also help make sense of the myriad exotic terms that swirl through news reports about directions in computing technology—terms such as HTTP and HTML, TCP/IP, POP3, backbone, fiber optics, Java, ActiveX, and more. And when you emerge at the other end, you should be able to see networks, group computing, and the Internet in a new and comprehensible light.

Bear in mind, however, that change is rapid

As you wade into this fascinating sea of technology, however, bear in mind that computing is never static. If you've paid attention to the growth of the computer industry, you know that it's famed for its rapid pace of development. Microprocessors annually bound past their previous limits of speed and number of transistors. New versions of software products are famous (or infamous, depending on your point of view) for appearing one right after the other.

Where the Internet is concerned, change is *very* rapid

Nowhere is the speed of development more noticeable than in areas covered by this book. Internet technology in particular is moving so rapidly that it has given rise to a new chronological term, *Web time.* The upshot of all this speed and change is that, although this book was written far from the eye of the hurricane and although it is meant to introduce new developments, time passes. What was current in early 1997 might well be dated a few months later.

But understanding the current foundations of groupware can only help you in the future

That's not to say, however, that this book will provide value only when "hot off the press." Remember that new developments are based on older ones. By gaining an understanding of existing technology, you will build the foundation of knowledge you need to keep pace with new developments in the future. There will be many of them.

Chapter One

The Evolution of Group Computing

Half a millennium ago, John Donne wrote that "no man is an island." To this day, no one has better stated the need for people to have and maintain contact with the rest of society. Hermits and prophets might argue differently, but they seem to have been touched by a different hand. For most of us, there is a real need to interact with others. And oddly—or maybe not—Donne's poetic statement is now the best way to introduce a book on using computers to eliminate human islandhood, even though the poet himself never heard of electric light, microchips, C++ programming, or, for that matter, gender equality.

Here you are at the beginning of a book about the hardware and software environment that makes group computing happen. The assumption is that you and most of those in your organization want and need to interact with one another, but there's a question to be answered before you start off. What *is* group computing? Is it e-mail? Is it electronic scheduling? Is it document-sharing? Is it that collection of software commonly described as "groupware"? Or is it the much-vaunted Internet, the even-more-vaunted intranet, or the latest in hot technologies, the extranet? Is group computing more than these parts, or less?

What is group computing?

How do you collaborate?

Sophomoric as it sounds, how you *define* group or collaborative computing depends on what you *mean* by it. Certainly, you're collaborating when you set up a video conference or a conference call. But are you collaborating when you send e-mail to a colleague, or are you simply communicating sans telephone? Are you collaborating when you use Microsoft Word to route your memo to other department heads, or are you distributing information sans paper? Are you and others collaborating when you access profit statements or inventory or design specs or price lists, or are you gathering data sans printout? Where does group computing begin and end?

In the narrowest sense, group computing happens in real time

In the narrowest sense, *group computing* is limited only to computer telephony and conferencing that happens in *real time*. That's true collaboration, when people meet electronically to talk out a problem, work jointly on a budget or a contract, or gather together for some other reason when geography says it's the only way to go. Real-time collaboration is the equivalent of the boardroom, conference room, or water cooler.

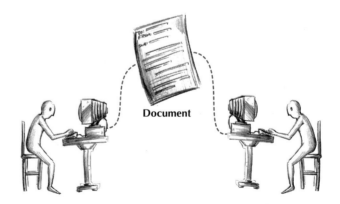

Document

But asynchronous interaction is equally important

But in the real world, real-time collaboration makes up only part of the picture. There's an entire alternative way of collaborating—one that isn't quite so immediate but that definitely has a great deal to do with working together to get things done. That's *asynchronous* collaboration, which is no doubt better defined as *communication,* but which is still invaluable in connecting one human island to another, whether the purpose is to move the mail, sell a product, request a price quote, set up a meeting, gather opinions…whatever.

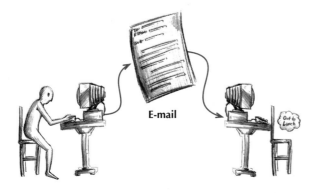

E-mail

Unless you are forever running between one meeting and another, in fact, this asynchronous mode of operation is how most people get most things done, whether it's because they're not available when the other person is, because they need information from a number of people who work in different departments or even different cities or time zones, or because they work best when they have the freedom to decide what to do and when to do it.

In fact, it's the way most things get done

This is where e-mail and scheduling software, public posting of important documents, and Internet/intranet connectivity take precedence. All of these help you, at your convenience, to collaborate with other people, at theirs. While the inter-action does not happen in the here and now, it happens nonetheless. So in the broader sense, all the possible asyn-chronous ways of working, from sending letters via "snail mail" to playing telephone tag to typing a message once and sending it to your entire workgroup with a single mouse click, can be—and in this book are—defined as forms of collaboration. The only distinction made here is that net-works, computer hardware, and computer software define the limits of the book.

There's a lot
of technology
under the hood

But suppose you already know how to use e-mail, and perhaps your department already has an intranet web site. Your company routinely maintains one or more databases that give you prices, schedules, suppliers, customers, and all the other information you need. What more do you need to know? It might help to know what other technology exists and what new developments are galloping down the information turnpike. More to the point, have you sometimes felt a little like a backward student when colleagues with a higher technical comfort level toss around terms like Ethernet, backbone, HTML, T1, ISDN, and even more abstract terms like TCP/IP, scalability, and API? How about when they rave about Java, but coffee is the last thing on their minds? All this stuff forms the environment that makes group computing possible. Despite the terminology, it's comprehensible by any reasonably informed person. It is not, however, readily comprehensible in the kind of detail you would need to sit down at your computer and start whaling away at developing your own communications program. A lot of thought—indeed, a lot of creativity and even artistry—goes into actually producing a working piece of software, much less establishing a new branch of computing technology.

But you're presumably not seeking such in-depth knowledge. If you were, you would be on your way to certification as a computer professional in networking, web-site creation, technological support, or applications development. And you would not have picked up this book. Instead, the assumption is that you want or possibly need to know more about the technological underpinnings of the computers, networks, and software that enable collaboration in your organization. Perhaps you need to make informed decisions. Perhaps you're simply curious. Perhaps you've been assigned to investigate the feasibility of turning existing computer facilities to supporting Internet and intranet accessibility. Whatever the reason, this book is designed to help you understand the technologies that enable group computing, which is probably the fastest-growing, most influential, and most intriguing side of an industry that runs on its own highly accelerated time scale.

Group computing encompasses a little of this and a lot of that, essentially ranging across vast areas of computer technology. Given such a landscape, where do you begin? Start with a look at the road behind. By understanding how the current computing environment came to be, you can more easily see where group computing fits in and you can try peering into your own crystal ball to see where it might be going.

Start with a look backward

The Need for Community

As already mentioned, collaboration of any kind exists because it satisfies a basic human need. That's why, in this information age—this age of superfast computers—the tools that we use still support the age-old needs of the community.

But what's so special about the communal *computing* environment? What distinguishes communities of computers from communities of, say, Camp Fire Girls? Two things: networks and communications. Together, they form the interconnected sets of machines, phone lines, satellites, cables, and software that make group computing and collaboration possible. In that sense, networks and communications even define group computing, because without either there would be no online community and no interaction.

Networks and communications make group computing happen

This book focuses on the computing half of the network and communications partnership. For an in-depth look at the communications side, refer to a companion volume in this series, *Understanding Bandwidth,* by Cary Lu (Microsoft Press, summer 1997). You'll both enjoy and profit from what he has to say.

This book is about networks and their software

Group Computing, Then and Now

The circular history of computing: networked to stand-alone, and back to networked

At the dawn of computing history—business-related computing, at any rate—everyone relied on mainframe computers. Huge machines sitting in air-conditioned splendor, these mainframes were tended by cadres of elite professionals trained to groom and pamper them, and to feed them boxes of neatly punched cards.

Terminals and phone lines enabled early networking

Over time, lesser mortals gained the ability to communicate with mainframes via desktop devices known as *dumb terminals.* These terminals had no processing ability of their own, but people could use the terminals' keyboards and display screens to transmit and receive information stored on the mainframes.

Soon the reach of the mainframe extended farther. With the help of *acoustic couplers*, into which you plugged the handset of a phone, computing went "on line." Once communications entered the picture, time sharing became possible. And time sharing, by allocating computing time to different clients, made computerized operations possible for companies that could not afford the expense of maintaining mainframes and software on their own.

Even though the tools and methods differed significantly, these old ways of accessing information stores, communicating, and using a remote computer were, if you think about it, the early equivalents of today's server-based local area networks (LANs) and wide area networks (WANs) and, yes, even the Internet.

Mainframes, terminals, shared software, and—most importantly—shared data are obviously still in widespread use today. Their sphere of influence, however, has been both augmented and heavily impacted by the arrival and evolution of the upstart personal, or desktop, computer.

In the early 1980s, the so-called "information revolution" arrived with the IBM PC, the first widely accepted business computer, and—soon—its many imitators, or clones. With the IBM PC, computing power appeared on individual desktops. And such power it was. People could choose their own brands of hardware and software and even, if they had the necessary skills, build their own applications. (Never mind that an eruption of options in hardware and software brought with it a firestorm of compatibility issues. That's another topic entirely.)

The PC added a new branch to the evolutionary tree

With a PC, you could create error-free correspondence. You could build and query a database and receive the results immediately. And you could easily store and transport information on disks no bigger than a pancake. Stand-alone computing was great. People dizzied by the heady thrill of controlling a responsive, interactive, efficient servant could create individually tailored environments in which their preferences ruled their own electronic universes.

Stand-alone computing came to the fore…

When personal computing reached critical mass, however, meaning that there were enough desktop computers around to make people want and need to share files and information, there began a slow but steady about-face. Suddenly, floppy swapping and "sneakernet" became less a fraternal ritual binding technological acolytes than a pure and simple pain in the business backside. Copying files. Formatting

…but the need to share reasserted itself

disks. Recopying files. Maintaining records of who got what and when. Keeping track of revisions. As they say, "oy, vey." There had to be a better way. And there was: networks.

Collaboration was limited at first, but change has been rapid

Early networking and group computing were primitive by today's standards. Text-based e-mail. Shared directories on a network server. Shared printers. Three-hundred bps (bits per second) modems. But hardware has evolved at an incredible pace. Processors have increased in speed and power so rapidly that, had automobiles developed at the same pace, you might very well be driving a car that never heard of fossil fuels. Along with advances in processing have come huge improvements in disk storage and communications capabilities. In the space of about 15 years, processors have leaped from speeds of about 7 megahertz (7 million cycles per second) to 200 megahertz. Hard drives have increased from the PC XT's 10 megabytes (roughly 10 million characters) to 2 gigabytes (roughly 2+ billion characters) and more. Modems have mutated from clunky, plug-in 300 bps models to the 28,800 bps PCMCIA "credit" card sitting in your laptop. And with the recent burgeoning of the Internet and increasing acceptance of PCs as consumer electronics devices, development of products such as Intel's Pentium MMX processor have turned animation, 3-D graphics, sound, and TV-quality video into a thing of today and not of tomorrow.

Software development has kept pace with the hardware

And software has grown to match the abilities of all this new hardware. Years ago, as the software industry began to mature, it became more and more responsive to the diversifying needs of its customers. And the response continues, even faster than before. On the personal desktop, operating systems, languages, and applications have become increasingly sophisticated and at the same time easier for new users to understand. (Compare the MS-DOS command *xcopy a:*.*c:\mydocs* to the Microsoft Windows 95 action of dragging a floppy disk icon to a folder on your hard drive.) For work and home, Internet technology in the last year or so has driven the development and release of a truly dizzying parade of new, highly graphical, easy-to-use products for accessing, navigating, creating, and maintaining sites on the World Wide Web.

Of course, computing designed for enterprise-wide use has not languished during this time, but its growth and development have in many respects been less glamorous and less well publicized than the spectacular evolution of desktop operating systems and applications. Mainframe-based networks, often referred to as *host-based* or *legacy systems*, have continued functioning and distributing information enterprise-wide very well, thank you. In fact, such networks still retain their primacy in areas, such as transaction processing, that require security, real-time accuracy, and proven reliability.

And computing has moved full circle, in a way, back to relying on centralized processing power

But to much of the business world these days, collaboration and information sharing, not to mention the ubiquitous Internet, is *distributed*—that is, the computing power sits atop server-based networks, which are configurations of one to many high-storage, high-performance "personal" computers (servers) that act as transfer and distribution centers for information and messages moving among individual desktop PCs (clients). In some cases, these networks provide all the computing power for an organization. In other cases, particularly in large enterprises, they supplement or interact with mainframes and with other networks, including the Internet.

1946	1960s	1970s	1980s	Late 1980s, 1990s	Mid-1990s	1997 & beyond
		Remote access ▶			Internet/intranets	Network computers, PDAs, etc.
	Centralized ▶			Client-server computing		
			Personal computers		Remote access ▶	
Stand-alone		Timeshare services		Centralized ▶		
	Mainframes / Mainframes + dumb terminals		Stand-alone ▶			
ENIAC						

However, if both mainframe-based and server-based computing rely on centralized processing, is there a difference between the two, other than in machine size? There is, and it's a big one: the distribution of computer *intelligence,* or processing power.

In a server-based environment, intelligence exists on both the server and the client, and you can use whichever suits your needs

In mainframe-based networks, intelligence resides on the host. In server-based networks, all the smarts are no longer on a central computer. In a server-based environment, processing can occur either on the desktop or on the server, depending on what needs to be done. For example, you might use the intelligence on your desktop computer to write a memo with a word processor installed on your hard disk. Later on, you might gather sales figures by connecting to a network server and running a server-based query program that searches a server-based database. Throughout the day, you can use the e-mail client on your desktop to route mail through an e-mail server somewhere on the network. And don't forget, at 2 p.m. on the dot, you can rely on the same desktop machine to work with a communications server somewhere on the network to set up teleconferencing and document sharing with your peers in other cities. Same client plus different processes equals increased flexibility and the best of all possible business worlds to date.

Some people envision alternate systems—e.g., network computers

This is something of an aside, but you've probably read that there's some debate about whether the type of network described here will eventually give way—or revert to—a closer representation of the mainframe-based systems of old. Some people argue that current desktop systems will be replaced by "dumb," diskless *network computers* that connect to servers acting both as information stores and as distribution centers for small, task-specific applications that people can download and use on an as-needed basis. The issue has taken on a religious heat in some circles. Current (that is, early 1997) thinking, however, assumes that (1) client-server networks will probably not go away; (2) people will continue to like being able to store

confidential information on their own desktop machines;
(3) full-service, integrated applications and application
suites will remain useful; (4) prices for moderately powerful
PCs will be competitive with prices for network computers;
and (5) in computing, as in politics, the majority will make
sure that there is room in the world for everyone and everything, including *both* network computers, which are now
expected to occupy the niche formerly occupied by dumb
terminals, and desktop machines.

Although network support, in the form of servers, communications lines, maintenance, and administration, remains in
the hands of dedicated and highly trained experts, just as is
(and was) the case with mainframe systems, group computing, in the form of sending and receiving e-mail, posting
information, routing documents, scheduling projects, and
even developing limited-use applications, is solidly in the
hands of the people. Someone who accesses resources on
a server does not approach as a supplicant would a minor
deity but as a customer seeking service. Even though the
network infrastructure is managed and supported by a few,
the task-oriented software that runs on the network creates a
person-to-person environment that essentially democratizes
the whole concept of network computing. Its sole purpose
is to enable communication in which any individual can
interact with any other, at any given time, to find and share
information, solve problems, brainstorm—whatever is required to help a business run smoothly and more efficiently.
Besides, e-mailing the office of the president is a lot more
satisfying (for the lower-downs) than routing a memo up
through the corporate ranks.

The environment creates the culture: Collaborative computing flattens the corporate hierarchy

The Network Foundation

Whether people use computers and networks to collaborate
asynchronously or in real time, the technology that enables
their interaction sits on top of the foundation provided by
the network.

For asynchronous
communication,
you use a messaging
system that takes
care of e-mail,
scheduling, and—
to some degree—
document sharing
and routing

Microsoft, for
example, wouldn't
run nearly as well
without e-mail

The best known, and probably most widely used, method
of asynchronous communication is e-mail, the electronic
equivalent of—some some would replacement for—snail
mail delivered by the post office. Related to e-mail, and
actually different aspects of the same communications
technology, are scheduling, faxing, and remote, or dial-up,
phone access. All these capabilities enable people to coordinate and communicate as their own schedules allow.

For example, employees at Microsoft and, probably, at other
companies, live by—and sometimes for—e-mail. Perhaps
the ultimate facilitator of asynchronous communication,
e-mail can be routed to one person or to many. It can be
read and answered whenever time allows. At Microsoft,
e-mail means Microsoft Exchange. With Exchange, mail can
be "stamped" with an *urgent* symbol or sent with a request
for a return receipt. Senders can mail an entire group, cc:
one or many individuals, or send a "blind copy" to selected
recipients. Respondents can include all or part of an original
message in their replies. Everyone can request and schedule
meetings via e-mail, attach documents and graphics to a
message, and file related correspondence in one or more
private electronic folders. In the fun-but-not-necessary
category, they can also add emphasis and aesthetics with
different fonts, use color, add "smileys" to take the place
of face-to-face expression, and create personalized—
sometimes irritating—signatures.

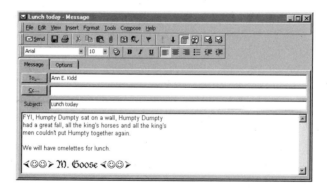

But, of course, people need to collaborate synchronously, in real time, as well. Both hardware and software are growing to support such functions as telephone conferencing and live, chat-type sessions, although this technology is not as advanced as the technology for e-mail and scheduling. Computer audio and telephony are well developed, growing quickly, and well supported in products like Windows 95 and Microsoft Windows NT. Video, because it requires substantial amounts of processing and graphics capability, has been slower to result in released products, but especially with the recent emphasis on Internet/intranet interactivity, the technology is quickly advancing to match demand.

For collaboration in real time, you need person-to-person communications services such as the phone system and conferencing

Real-time collaboration, even though it is not an everyday feature of group computing, isn't just pie in the future sky. A number of hardware and software solutions are available that help with virtual "face-to-face" communications. Numerous articles, for instance, have been written recently on video and phone technologies that enable people to bypass the traditional telephone system and make long-distance calls via the Internet. For group communication, there are also programs like Microsoft's real-time conferencing program, NetMeeting, which turns the Internet into a virtual boardroom. With NetMeeting, people can talk, share applications and files, and even collaborate via a "whiteboard" on their computers. And in the hardware arena, there are products like Intel's ProShare Conferencing Video System, which lets as many as 24 people share ideas and documents at the same time via their PCs.

Conferencing programs such as NetMeeting enable "face-to-face" interaction even when there are miles between you and your peers

The Case for Collaboration

E-mail and conferencing, attractive though they are, might not, on their own, seem like compelling enough reasons to invest anywhere from five to seven digits' worth of dollars in the hardware and software needed to create a group computing environment. But there's more to the collaborative

Group computing is worth the investment, and here are a few reasons why

life than e-mail. Assume that you have the needed networking infrastructure in place and that it's functioning like the proverbial Swiss watch. What are some of the areas in which it can help the company perform as a lean, mean, earning machine? Given a corporate culture in which openness is valued and encouraged, here are some broad categories in which networked, group computing can save time, money, and frustration:

Software can keep track of schedules

- Interacting. You've already seen e-mail and conferencing. There's also individual and group scheduling, both of which are easily managed with the help of a program such as Microsoft's Schedule+ (pronounced "schedule plus"). For instance, you want to meet with several busy people. Often, a meeting request generates multiple rounds of "Gee, I can't make it then, but how about…?" With scheduling software, you can check each individual's upcoming schedule to find a time when everyone is free *before* sending out the formal request for a meeting. Once you know when everyone is available, all you do is send a standard e-mail form giving the date, time, and location of your proposed meeting and then wait for the enthusiastic "ayes" to arrive in your electronic mailbox. At Microsoft, in fact, "Schedule Plus me" is a shorthand way of telling someone to check your schedule and choose a time for you to get together.

It's easy to get the word out

- Finding and sharing information. Every organization has information that needs to reach anywhere from a few to many people: company goals, sales figures, personnel policies, inventories, budgets, and short-term and long-term plans. Some types of information, such as company guidelines, rarely change; some, such as inventories and sales figures, are moving targets, constantly being updated. All can affect not only the way people do their jobs but also the very quality of the work they do. And the larger the organization or group, the more important it is to be sure that essential information reaches those who need it. The answer: Put it out on the "net." The current move in large organizations is to make use of the page-based metaphor of the Internet to create private or semiprivate intranets that allow people to follow *links* from one document (page) to another, gathering the information they need in a natural, intuitive, connect-the-dots kind of way.

But there are other ways too. Information sharing is the arena in which Lotus Notes made its reputation. A network database consisting of server and client applications, Notes uses elements called *documents* as a vehicle for people to exchange information via messages, automatic links to specific documents, and attachments. To make such public information easier to find, Notes also allows these documents to be grouped in *views*. In a similar way, Exchange supports information "containers" called *public folders* that allow people to post and distribute documents, links to documents, and even forms for surveys, discussions, and reports on everything from day care to restaurants.

- Collaborating on documents. Suppose you and your peers are asked to come up with the annual budget or, perhaps, to evaluate the costs of implementing group computing. Suppose further that you do not all work in the same office. One easy way to communicate and coordinate your work is by publishing links to your efforts via the documents or public folders provided by Notes or Exchange. (Posting links instead of the actual files means that the original remains in the location you choose, so you can update it at will and others can add to it whenever they want, and no one has to worry about working with an outdated copy.) Another way, which also

People can contribute to, revise, and finalize documents as a group

ensures that everyone sees the same version of a document, is to add an electronic twist to interoffice mail and circulate a work in progress to all interested parties with a "routing slip" like this:

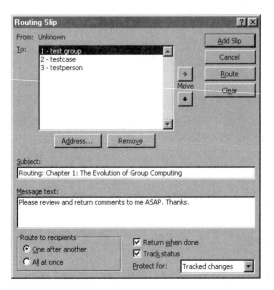

In both cases, the documents remain in the hands of one owner, who can track revisions and make the final decisions about which changes to accept and which to reject. Neat, clean, and no worries about different time zones or who's in or out of the office. And you save trees. And copier time. And postage.

You can institute the "publishing" environment everyone is talking about—with little additional expense

- Publishing on the Internet or an intranet. This is the big one. The hot topic of the year, and justifiably so. The Internet, as you probably know, was created by the United States Department of Defense. Its original purpose was to enable computers at different universities and research institutions to exchange information and to protect military communications in case of war. These days the Internet, or rather the graphical offshoot known as the World Wide Web, is fast becoming *the* means for people to publish and exchange information on topics ranging from the sublime to the ridiculous and, sadly, even the offensive.

Nonetheless, the Internet is in, and in many businesses intranets are even "in-er." Intranets are private "Corporate Wide Webs" that rely on Internet technology and its intuitive page-and-link navigation techniques to create an environment in which employees can distribute and exchange information. Intranet technology at present is more distributive than interactive, and real-time collaboration of the sort offered by NetMeeting is not yet much of a reality, but intranets, like the Internet, offer huge potential for marketing, sales, product tracking, and other activities that rely on interactivity. Indeed, Microsoft, Netscape, and many other companies are hard at work developing new tools to make intranets more compelling, more interactive, and easier to create and maintain.

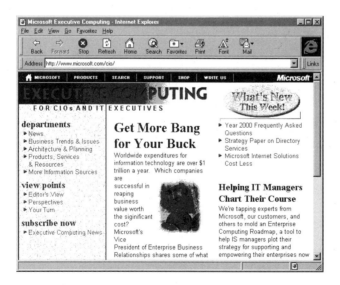

If nothing else, it seems safe to say that the Internet and intranets will only grow and get stronger. Witness the massive quantities of ink and paper devoted to articles and news releases about the major players, their so-called "browser wars," and the Java programming language. Indeed, it sometimes seems that it's only a matter of time before an alien invasion of the Internet will rival garlic cures and movie stars for tabloid attention. But that's personal opinion. Far more important to consider are the following statements by Bill Gates in his weekly *New York Times* column dated April 24, 1996. "From a manager's point of view, perhaps the best aspect of an intranet is that it doesn't take much effort or investment to get one going. Businesses that have networked computers already have everything they need. The only expense is to have an employee write the descriptive pages and links." And "So perhaps my most timely general advice is: Get an intranet going in your company. It's a great tool, and you've already paid for it." (If, of course, you've got a functioning network.)

Paranickels, Paradigms

Even though you can view the Internet/intranet environment in terms of a new, easy-to-understand Web or page-based metaphor, that metaphor currently applies mostly to Internet and intranet publishing. Collaboration, however, is made up of many technologies. Is there also a metaphor that can be applied to the whole thing? Certainly. All you need is a simple paradigm.

Paradigms simplify descriptions of complex processes

A paradigm is a model, pattern, or example that clearly describes or explains something in the real world. The "law of the jungle," for instance, is a paradigm that helps make sense of the numerous and highly complex interactions that define nature. And because it is so clear, the same paradigm is often used to help explain similar complex systems from Wall Street to the White House (nonpartisan reference).

Given the way collaboration works, if your mind tends to the dark side, it's easy to begin envisioning masses of people "interfacing" via keyboard. With such a mental image, you're likely to come up with a paradigm based on concepts like *sweatshop, hive,* or even *Brave New World.* But there is a more appealing image, and one that will serve you better.

Assume, as is true, that collaborative computing is not so much a brand-new form of technology arising to serve brand-new needs as it is simply the next logical step in computing evolution. New technologies can, and do, arise as they are needed, but generally speaking, group comput- ing is based on the extension and further development of existing technology to serve expanding needs. Furthermore, computers are simply tools for getting things done, and collaboration is simply a shift away from stand-alone desk- top computing toward a more efficient and compelling *mix* of stand-alone and network-based group activity.

Don't say this to an engineer, but technology is not an end in itself; it is a means to an end

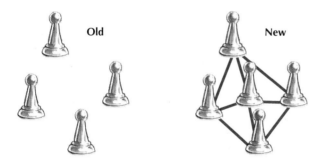

Ever since primitive people banded together to hunt the woolly mammoth, civilization has tended toward just such group interaction. And there's the paradigm to apply to collaborative computing: the power of the group. "Old- style" (stand-alone, 1980s) computing was comparable to islands in the sea or castles surrounded by moats. "New- style," collaborative computing takes those same islands or

The new paradigm is all about connections

castles and connects them with bridges, roads, sea lanes, flight routes…whatever works to connect one to the other so that people can interact when and how they choose.

Just as societies are collections of individuals, collaborative computing is the collection of existing and new hardware and software that enables people to communicate, share information, and work together. And thanks to the magic of communications and electronics, collaboration can happen no matter where people are physically located and no matter whether they interact in real time or asynchronously. When, or if, you feel overwhelmed by the acronym soup or connectivity overload associated with networking and group computing, just remind yourself that all you're doing is studying an environment created by a bunch of computers linked through electronic pathways. True, the engineering is a tribute to human ingenuity, but you're not seeking mastery. You're just signing up for a tour of the landscape. That begins in the next chapter.

Chapter Two

Networks: The Basis of Group Computing

On a typical networked morning, you walk into the office, grab a cup of coffee, and switch on your PC. Your screen prompts you for a password, your ticket to the corporate net. You type the password, the input flows into the wall through the tangle of wires and cables behind your desk, and a few seconds later the door to the network's resources is open, all because the electronic gatekeeper now knows who you are and has verified that you are a valid member of the group.

As simply as that, you gain the ability to communicate with any other computer reachable through the network. You can send e-mail, schedule a meeting, route the final draft of your latest report, fax a message to a client, download the slide show put together by a colleague, check the stock market, reserve airline tickets, read news articles selected by your Internet browser software…even run through video training via the corporate intranet.

Of course, to support such capabilities, there must be a lot going on behind the walls. You see network maintenance crews periodically roaming the halls, fiddling with miles of cabling, and anyone can see that the computer plugs into it all in some way. But how? And where does everything go? What keeps the bits and bytes flying in formation? What makes it possible for your computer to talk so easily to another that can be thousands of miles away?

Everything begins with the hardware and software that comprise the network. First, the hardware.

Networks and Nodes

The most tangible part of a network, to end users, is the computer—known as a *node* in network terminology—that makes the connection. To distinguish it from all others, a network node is assigned a unique electronic "label" called an *address*. This address enables the node to actively, and accurately, communicate and swap information with other nodes on the network.

The illustration below shows a typical client computer. Vast as network capabilities are, they're founded on only two pieces of network hardware: the highly visible *cabling* and the far less visible *network adapter*.

The Cables

Currently the majority of networked computers rely on cabling rather than on an alternative, wireless form of transmission such as radio or infrared light. On such cable-based networks, the connection is generally made with either *twisted-pair wiring* or *coaxial cable,* although much faster *fiber-optic cable* might well form the hidden *backbone* that connects groups of nodes on large networks. Both twisted-pair and coaxial cable transmit signals in electrical form, and both are widely used in building networks. You can find out which type of cabling is used to connect your computer to the network by looking at the ends of the cables: Twisted-pair cable uses telephone-like (but larger) *RJ-45 jacks* for plugging into the computer and the wall; coaxial cable relies on round *BNC (British Naval Connector)* hardware like the connectors that tie your home cable box to your television and wall outlet.

Cabling is typically either twisted-pair wiring or coaxial cable

RJ-45 connector and jack

BNC connector

On a fiber-optic cable, signals travel as light, rather than as electricity or sound, through a thin, flexible fiber made of glass (preferable) or plastic (not as effective). This fiber is surrounded by a protective sheath, or *cladding;* the signal itself is a beam, generated either by an *LED (light-emitting diode)* or by a laser, and it moves at, well, the speed of light. Fiber-optic signals, in addition to travelling much faster and being less prone to degeneration than electrical or sound signals, are more secure because they cannot be tapped by outside intruders. Fiber-optic cable is expensive, however, and is generally used behind the scenes in high-speed, high-security, and/or high-performance situations, such as connecting whole networks or network segments.

How does fiber optics fit in?

The Adapter

The network adapter enables the computer to access the network

In addition to wireless or cable connections, a networked computer requires a specialized *network adapter card* or *network interface card (NIC)*, which typically plugs into an expansion slot inside the machine and is needed to connect the PC to the network itself. About the size of a small paperback, the adapter looks like a typical circuit board. It's made of nonconducting material covered with a grid of metallic circuitry, and it has a one-section or two-section tablike edge on one side that slides into the computer's expansion slot. This edge is the part that makes contact with the computer's main internal circuitry, which is located on the *motherboard* (the big green thing covering the bottom of the computer).

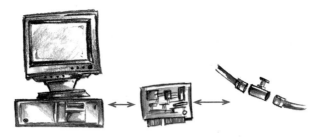

The adapter's job is to mediate between the PC and the network

The network adapter converts outgoing information to a form that can travel over network cables, and it also converts incoming information into a form that the computer can readily use. These two data forms are so different, and the conversion process is so rapid, that the whole thing seems almost magical.

Bytes to bits...

To understand what the adapter does, picture traffic on a multilane freeway. Rush hour will do perfectly, because you want to imagine row upon row of cars (bytes of information in the PC) traveling side by side. That's the situation in the PC. Information gets shunted around—for example, to and from memory—in *parallel* as it travels on internal *buses*, which are pathways, not vehicles, despite the name. (Buses are actually some of the silvery "threads" you see connecting to the processor in the Intel commercials on television.)

Network cables, however, are not equipped for parallel transmission. They must move everything *serially,* and so those bytes must be turned into a single *bit* stream in which the individual bits making up each byte travel in single file. Essentially, this conversion is the equivalent of funneling all rush-hour freeway traffic onto a one-lane, one-way road and ensuring that the cars maintain the same relative relationship they had on the freeway. In the case of the network adapter, however, there's an added wrinkle in that the adapter not only handles the parallel-to-serial conversion, it also transforms the information from the digital format used in the computer to a signal that can travel over the network cables.

…and back again

Parallel transmission   **Network adapter**   **Serial transmission**

Converting parallel to serial and vice versa is one part of the job performed by the network adapter, but there are two others, which are just as intriguing. When a PC sends information over the network, the message can't simply go out in a single stream. For traffic control and other reasons, the message is broken into smaller pieces called *packets.* The difference is rather like that between a train or convoy and a line of cars; the cars (packets) can travel faster and take different routes to the same destination. The network adapter is the hardware responsible for "packetizing" messages before transmission.

The network adapter also packages messages

When a network node receives information, the adapter follows almost the reverse course. First it determines whether the address on an incoming message matches the address of its node. If the addresses match, the adapter then "de-packetizes" the message. At this point, it also removes

And it "listens" for incoming messages

error-control information required by the network's transmission procedures, and it converts the serial transmission to the parallel form needed by the computer and the application that eventually works with the received information.

LANs

A network
by any name...

A network is created whenever two or more computers are connected to one another. Once you get beyond this easy-enough-for-a-two-year-old concept, however, you find that there are many ways to define the resulting network. For instance, you can define it by:

- Size: as in workgroup, LAN, or WAN
- Functionality: as in peer-to-peer vs. client-server
- Shape: as in bus, ring, or star
- Bandwidth: as in baseband vs. broadband and megabits vs. gigabits per second
- Architecture: as in Ethernet or Token Ring

These are the most common categories. The following sections explain what they mean.

Size

LANs cover a
restricted area;
WANs reach
farther afield

PC-based networks come in all sizes. Not only that: Like the amazing Alice with her Wonderland cookies, they can be *scalable*—that is, they can grow or shrink depending on how many people they need to support. On the broadest level, however, you can divide PC-based networks into two major categories: *local area networks,* or LANs, which require cabling and cover a relatively limited area, such as a floor, a building, or a small office campus; and *wide area networks,* or WANs, which use telecommunications facilities to reach much farther, even to other countries. The difference between the two isn't always clear to the naked eye, since multiple LANs can be linked to form what might appear to be a WAN, but the basic distinctions hold true.

This chapter is LAN-oriented. The next chapter deals with issues and terminology specific to WANs.

Functionality

LANs, which are pretty much synonymous with PC-based networks, break down into two additional types: peer-to-peer and client-server. Chapter 1 covered some of this.

LANs can be peer-to-peer or client-server

In a peer-to-peer network, each computer can communicate and share files and printers with every other computer on the network. Peer-to-peer is very democratic, but it is limited to small groups of computers, say 10 or so. This is the type of network you can set up with Microsoft Windows 95 and that works very well in a workgroup situation, such as a small office. In a peer-to-peer situation, each computer can act as either client or server, depending on whether it is providing or receiving information.

Peer-to-peer is for small networks

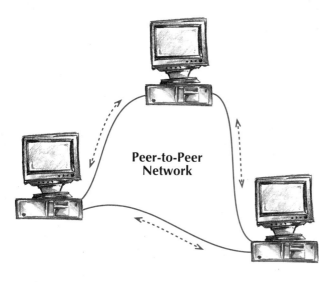

Peer-to-Peer Network

For larger numbers of computers—hundreds, thousands, or even tens of thousands—businesses rely increasingly on client-server networks. Although it is massively oversimplifying a complex situation to say so, a client-server network is essentially one in which individual computers connect to,

Client-server is for larger ones

and through, one or more larger machines that act as intermediaries. Servers in such an environment are generally equipped with one or more processors in the Pentium or *RISC (Reduced Instruction Set Computing,* such as the DEC Alpha AXP) class, and they run a *network operating system,* or *NOS,* such as Microsoft Windows NT Server, a more powerful relative of Windows 95 that has been designed and optimized to hold a network environment together.

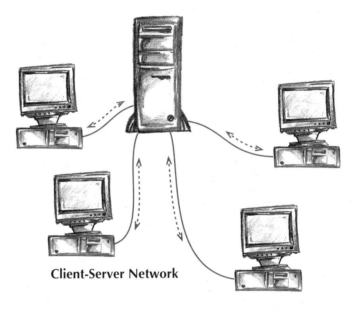

Client-Server Network

Servers and clients
work together

The servers' role is to centralize security, manage traffic, and hand out resources, including information, applications, and access to shared devices, such as printers, as requested by the clients. The clients in this environment are desktop computers (rather than dumb terminals) that run a desktop operating system such as Windows 95 or Windows NT Workstation. These clients usually use their own processing ability to manipulate the information received from the server, but they rely on the server to provide the information or programs they require. When the processing is shared between client and server, the client's share of the work is known as *front-end processing* and the server's labors are called *back-end processing.*

Client-server networks, in addition to working in their own closed, "native" environment, can also be set up to work with minicomputers and mainframes. This flexibility, when combined with a relatively low cost compared to host-based systems, forms part of the appeal of client-server networking. In such an environment, the people working on client machines can reap the benefits of three distinct "modes" of information processing: stand-alone work, collaboration with others via the network, and a mode you might think of as information harvesting, through connection to mainframe hosts and the wealth of information stored on them.

Client-server networks can be linked to each other and to mainframes

Shape

The shape of a network is called its *topology* and refers to the way the network is laid out. Topology describes the connections between the computers. There are three basic topologies—*bus, ring,* and *star*—each of which defines the ways computers are cabled to one another and to their server(s). Despite the descriptive names, however, the actual layout of a bus, ring, or star network generally bears about as much resemblance to its namesake as a toddler's art does to the real world. The beauty here is often in the mind of the technical beholder.

Topology refers to the "shape" of a network

Bus networks The simplest of the three, a bus topology hangs computers like laundry on a line from a single cable known as the *trunk* or *backbone.* The Ethernet network described later is a common and widely used LAN network that relies on this topology.

The backbone of a bus network is a single line

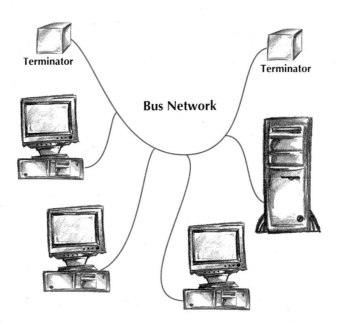

Bus Network

Terminator

Terminator

On a bus network, all messages are *broadcast* along the trunk, and each computer sits listening for broadcasts directed to its own unique address. The trunk carries messages one at a time. To keep signals from *bouncing* or being *echoed back* from the end of the line and thus preventing other messages from being transmitted, each section of cable ends in a computer, a connector to another section of cable, or a special piece of hardware called a *terminator,* which absorbs the signal before it can bounce back along the trunk. In other words, no piece of cable in a bus network can simply end; it must end in appropriate hardware.

Bus topologies are easy to manage and to extend, and they use less cable than other topologies. However, because all computers are connected to a single cable, a break in that cable can bring down all or a large part of the network. In addition, because only one computer at a time can send a message over the trunk, bus networks with too many computers and too much traffic are subject to slowdowns. Like people on a party line, computers attached to a too-busy bus network may have to sit drumming their virtual fingers, waiting for a chance to transmit.

Ring networks Easy to envision, a ring topology is a group of computers connected, one to the next, in a circular pattern. The ring itself can be either *physical* (an actual ring) or *logical* (circular in the direction messages travel). In either case, the computers in a ring network communicate by passing transmissions, always in the same direction, around the ring. Because the network nodes participate in keeping the network going, a ring represents an *active* topology, as opposed to the *passive* broadcast type of arrangement typical of a bus topology.

Round and round and round she goes

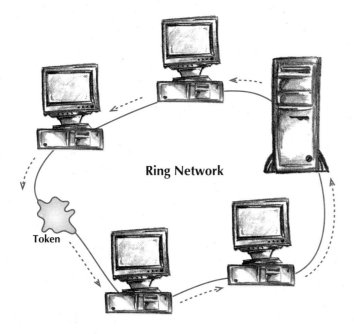

Ring Network

Token

To ensure that messages reach their correct destination, and to ensure that all nodes on the network have equal access, a ring topology operates a little like a kids' game of Pass the Beanbag, in which an electronic packet is handed from one node to the next. Each computer on the network interacts only with its immediate neighbors to the left and right, receiving the packet from one and passing it to the next.

Messages travel in packets

The best-known form of ring topology is known as *token ring,* named after the small, 3-byte bundle, or *token,* that the nodes in the network pass around. Each node receives the token in its turn, and only the node with the token has permission to transmit a message. If the node with the token has information to place on the network, it attaches the message and the address of the receiving node and sends the modified token on its way around the ring. Each node receiving the token then examines the address and, if the message is addressed to another node, sends the message on its way. When a receiving node recognizes the address as its own, it extracts the message, attaches a "got it" acknowledgment to the token, and sends the revised token on around the circle, where it eventually reaches the originating node. At that point, the originator releases control by passing a "free for use" version of the token to the next node in the ring, and the whole process begins again.

Although the idea of passing information around in a circle sounds somewhat ungainly and time-consuming, in actuality a ring network is not inefficient, because transmissions *fly*—at about the speed of light—around the ring. (The fact that the computers manage to examine and grab what they need at such speeds is really wondrous when you consider that the capability is packaged in a few thousand dollars worth of hardware.) The great advantage of a ring topology is that each computer has an equal opportunity to transmit information. Problems, however, can be difficult to locate because transmission is one-way and circular. In addition, the failure of one node can break the circle and can require *reconfiguring* the network by adding or removing nodes.

Star networks Star networks originated when terminals were connected to mainframes. Like the arms of an octopus, the cables and connected computers on a star network radiate out from a central point, the *hub.* This hub can be a server computer, but more often it is a wiring center to which the computers in the star are cabled individually. The hub itself (which is also used in other network topologies but is the distinguishing characteristic of the star formation) can simply sit at the center of the star, passively transferring signals, or it can be an active device that *boosts* (strengthens) the signal or transmits selectively. In the most common type of star network, however, known as *low-impedance ArcNet,* the hub is passive and simply broadcasts incoming signals to the nodes.

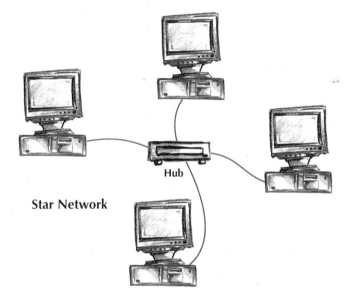

Hub

Star Network

Star networks require considerably more cabling than bus networks do, but because each node is connected separately to the hub, the network continues functioning if one node fails. On the flip side, however, failure of the central server or hub causes the entire network to go kaput until the problem is fixed. (In this situation, you *can* take a positive view, however, and remind yourself that the source is, at least, easy to find.)

The pluses and minuses

Bandwidth

Bandwidth is needed for communication

All networks, no matter what their topology, have one feature in common: bandwidth. It's a feature they share with television, radio, cellular phones, and your microwave, and the term itself seems to have become the high-tech word *du jour*, even among people who don't completely understand what they're talking about. "Everyone," for instance, says that for the Internet to grow and thrive, there must be more bandwidth. As with many things in life, "everyone" also knows that more is better. But why?

The definition depends to some degree on what you're talking about

Bandwidth has to do with sound, light, and other occupants of the electromagnetic spectrum. That sounds like Physics 101 because it is, but even if you're uncomfortable with close encounters of the scientific kind, take heart. Although bandwidth is mostly about waves and frequencies, the key to understanding its importance in networking and communications is in the two ways people usually define bandwidth—what you can think of as the "traditional" and the "electronic" definitions.

Sound, light, and other forms of energy are usually pictured as waves

The traditional definition As you probably remember from school, electromagnetic radiation, such as electricity, light, and radio, is generally spoken of as traveling in a wave form. Each wave, like any in the ocean, has a high point, or *crest*, and a low point, or *trough*, like this:

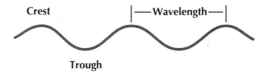

The distance between one crest and the next is known as the *wavelength*, and different forms of radiation are characterized by different wavelengths. Radio, for instance, at the low end of the electromagnetic spectrum, has a long wavelength of 1 meter or more. Gamma rays, at the other extreme, have

very short wavelengths of less than 0.01 nanometer (a nanometer itself being a dinky one-billionth of a meter).

One way to define these waves is in terms of their *frequency*—how often a particular wave cycles from crest to
crest in one second. Obviously, the longer the wave, the
fewer cycles per second, so the longer the wavelength, the
lower the frequency. Even a dedicated landlubber knows
that long, rolling swells hit the side of a boat with less frequency than do short, choppy waves. The situation is the
same with radio, visible light, X-rays, and all other forms of
electromagnetic radiation.

Frequency is the
number of times the
wave crests in one
second

Frequencies are measured in *hertz* (Hz), or cycles per second. Because there's a vast range between the bottom and
top of the electromagnetic spectrum, short and very short
wavelengths with high and very high frequencies are measured in powers of hertz—kilohertz (kHz), or thousands of
cycles per second; megahertz (mHz), or millions of cycles
per second; gigahertz (gHz), or billions of cycles per second;
and even terahertz (tHz), or trillions of cycles per second.

Frequency is
measured in hertz

Electromagnetic frequencies are thus charted over a continuous spectrum that ranges from extremely low (subsonic)
through degrees of low, medium, high, very high (radio, TV,
shortwave, microwave) and mind-bogglingly high (X-rays
and gamma rays). Each of these categories has its own
bandwidth, or range of frequencies, and this reference to
kilo/mega/giga/terahertz is the way you usually see bandwidth defined in science texts.

Traditionally, band-
width refers to a
range of frequencies

The "new" definition In the world of computers, networks,
and communications, bandwidth is still bandwidth. For
example, you've probably seen articles or heard news reports referring to the greater bandwidth of fiber-optic cable
over coaxial or twisted-pair copper telephone cable. Wide
bandwidth here, at least in cable-based networks and communications venues, still refers to a range of frequencies,

The electronic
definition is just
another way of
seeing the same
thing

just as in the "traditional" definition. But the reason wide bandwidth is so important is that the wider the bandwidth, the greater the possible information flow. Wider bandwidth allows multiple signals to flow simultaneously through the same pipeline by dividing the available frequencies into separate *channels,* each of which can carry a different stream of information. And, of course, the more streams you have, the more information that flows. And the more information, the better the world, all because of more bandwidth.

Narrow bandwidth

10101010100010	one channel carries all data	10101010100

Wide bandwidth

10101010100010	Data channel	10101010100010
a b c d e f g	Voice channel	a b c d e f g
🍾🍾🍾🍾🍾🍾🍾	Video channel	🍾🍾🍾🍾🍾🍾🍾

"Guard" bands of unused
frequencies buffer channels

In electronics and telecommunications, speed is more meaningful than frequency

In the world of networks and telecommunications, everything seems to run on an accelerated timescale, so it's only natural that "traditional" measures of frequency and wavelength should give way to "electronic" measures of speed and information-carrying capacity. And they do. Even though the electronic freight rolls on the rails of frequency traditionally defined as "bandwidth," engineers are more concerned with the speed of the train than with the gauge of the tracks, and so even though the frequencies that make up a given bandwidth are still measured in some variant of the traditional kilo/mega/giga*hertz,* networks prefer to measure bandwidth in some variant of kilo/mega/giga*bits* per second. This shift from cycles per second to bits per second can be a little disconcerting, but there actually is a connection between the two: Higher frequencies can carry more information than lower frequencies can.

There are a few wrinkles in this simplified explanation, of course. Fiber-optic cable, for instance, relies on very narrow beams of light, and the narrower the beam the better the quality of transmission. But even in this situation, carrying capacity is still a matter of how many light waves can be transmitted through the cable simultaneously, and speed is still a matter of how fast the information flows—in gigabits per second—through the line. Now, how does this apply to networks?

Channel capacity is another "measure" of bandwidth

Network bandwidth Different types of networks have different bandwidths, but whether a network takes the shape of a ring, star, or straight-line bus or, for that matter, a global entity like the Internet's World Wide Web, it is still at least partially defined by its bandwidth.

Baseband vs. broadband PC-based networks are divided into two categories, *baseband* (also called *narrowband*) and *broadband* (also called *wideband*). Baseband is slower than broadband for the reasons decribed earlier. Don't, however, make the mistake of assuming that stated transmission speeds, whether for baseband or broadband networks, are gospel. The speed at which a network *can* function is not necessarily the speed at which it *does* function, at least not all the time. Traffic volume and other factors can, and do, affect the actual operating speed, or *throughput,* and in the end it's throughput that determines how effective a network is.

Network bandwidth can be narrow (baseband) or broad (broadband)

Baseband networks devote the entire bandwidth to a single channel over which electrical or light signals travel in two directions, to and from network nodes and servers, rather like cars on a reversible lane on a freeway. Transmissions are broken into packets, and all information travels in *digital* form, meaning that each bit—the smallest possible unit of information in each transmission—is represented by one of two states: 0 or 1 (basically, on or off). A typical baseband

Baseband networks use the entire bandwidth as a single channel network, such as plain Ethernet, operates at about 10 mega-bits per second (Mbps), but considerably higher speeds are possible, including some forecasted for the gigabit range.

Multiplexing
allows multiple
transmissions at the
same time

At its simplest, a baseband network carries one transmission at a time, with network nodes waiting until the channel is free before they can use it. Baseband networks can, how-ever, carry multiple transmissions at the same time with the help of a communications technique called *multiplexing,* in which the transmission channel is divided into segments called *time slices.* These time slices can then be loaded with packets—one per slice—from one or many transmissions. At the receiving end, a "demultiplexer" takes care of restor-ing a received transmission to its original, whole form.

Broadband networks
use analog signals,
wider bandwidth,
and multiple
channels

Broadband networks, which represent a newer and much faster technology, use a range of frequencies dedicated to two or more channels separated by buffer zones of unused frequencies known as *guard bands.* Broadband networks have dedicated channels for incoming and outgoing trans-missions, and they move traffic in *analog* form, meaning that the signal is continuously variable, like a song or the read-out on a seismograph, rather than being two-state, pulsed, and digital, as on a baseband network.

What will the
networks of the
future be like?

Broadband networks are fast and flexible, operating at speeds of 100 Mbps and, theoretically, at speeds in the multiple-gigabit range. They are also more complex and expensive than baseband networks. As already mentioned, the overall bandwidth in a broadband network is divided into a number of channels, each used for a different pur-pose. Although a broadband network at its simplest uses only two channels—one outgoing and the other incoming, broadband channels can be used for different forms of information, such as voice, video, and data, so this type of network has the potential to carry a richer and more varied information stream than can a baseband network. You see broadband technology at work whenever you tune into cable television. Perhaps it won't be long until you see it emerge as a force on the corporate computing scene too. At the moment, however, broadband is still more potential than reality.

Architecture Standards

In the computer world, the word *architecture* refers to different things, depending on what you're talking about. Always, however, the word refers to the way a piece of hardware or software is constructed or to the way it works. Thus, talk about a PC's architecture is not the same thing as conversation about the architecture of an operating system or of a network. But regardless of the subject, the talk is always about the bones that hold the technology together and make it function.

Architecture refers to the way something is built or the way it works

Network architecture refers partly to the way a network is laid out and moves information around and partly to the way software implementations of rules known as *protocols* work—that is, the many and varied rules this software follows in maintaining order and transmitting information. Historically, the tried-and-true network architectures have relied on relatively restricted baseband transmission; the forward-looking architectures of tomorrow require broadband to carry the data, voice, fax, video, and other goodies of today's and tomorrow's collaborative society.

Network architecture is about rules

Despite the specifics of individual layout and implementation, to ensure that everyone plays by the same rules, network architectures follow the standards set out in two sets of guidelines known as *IEEE 802* and the *ISO/OSI networking model.* Like the rules of chess or bridge, these guidelines

The physical rules everyone follows are known as IEEE 802 and the ISO/OSI model

help impose structure and uniformity on a potentially vast array of networking solutions so that even markedly different approaches are based on the same principles during design, development, and implementation and can, to some extent or another, be interconnected.

IEEE 802 is primarily concerned with the hardware

IEEE 802 The IEEE 802 specifications are named for standards defined, beginning in the late 1970s, by committees of the Institute of Electrical and Electronic Engineers. IEEE 802 concentrates on the hardware and data transmission (coding, addressing, and sending) that comprise the foundation layers of any communications network, and it defines the standards to be followed in the design and deployment of such items as network adapters, cabling, and connectors. When people talk about different network architectures, such as ARCnet, Ethernet, and Token Ring, as described a little later, you might hear references to IEEE 802. Token Ring, for instance, is a widely implemented network architecture that conforms to the IEEE 802.5 specification.

Hardware and transmission are part of the ISO/OSI model

The ISO/OSI model The hardware and data transmission, or *data link* specifications, of IEEE 802 correspond to the two lowest layers of a larger, seven-layer network cake known as the ISO/OSI (International Organization for Standardization/ Open Systems Interconnect) networking model. Altogether, these seven layers address all the different ways in which networks and their software must work together to enable communication. Starting with the software and moving successively closer to the hardware, these layers and what they refer to, along with some rough noncomputer "real-world" equivalents, are as follows:

ISO/OSI layer	Responsible for	Business equivalent
Application	Information transfer between application programs	Sales and service
Presentation	Appearance and display of information	Merchandising or showroom
Session	Setting up and maintaining smooth communications	Switchboard
Transport	Controlling service quality and message delivery	Scheduling and delivery
Network	Message routing and handling	Dispatch
Data-link	Message packaging (coding and addressing) and transmission	Shipping
Physical	Hardware, including cabling and connectors	Motor pool or physical plant

A good way to remember the layers (from the bottom up) is Please Do Not Throw Sausage Pizza Away.

Protocols

IEEE and OSI are terms you're likely to hear bandied about by network professionals. So, too, especially if your company is following the intranet path, are the terms related to the next, somewhat overwhelming, set of networking standards: *protocols.* Protocols operate across the OSI layers from top to bottom, so they are not as narrowly defined as the IEEE 802 specifications. They are, however, just as essential in communications and collaboration.

Protocols are less tangible than hardware but just as necessary

Everyone who reads the paper or tunes in to the news hears about protocols in terms of the rules that politicians and diplomats do—and sometimes don't—follow when dealing with one another. Protocols at these exalted levels are what etiquette is to the rest of humanity: a means of ensuring that all parties involved follow the same code of behavior so that effective communication takes place. Networks have protocols too—rules that help one process (roughly, program) communicate with another operating at the same OSI level. Network protocols, unlike the rules of Emily Post or the Marquis of Queensberry, go by some jaw-cracking monikers.

Different protocols work at different OSI levels

Quite specific in what they do, network protocols govern the way actual transmissions are handled. Some determine how a message is packaged. Others control how the message is delivered, routed, checked for errors, and so on. Because each of these tasks occurs at a different level in the OSI model, different protocols correspond to different layers, and groups of similar protocols go by names that map at least roughly to the OSI level at which they work. A set of related protocols designed to work together at the various network levels is known as a *suite* or, when implemented on a particular type of network, a *stack.* Protocol suites/stacks include individually named protocols that are also categorized by the type of work they do. For example, there are *transport* protocols for computer-to-computer communication; *application* protocols for application-to-application communication; *session* protocols for managing communication sessions; and *network* (OSI network layer, that is) protocols for lower-level work such as addressing, routing, and error-checking.

Protocol suites A number of protocol stacks or suites are well known and widely used on current networks, including those that provide access to the Internet. The following are the most common ones—those you are most likely to hear or read about.

TCP/IP: To verbalize this one, pronounce each letter: "tea sea pea aye pea." The letters stand for *Transmission Control Protocol/Internet Protocol* and refer to a suite of protocols originally developed for use on the Internet (that is, the Internet as it existed before the graphical World Wide Web became the media and business darling of today). TCP/IP not only enables transmission within an enterprise, it also provides access to the Internet and to the World Wide Web. Flexible and fast, TCP/IP has long been the standard protocol suite on UNIX networks and is now rapidly attaining the same status on PC-based LANs and WANs. There are a number of advantages to using TCP/IP, but the two most significant are its *interoperability* and its *routability*. Interoperability means that TCP/IP (or any other interoperable protocol suite) can work with a mix of different types of computers, such as Macintoshes and PCs. Being routable means that TCP/IP can make use of different paths to transmit messages between separate LANs—in other words, TCP/IP is "intelligent" in the routes it follows to deliver messages and so can be used to connect multiple LANs to create a larger network or even a wide area network.

TCP/IP is fast, flexible, and rapidly becoming the standard set of protocols for communications

IPX/SPX: *IPX/SPX*, pronounced letter-by-letter, stands for *Internetwork Packet Exchange/Sequenced Packet Exchange* and is a small, fast, routable protocol stack used in Novell NetWare networks. The IPX portion of the stack handles lower-level network services, such as addressing and routing. The SPX portion handles the transport work required to send and verify accurate transmission of messages from one node to another. IPX/SPX is the descendant of an older, slower set of protocols called XNS, short for Xerox Network System.

IPX/SPX is a routable protocol stack for Novell NetWare networks

NetBEUI: *NetBEUI,* variously pronounced "net byooie" or "net booey," stands for *NetBIOS Basic Extended User Interface.* A small and fast but nonroutable protocol, NetBEUI was designed to work at the transport level and, as the beginning of its name implies, was closely allied with a session layer protocol named *NetBIOS (Network Basic Input/Output System).* NetBIOS was eventually made a separate entity, however, so that it could work with other transport protocols. NetBEUI has been available for years—since about the mid-1980s—in Microsoft networking products such as LAN Manager. Despite its speed, NetBEUI's inability to support routing has relegated it to the backwaters of 21st-century Internet/intranet development.

Individual protocols Individual protocols within these and other protocol stacks and suites go by names that range through most of the alphabet. To give you an idea of their (almost) infinite variety, the following list provides a sampling of TCP/IP protocols. There are, of course, many others, including a number that are familiar to users of the Apple-Talk network used with Macintosh computers. This list is restricted to TCP/IP, however, because TCP/IP is pretty much the current standard and these names have more currency than others that are or have been equally significant.

- *DHCP,* short for *Dynamic Host Configuration Protocol,* works with a special DHCP server to assign addresses dynamically, or "on the fly," to clients that connect to the network. You might encounter a reference to this protocol if you access the Internet through an *Internet Service Provider,* or *ISP.*
- *FTP,* short for *File Transfer Protocol,* deals with file exchange between computers. It is a standard for transferring files on the original, text-based Internet.

- *HTTP,* short for *Hypertext Transfer Protocol,* enables interaction on the World Wide Web. (These are the letters you see and type at the beginning of every Web location, or address, that you go to, as in *http://www.microsoft.com.*)

- *PPP,* short for *Point-to-Point Protocol,* is the TCP/IP protocol that deals with telephone transmissions.

- *SMTP,* short for *Simple Mail Transfer Protocol,* is the TCP/IP protocol that handles e-mail. This is one of several similar-sounding protocols in the TCP/IP suite, others being *SNMP (Simple Network Management Protocol),* which monitors network traffic and operation, and *SNTP (Simple Network Time Protocol),* which is the official TCP/IP timekeeper.

As you can see, protocol designations are many and varied. If you need to understand them or learn about any one in particular, two very good if rather technical sources of information are *Networking Essentials* (Microsoft Press, 1996) and *Encyclopedia of Networking,* second edition, by Werner Feibel (Network Press/Sybex, 1996). But if a little knowledge is enough for you, just bear in mind that a protocol by any name is simply a set of rules that helps one machine or program "talk" to another in a way that both understand.

Common LANs

Once you know the various ways in which networks can be defined, and the terms used in defining them, you can make sense of the networks themselves. The three described in the next sections, ARCnet, Ethernet, and Token Ring, are all defined at and just above the hardware level, meaning at the lowest two levels in the OSI model. These networks are particularly well known and are widely used today in LANs. The original forms of all three were developed relatively long ago in computer years, in the 1970s and thereabouts. Newer forms, with faster transmission speeds and more capability, have been developed since those early days.

ARCnet is used for
small LANs but
is not as popular
at Ethernet

ARCnet *ARCnet* stands for *Attached Resource Computer network.* A baseband network that uses token passing to provide nodes with network access, ARCnet is inexpensive and, because it supports a limited number of nodes (255), is best suited for relatively small LANs. ARCnet uses either of two topologies: bus, which is known as high-impedance ARCnet; and star, which is known as low-impedance ARC-net. The original ARCnet operated at 2.5 Mbps, but newer forms run considerably faster. One, called ARCnet Plus, has a transmission speed of 20 Mbps. Another form, based on the ARCnet architecture but known as TCNS (Thomas-Conrad Network System), transmits at 100 Mbps over coaxial and fiber-optic cable.

ARCnet corresponds, though not exactly, to the IEEE 802.4 specification. It is not widely used outside workgroup types of connections.

Ethernet *Ethernet,* the most widespread network architecture of today, comes in a number of variations characterized by baseband transmission and either a linear (straight-line) bus topology or a star topology in which nodes are connected to central hubs that can then be linked together. All versions of Ethernet rely on a traffic-control and network-access mechanism known as *CSMA/CD (carrier-sense multiple access [with] collision detection).* Ethernet corresponds in most respects to the IEEE 802.3 specification.

CSMA/CD uses a
carrier signal as
a "busy" flag and
relies on collision
detection to
regulate access

Unlike token passing, CSMA/CD keeps the transmission line open for any node that wants to transmit, hence the *multiple access* part of the term. In return, however, the nodes must behave themselves by "listening" for a carrier signal (the *carrier-sense* part) that indicates the network is in use. When no signal is detected, any node that needs to transmit can do so. However, if two nodes transmit at the same time, the transmissions collide, the nodes detect it (the *collision detection* part), and both nodes must then back off and wait a random period of time before retransmitting. Although relying on collisions to regulate traffic sounds a little dangerous, in truth CSMA/CD works at least as well as, and probably better than, the U.S. freeway system.

Ethernet, like most good things, did not spring forth fully formed like Venus riding a scallop shell from the sea. It was based on a University of Hawaii WAN named ALOHA and further developed at the famed Xerox Palo Alto Research Center (PARC), also home of the graphical user interface and the mouse. The original Ethernet transmitted at 10 Mbps; newer forms, named AnyLAN and Fast Ethernet, support speeds of 100 Mbps.

Unlike ARCnet, Ethernet can be confusing simply because of the variety of terms used to distinguish one form of Ethernet from another. Some forms support larger numbers of nodes, some span wider geographic areas, and some are less expensive to implement. When you delve into this type of architecture, the following terms often crop up:

The forms of Ethernet

- *Thinnet* and *thicknet.* These terms refer to the thickness of the coaxial cable connecting network nodes.
- *10BaseX.* 10 Mbps topologies are distinguished, among other things, by the type of transmission, type of cable, and distance spanned. For instance: Standard Ethernet is known as 10Base5, meaning 10Mbps transmission, baseband, and 5 × 100 meter cable segments.

  10Base2 Ethernet transmits at 10Mbps, is also baseband, and carries a signal approximately 2 × 100 meters. (10Base2 is less expensive than 10Base5 but supports fewer nodes.)

100BaseX Ethernet, or Fast Ethernet, transmits at 100 Mbps, is baseband, and uses different types (X) of telephone-grade, data-grade, or fiber-optic cable.

- *Baseband* and *broadband*. Ethernet can support either type of transmission. Baseband, as noted earlier, is typical, but broadband can be used in newer Ethernet networks corresponding to the IEEE 802.3 specification.

Token Ring Token Ring was described earlier in this chapter as a topology in which nodes use a packet, called a token, to determine which node can transmit at a given time. In PC-based LANs, this architecture is more or less synonymous with IBM's Token Ring implementation, which was developed in the 1980s to allow connectivity between PCs, minicomputers, and mainframes based on the IBM networking standard known as SNA (Systems Network Architecture). IBM's Token Ring operates as a baseband network with transmission speeds of either 4 Mbps or 16 Mbps and, of course, relies on token passing for network access. This architecture is the basis for the IEEE 802.5 standard.

In PC LANs, Token Ring usually refers to IBM's implementation

The wiring is a little different

Whereas the original token ring structure cables nodes together in a ring, the IBM version is a little more complex. Groups of nodes are cabled in a star formation to a central hub known variously as an *MAU* or *MSAU (Multistation Access Unit)*. The ring around which the token passes is logical rather than physical. It exists, as you might say, in the "mind" of the MAU because the MAU passes the token in a one-way circle from node to node. Token passing does, therefore, move in a ring, but via the MAU rather than a physically circular cable.

Each MAU in a Token Ring network can support up to eight nodes. This does not mean, however, that a Token Ring network is limited to eight computers. Depending on the

type of cabling used, it's possible to connect up to 33
MAUs, each with its attached set of nodes, to support up to
260 computers per ring. The only caveat to bear in mind
with multiple connected MAUs is that the cables plugging
one to the next must ensure that a ring formation is maintained, as in the drawing below:

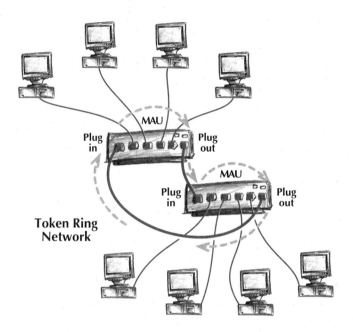

There's much more to know, of course, about LANs and
protocols and all manner of network hardware. There's
enough, in fact, to fill whole doorstop-size books. But this
chapter has given you a basic familiarity with common LAN
terminology. Now you can expand your world view and
move on to WANs.

Extending LANs: Remote Access and WANs

LANs, whether ARCnet, Ethernet, Token Ring, or any other architecture, are all confined to a relatively limited geographic area. With the advent of high-speed communications, the increasing importance of the global economy, and the branching of corporations into sometimes widely separated offices, businesses need bigger, better, more flexible, non–time-dependent methods of communication and collaboration to function efficiently and compete effectively. This is where remote access enters the picture and where WANs prove their mettle. By adding the ability to "call home," remote access opens a LAN or WAN to people working at home, in the field, or in branch offices away from corporate headquarters. And by linking widely separated LANs through long-distance communications, WANs extend the networking community across town, across the country, and around the globe.

In the age of global everything, LANs lead inevitably to remote access and to WANs

Remote Access

Remote access is supported by the operating system and is available by dialing in from outside

Remote access is all about opening up the capabilities of a LAN to people who are not hard-wired into the network. Through a simple telephone line and dial-up capability, remote access can connect one LAN to another or, more importantly, enable telecommuters, salespeople, and others to dial in and use group resources even when they cannot be physically present. Thanks to remote access, such individuals can send e-mail, schedule meetings, share documents, and consult public databases of inventories, prices, and other important information—all for the price of a telephone connection.

Remote access has two obvious and very basic requirements:

- A modem to mediate between the computer and the telephone line
- A telephone line through which people can make the connection

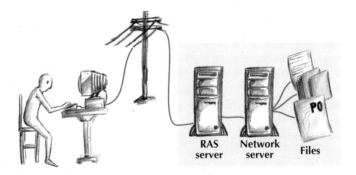

To these essentials, you add *client* software that enables the calling computer to connect to the network and *network* software that enables the network to support multiple client

computers dialing in via telephone. That done, stir in enthusiastic users and useful group-computing applications, such
as Microsoft Exchange, and remote access creates a "virtual"
home where geography becomes invisible and valid users
anywhere can use the network resources whenever and
wherever they wish.

Modems

You probably know that *modem* stands for *mo*dulate/
*dem*odulate. But what does a modem do, and how does it
do it? You can start by thinking about the modem's job,
which is to transmit and receive information over a telephone line. That sounds simple, until you remember that
PCs do all their work in digital form, while phone lines
carry signals—sound waves—in analog form. To transmit,
a modem must convert digital signals into analog so that the
information can flow through the communications conduit.
To receive, the modem must reverse the process by converting analog to digital.

These smart devices convert digital to analog and vice versa

To convert digital to analog, the modem loads the digital
information (bits) from the PC onto a carrier wave that can
travel over the phone line. To do this, it *modulates* the carrier signal, altering the form of the wave to represent the
actual bits of information. Depending on the way the modem works, it can use changes in frequency, amplitude
(wave crests and troughs), phase (location within the wave
cycle), or a combination of amplitude and phase to represent digital 1s and 0s. (The illustration below shows the
general idea, but it does not truly represent the way signals
"ride" on the analog wave.)

Modulating converts analog to digital; demodulating does the reverse

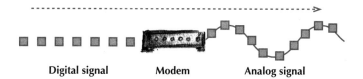

Digital signal   **Modem**   **Analog signal**

In the analog-to-digital conversion that is needed to receive a transmission, the modem reverses the process by *demodulating* the signal, unloading the bit information from the carrier wave and returning the information to digital form that can then be fed to the computer.

Modem Specifications

Modems operate in any of three ways and conform to standards known as the ITU specifications

Modems, like everything else in networking and communications, function in well-defined ways and conform to certain standards. In transmitting and receiving signals, they can operate in one of three modes:

- *Simplex,* which, like a one-way street, supports traffic in one direction only (either sending or receiving, but not both)
- *Half-duplex,* which, like a reversible freeway lane, supports bidirectional traffic, but not in both directions at the same time
- *Full-duplex,* which, like a divided highway, supports bidirectional traffic in both directions at the same time

Older standards include Hayes compatibility and the Bell specifications

Where standards are concerned, many modems in the past (and some today) announce that they are *Hayes compatible,* meaning that they use the same set of commands developed and used by Hayes, manufacturers of the modems that have long represented an industrywide though unofficial standard for modem hardware. In the 1980s in particular, modems were also characterized as conforming to certain *Bell specifications,* which described the speed and signaling used by the modem. For example, Bell specification 208B indicated a half-duplex modem operating at 4800 bps (slow by today's standards) over dial-up phone lines.

These days, you refer to the ITU (formerly CCITT) specifications

Currently, modems are most often identified as being "V.something," such as V.32, with perhaps a *bis* or a *ter* tacked onto the end. These somewhat cryptic identifiers indicate a modem's characteristics just as the Bell identifications did, but they refer to a set of specifications known as the *ITU specifications.* ITU stands for the International Telecommunications Union, a standard-setting body formerly known as the *CCITT,* for Consultative Committee for International Telegraphy and Telephony. Beginning in the late 1980s, the ITU began to categorize and set standards for more current, i.e., faster, modems than did the Bell specifications. ITU designations for modems currently in wide use are V.32bis, for full-duplex modems operating at 14,400 bps, and V.34, for modems operating at 28,800 bps over dial-up phone lines.

By the way, *bis* is French for "second," and *ter* is French for "third." A bis designation indicates a revised specification based on an earlier standard; a ter designation indicates a revision to the bis revision.

Phone Connections

At the very least, modems need something to communicate over. Although a variety of faster alternatives are available or under development, remote access generally means that the "something" is a telephone line, which often goes by the rather endearing name of *POTS* (plain old telephone service).

For modem connections, you use an analog line

POTS comes in two varieties: standard dial-up lines and leased lines. Dial-up lines, which most everyone uses when connecting to the office from home, are less expensive than leased lines, but they are also slower, they require making a new connection each time they are used, and they are poorer in quality because calls are routed through different switches to make the connection. Leased lines, often used to connect offices with high traffic volumes, are more expensive, but they are also faster, of higher quality, constantly open for use, and, at least on the local level, do not require switching by the telephone company. Long-distance calls might be routed through switches, but this is done in such a way that the caller perceives no difference from an unswitched, dedicated line.

WANs

WANs also offer remote access, but they are much broader in scope and essentially form a secure network that transcends geography

WANs are LANs connected by telecommunications. Where remote access can enable an employee in the field to communicate with the home office, a WAN enables multiple offices to communicate with each other and with headquarters. A WAN is to a national or international organization essentially what your own nervous system is to your hands and feet, head and heart: the connecting thread, the tie that binds.

WANs have their own requirements

Building a WAN, however, isn't a simple matter of running a cable or a phone line between two LANs. WANs do, in fact, introduce their own sets of hardware and standards into the networking equation. The complexity, as you might expect, is significant. The elements, however, are relatively few and fairly simple to understand, in theory if not in practice. To create a WAN, you need:

- Connectors to link different networks or network segments
- Connections—carrier lines—that enhance the efficiency and speed of transmission

Bridges and Routers, Brouters and Gateways

Politicians aren't the only ones who need a "big tent"

Although it might be nice to imagine idealized LANs and WANs composed of PCs and servers that can be connected effortlessly like Tinkertoys to swap information in complete harmony, the vision does not always correspond to what occurs in real life. At a minimum, networks tend to spread beyond their initial set of nodes, or else different segments must be linked together to enable one group in the organization to communicate and work with another. In addition, many networks, especially very large ones that have grown over the years, end up being a heterogeneous mixture of PC *platforms* (computers and operating systems), such as MS-DOS, Microsoft Windows, and Macintosh. They often run a variety of different protocols, as well, and may need to connect PCs with minicomputers or mainframes running their own software and occupying their own unique niches in the network ecology.

To enable these different types of connections and cross-connections, networks rely on different types of hardware that transfer information between LANs or segments of LANs. In increasing order of complexity, either in function or in the types of environments they connect, these devices are known as *repeaters, bridges, routers, brouters,* and *gateways.* Each device, befitting the tasks it performs, operates at a successively higher layer in the OSI model: repeaters at the physical layer, bridges at the data-link layer, routers (and brouters) at the network layer, and gateways typically at the top, or application, layer.

Different types of hardware bridge the gap from LAN to LAN

Repeaters A repeater, the simplest and least expensive means of extending a LAN, performs either or both of two jobs. Its basic function is to strengthen and retransmit signals so that messages can travel farther than they could otherwise. A repeater can also moonlight as a go-between, however, by transferring signals between two different types of cabling—for example, between coaxial and fiber-optic cable.

Repeaters are the simplest way to extend a LAN

Repeater

Normally, any signal transmitted over a standard network cable—coaxial or twisted-pair—can travel only a certain distance—say, 300 feet—before it begins to *degrade,* or lose its integrity. By refreshing these tired messages before sending them on their way, repeaters can extend the network either by connecting separate segments of cable or, more practically, by connecting similar, but separate, network segments to create a larger LAN. Repeaters are useful for increasing the physical area covered by a network, but they do not function well on networks with heavy traffic. In addition, they cannot be used to join network segments based on different topologies or access methods—for example, token ring and CSMA/CD.

Bridges span the gap
between networks
and also help control
traffic volume

Bridges Bridges, like repeaters, send transmissions from one network or network segment to another, but they are more intelligent devices. Where repeaters simply pass messages along, bridges are more selective, transferring only those messages destined for nodes on a different network. In so doing, bridges help control traffic flow by separating "local" from "long-distance" traffic.

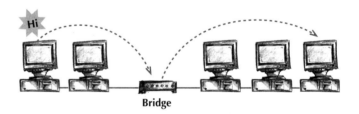

Bridge

Bridges filter traffic
as well as pass it
between LANs

To do its work, a bridge monitors all traffic on the networks it connects and checks the sending and receiving addresses on all transmissions (packets). If both addresses on a packet belong to nodes on the same network, the bridge lets the network do the delivering. If the addresses belong to nodes on different networks, the bridge spans the gap between the two and transfers the packet to the destination network. If the destination address is unknown, the bridge forwards the packet to all connected networks other than the one sending the message. A bridge also keeps track of all these nodes and their "home" networks by continually adding known addresses to a database called a *routing table.* Because it checks this routing table to determine who is local and who is long distance, as time passes fewer packets are sent to all possible destinations and the bridge becomes more successful at moderating traffic flow. Some bridges can connect only networks with the same topology; others can connect different types of networks, such as Ethernet and Token Ring.

Because bridges filter transmissions, they are more flexible than repeaters and can be used not only to connect network segments but to break a heavily used network into smaller, less heavily used clumps of computers. On networks that cannot be directly cabled together, devices known as *remote bridges* can be connected to modems and dedicated phone lines to connect widely separated groups of computers. Although bridges are smart, they are best suited to connecting relatively small numbers of nodes. Multiple bridges can, however, be used to link several LANs to create a larger network.

Bridges can connect either nearby or widely separated networks

Routers and Brouters

Q: What's a brouter?

A: A device that can act as either a router or a bridge.

Now that we have that out of the way…

In terms of forwarding transmissions, routers (and therefore brouters) sit at the top of the network food chain. Capable of connecting complex configurations of networks and subnetworks, routers are intelligent devices that not only forward packets from one network to another but are also able to figure out the best route and transfer packets through multiple intervening networks if necessary. As you can imagine, routers are needed for Internet connectivity.

Routers and brouters can connect complex network webs with different protocols and architectures

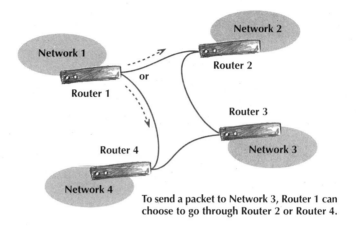

To send a packet to Network 3, Router 1 can choose to go through Router 2 or Router 4.

Routers can be used to connect both LANs and WANs and can move packets through networks based on different protocols and different topologies. Although some *(static)* routers must be told by a human which routes are available, more sophisticated *(dynamic)* routers maintain and constantly update routing information that tells them not only the number of *hops* a packet must take to reach a particular network but also which intervening networks to avoid because they are busier than others. The actual details of how they work are filled with acronyms, protocols, and routing algorithms, but essentially routers do the following: They "stuff" information-laden packets into transportation "envelopes"; they address those envelopes with specific network addresses (more detailed than those used by bridges); and they determine which routes to use for delivery by communicating and sharing routing information with neighboring routers. The nitty-gritty is endlessly fascinating. If you want or need to know more, any good networking book should cover network addresses, router protocols, routing algorithms, and other details.

Gateways are links between dissimilar network environments

Gateways As mentioned earlier, not all networks are homogeneous in their components. In some instances, especially in large corporations, the network not only must include

PCs joined by, say, a Token Ring architecture, it must also enable those PCs to communicate easily with Macs on an AppleTalk network or, often, with a minicomputer or a mainframe that is completely unaware of its lesser relatives. In these situations, the network requires a dedicated server known as a *gateway,* which passes information between the two dissimilar environments. To do this work, the gateway not only forwards information but transforms messages to put them in the format each environment requires.

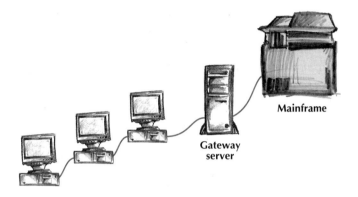

Mainframe

Gateway server

The transformation performed by a gateway involves stripping messages of the protocols specific to one environment and substituting those of the other. In some instances, the alteration requires converting e-mail from one format to another or even requires morphing content from one "alphabet" to another—for example, from the ASCII used universally by PCs to the EBCDIC (Extended Binary Coded Decimal Interchange Code) that is the mainstay of the IBM mainframe world. In effect, a gateway connecting, say, a Token Ring PC network with an IBM mainframe camouflages the true nature of the other network. Because the gateway gives each connected network information in the form it needs, the PC network "sees" the mainframe as just another Token Ring environment and the mainframe "sees" the PC network as just another part of the unique SNA (Systems Network Architecture) environment it calls home— a home, by the way, in which either the gateway or the

To do their work, gateways convert information from one network format to the other

clients require hardware or software emulation that enables them to pretend they are dumb terminals.

Gateways are focused on specific environments

Gateways, because of the unique nature of their work, are not simply freelance nodes on a network that can be turned at will to gateway functionality. Because they are so task-specific, they must be dedicated to the networks they connect. In fact, different types of gateways are identified by the type of work they do. For example, an e-mail or fax gateway handles only e-mail or faxes for a particular network; a Microsoft Windows NT to SNA mainframe gateway connects a PC LAN running Windows NT to an IBM mainframe based on the SNA architecture, protocols, and data format. Gateways, because of the amount of work they must do, can be slow and do require a considerable amount of memory. They are also expensive.

Note: *Gateway* is sometimes used to refer to less task-specific servers providing access to a network. Perhaps this usage will gain currency, especially with the increasing importance of the Internet. Generally, however, gateways are the machines described above.

Packet Switching and the X.25 Standard

Relaying packets is more efficient than relaying whole messages

A WAN, whether it uses routers, bridges, brouters, gateways, or all of the above, can potentially span great distances. For reasons of both cost and effectiveness, it obviously behooves the network to move information to the farthest-flung outposts as efficiently as possible. Certainly, the *medium*—analog or digital, wire or fiber-optic—has a lot to do with efficiency. So, too, does the *method* used to ship the information. Here, the best way to get information from A to Z is often not via a direct connection but by breaking the information into small packets and shipping those packets on the chosen medium through the best and fastest routes available through B, C, D, and so on. Why are little pieces better than big ones?

- Transmitting small packets, all of the same size, ensures that no single message takes up a disproportionate amount of transmission time.
- Resending a damaged packet is faster and easier than resending an entire transmission. (Yes, errors can happen, but it's the network's job to take care of them.)
- Traffic volume on the network varies throughout the day (and night). Differing time zones, for example, have an impact on the amount of traffic at different locations.

The technique used to deconstruct and route messages on WANs is known as *packet switching.*

Packet switching is exactly what it sounds like: In order to move transmitted "freight" across a mosaic of linked LANs or a WAN, the network breaks each message into equal-sized packets and then ships those packets to their destination, relying on either *virtual* (temporary) or *permanent* circuits that switch the packets from connection to connection en route. Packet switching is complex, and the actual technology is full of technical acronyms and protocols. For example, the network that the packet travels through is known as the *PDN,* or *public data network;* the component that interfaces with the PDN is called a *DTE* (for *data terminal equipment*); and packets themselves are created and reassembled by a *PAD,* or *packet assembler/disassembler.* To the bystander, however, one of the most fascinating aspects of packet switching is the way the packets actually travel.

Packet switching resembles cargo shipping on trucks, trains, and planes

When a message is broken into multiple packets, the bundles making up the message don't necessarily take the same route to their destination. Like passengers on different airlines, one packet might, for instance, travel through Chicago on its way to Los Angeles; another might be shunted through Dallas or St. Louis instead. The switching routes are determined entirely by the transmitting and

You can think of packets as entering the network "cloud"

receiving computers—so much so that in diagrams of packet-switched networks, packets are typically shown as entering a picture of a cloud at the beginning of their journey and exiting from that cloud at the end.

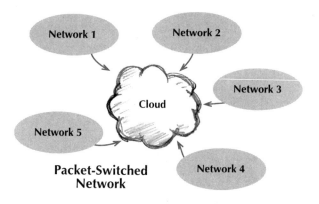

Packet-Switched Network

The humpty-dumpty factor

Because packet switching means that a single message can be broken into multiple packets and shipped via multiple routes, the packets comprising a message can arrive at their destination out of order and at different times. To humans, this would represent a jigsaw puzzle of seemingly titanic proportions when you consider the speed of a WAN (upwards of 64 Kbps) and the number of messages flying across it. To the computers and their PADs, however, it's all in a day's work, for they manage not only to create and transmit packets but to catch and reconnect arriving packets, in the proper order, at their correct destinations.

As you can imagine, the process of breaking up messages, routing the packets, and putting arriving transmissions back together requires a tremendous amount of work, all of which happens rapidly and away from human eyes. Before transmitting, for instance, the sending and receiving computers must exchange *parameters* that set the size of the message and must agree on certain communication procedures, including the way errors will be checked for and handled.

Packet-switching technology, like just about everything else related to networking, is described in a set of protocols. Set up by the CCITT, these protocols are known as the *X.25* standard, and they cover all aspects of packet switching related to the actual interface connecting a host computer to the packet-switched network—that is, X.25 covers everything but the cloud. It is X.25, for instance, that defines the DTE, the OSI layers at which packet switching functions, and the speed at which the network transmits. But X.25 does not cover the actual switching of packets on the PDN, nor does it define the carrier or the type of service required, because all of that happens in the cloud. X.25 is concerned only with how packets get onto the PDN and how they get off.

X.25 defines the ground rules

Digital Phone Connections

WANs, because they are bigger and busier than LANs, often rely on digital, rather than analog, connections. Standard digital lines, such as T1, which you've no doubt heard about in relation to Internet Service Providers, are available from telecommunications carriers and are not only faster than analog phone lines, they are far less prone to transmission error. Several forms of digital transmission are available, but they break down into two major categories:

Better and faster connections can be made through digital lines

- *DDS (digital data service)* is a *point-to-point* digital transmission service—that is, a service that forms a direct connection between two networks over a leased line. DDS transmissions are transferred between one network and the other by routers or bridges at each end. Each router or bridge is, in turn, connected to a device called a *DSU/CSU (data service unit/channel service unit),* which mediates between the network, with its standard, essentially on/off digital data format, and the digital line, with its somewhat different digital format, which is

DDS forms dedicated high-speed links between networks and is available from phone companies

bipolar, meaning that a 1 can be represented by either positive or negative voltage. One form of DDS, known as *switched 56,* transmits at 56 Kbps over a dial-up line. Switched 56 is less expensive than a dedicated DDS line and is widely used to connect LANs.

T1 is expensive but may be the only way to go on high-volume WANs

- *T1* is a digital line that can be used to transmit not only data but voice and graphics or video. A T1 line operates at 1.544 Mbps (megabits per second), a speed known as DS-1. To carry information, this 1.544 Mbps bandwidth is divided into 24 individual channels, each operating at 64 Kbps, or the DS-0 (zero) level. For even higher speeds, transmissions are *multiplexed*—interleaved—onto a T1 line at levels known as DS-2, DS-3, and the maximum, DS-4, which runs a little over a whopping 274 Mbps. T1 is an expensive service to install and run, but it is nonetheless widely used when high-speed, high-volume transmissions are required. A less expensive alternative known as *fractional T1* provides for leasing some, rather than all, channels in the T1 bandwidth. T1 is available in North America, Japan, and Australia. A comparable technology known as E1 is available in Europe and in Mexico and South America. The fastest lines you're likely to encounter here are multiplexed T3, or DS-3, lines, which carry 45 Mbps and might be used in exceptionally demanding situations.

ISDN is described a little later

ISDN, which is probably more familiar to you than T1, is another form of digital transmission but is described in the next section, rather than here, because it is an on-demand (dial-up) service and because it is viewed as one of several technologies that can or will form the basis for a broad global communications structure that affects private individuals as well as corporate WANs.

Up-and-Coming WAN Technologies

Two aspects of networking technology are garnering tremendous interest, both conceptual and financial. One is the server software dedicated to building and supporting corporate intranets (described in Chapter 5). The other aspect, of more relevance in this chapter, is the communications technology of the near future. Both are likely to have enormous impact on the way people live and conduct business in the 21st century.

The Graduate pushed plastics; now we are starry-eyed over intranets and communications

If you've been keeping up with telecommunications and computer news, you've certainly heard about ISDN, the high-speed digital phone service that can make the Internet a joy. You might also have heard about developments such as cable modems and a modemlike technology known as *ADSL (Asymmetrical Digital Subscriber Line)*. All these are harbingers of a rosy global future in which sound and movie-quality video will stream into homes and businesses in the same way that data does now.

Some technology is already here but not yet common; some is still under development

Why They Are Needed

Recent growth of the World Wide Web (which, remember, is becoming integral to business communications, marketing, sales, and the like) has been phenomenal. Although a majority of computer users, especially home users, have yet to go on line with the world, current Web subscribers testify—often loudly—that "surfing" the net is usually closer to "slogging," "trudging," or "sludging" the net. Part of the problem is the sheer amount of time required to find what you want on this massive network. The more visible problem, however, is getting the information quickly when you do find it. Bandwidth again.

It's the Web, stupid

The Web is great,
and it holds great
promise, but too
much information
is being pumped
through pipes that
are too small

The World Wide Web, as opposed to the original text-based Internet, is characterized by a lot of flash: graphics, sound, animation, video. All of these things are big not only in appeal but in the number of bytes they require for storage and playback or display. Obviously the colorful whizbang is not going to go away. Equally obviously, all that information needs to be funneled to computers through existing, often years-old telecommunications media that all too often prove to be sadly lacking.

The technology has
exploded; now the
infrastructure must
grow to match it

Of course it would be unfair to blame the medium for the slowness of the message. The World Wide Web has gained popularity far more quickly than many—perhaps most— people imagined it could or would. Condemning existing telecommunications facilities (which, remember, have served the telephone world quite well) would be a lot like shooting the messenger for riding in on a horse when no other transportation was available. Granted, the infrastructure needs to catch up with the capabilities of Internet-aware computers, networks, and software. No one debates that. The question is how. And who will pay. And how long it will take. And who is responsible. And what direction development should take. Satellites? Fiber optics? Digital communications such as ISDN or the newly developed ADSL?

Cable Modems

One current move toward global computing is the development of cable modems. The impetus behind the development of cable modems is the very same as the one responsible for telephone companies' current offerings of high-speed ISDN lines: bandwidth. In the quickly changing environment of the Internet, cable modems are seen as one solution with the potential to become reality in the near future. Among the organizations that have announced work on developing, supporting, and even field-testing cable modems are Intel, TCI, AT&T, Hewlett-Packard, the cable television research unit called CableLabs, Time Warner, Zenith, and Motorola. This impressive list adds considerable credibility to the technology, but as of January 1997, availability is still awaiting the rosy-fingered dawn.

Cable modems are essentially mediators that connect existing cable systems to PCs and LANs through an Ethernet connection that plugs into the computer. By using part of the broader bandwidth available through cable television facilities, they can move large quantities of information to and from computers and net servers faster than is currently possible with telephone lines and standard modems. Current fast modems operate at 28,800 bps (28.8 Kbps). U.S. Robotics, a well-known modem developer and manufacturer, has recently announced an x2 modem with a speed of 56 Kbps, but despite this advance, the probable maximum for analog modems is probably not much higher and almost certainly not in the megabit range. Cable modems, on the other hand, transfer information at speeds from 10 Mbps to 30 Mbps— several hundred times faster than a standard 28,800 bps modem.

Speed is the goal

Of course, saying a cable modem operates at 10 to 30 Mbps is a little like saying a sports car goes 150 miles per hour. It *can,* but that doesn't mean it does so all the time. Just as traffic volume affects the throughput of a network, the existing cable facilities (which are used primarily for television broadcasts, remember) and Internet traffic conditions have the same effect on the actual speed of a cable modem. There are, in fact, a number of issues that must be resolved before cable modems have the potential to become as ubiquitous as toasters:

As with networks, maximum speed is not actual speed

- Cable, the television service, is designed for one-way broadcasting. Signals received by the cable company are fed to a *head end,* which then delivers the signals through the wires that run to customers' homes. For true Internet or any other networking accessibility, however, cable must become a two-way connection that sets aside bandwidth for information both flowing to a computer (*downstream,* as it's called) and from a computer *(upstream).*

- Currently, speeds in the megabit range are for downstream data flow. Upstream rates are closer to those for standard modems—about 20 Kbps. This discrepancy is not seen as a serious problem, because home users in particular are expected to receive far more often than they give. E-mail, however, does flow in two directions, often with substantial files attached, so the issue does need attention.

- Cable is a *broadcast* medium, meaning that information is not funneled directly to a single recipient. Although broadcast is fine for television, Internet access speed could be slowed substantially if many subscribers "tuned in" to the same broadcast at the same time—especially if some downloads involved videos or similar large files.

- Most likely, cable companies supporting cable modems will need to install routers and other networking equipment needed to manage the transition to the Internet's TCP/IP-based traffic from a system originally designed to support television broadcasts.

Cable modems are mostly seen as home devices, but speed is speed and WANs use modems too

Cable modems are currently viewed primarily as high-speed devices for home use, but certainly they have the potential to become a source of fast Internet connections for some businesses. Today, for example, businesses can install high-speed ISDN phone lines to improve incoming and outgoing speed between the Internet and corporate servers. Cable modems, operating at many times the speed of ISDN, could improve the situation by offering not only faster access but also the ability to use more and better sound, graphics, animation, and video. There is no way to see the future, however, and other promising technologies, especially ADSL and ATM (both described later) are also close on the horizon.

Chapter Three

ISDN

ISDN, or Integrated Services Digital Network, is a technology that's been talked about—off and on—at least since the early 1980s. Idealized as the one-stop solution for the world's data, sound, video, and (later) computing and fax requirements, ISDN is a standard for delivering all kinds of information over a single line; it doesn't require separate voice-only (telephone), data-only (modem/phone computer and fax communications), and sound-and-video–only (television and imaging) circuits. Until recently, ISDN was implemented more in Europe than in North America.

ISDN has been around awhile, but more in theory than in fact in North America

These days, ISDN is gaining popularity as a relatively inexpensive (compared to T1) means of enabling fast access to networks (as in remote access computing) and, of course, to the ever-present Internet. ISDN makes dial-up connections rather than being "live" at all times as leased lines are, but the dial-up is so much faster than with standard modems that it can be hardly noticeable. Although fully digital, just as computers are, ISDN still requires some type of device to mediate between the computer and the ISDN line itself. Devices available include ISDN modems (which are inappropriately named because there's no modulation involved, but which do plug into a computer's serial, or communications, port like modems do); ISDN adapters, which connect directly to the computer's bus; and ISDN routers or bridges, which, as you would expect, are used to connect remote LANs.

Now, ISDN means fast connectivity to networks and the Internet

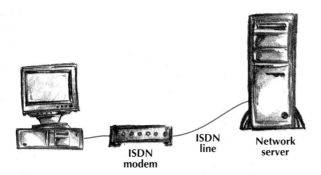

ISDN modem   ISDN line   Network server

ISDN comes in two forms, known as *BRI (Basic Rate Interface)* and *PRI (Primary Rate Interface)*. BRI transmissions move at 128 Kbps over two *bearer* channels, or *B* channels, on which the actual information is loaded, plus one *data* channel, or *D* channel, that carries control and other signals, such as phone numbers. PRI transmissions make use of 1 data channel and either 23 (in the United States) or 30 bearer channels (in Europe and Japan). The 23-channel lines run at 1.544 Mbps, the 30-channel jobs at 2.048 Mbps. PRI is preferable, for obvious reasons, to BRI lines for connecting high-volume WANs.

ADSL

ADSL (Asymmetric Digital Subscriber Line) and some interesting future offshoots represent the "new" news in high-speed communications and Internet connectivity. Developed as a means of enabling multimegabit transmissions over standard telephone lines, ADSL is a full-duplex (transmission in both directions) system that uses three channels: one for downstream data from the server to the client, one for upstream data from the client to the server, and one for normal telephone service. The two data channels operate at different speeds: 1.5 Mbps to 10 Mbps downstream and a slower 16 Kbps to 640 Kbps upstream. Because the technology uses existing phone lines, however, actual speed varies with the distance traveled—the greater the distance, the slower the speed.

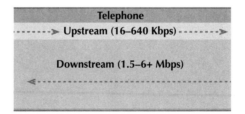

Although the speed difference between the upstream and downstream channels is substantial, as it is with the cable modems currently being tested, the effect is not as significant as it sounds, and for the same reason—downstream sluggishness can seem interminable while upstream pokiness, especially because less information moves up than down, is perceived as far more tolerable. ADSL has one additional advantage that is not shared with other telecommunications services: Because the telephone channel is both separate and on a different frequency from the two data channels, a breakdown in the data channels does not affect the subscriber's ability to use the telephone.

ADSL was still under development and testing as of early 1997. The GTE telephone company, however, conducted an initial field trial in Texas in early 1996, and in August of that year it joined with Microsoft in Redmond, Washington, to conduct a two-phase trial. The first phase, involving about 40 GTE and Microsoft staff members, combined ADSL technology and hardware with Windows NT servers to provide remote and Internet access. The second phase, scheduled to start later, is expected to expand the trial to the University of Washington and a number of local businesses, with extended applications-testing to include e-mail, chats, conferencing, and so on. Commercial availability is expected from GTE in about mid-1997.

ADSL isn't ready yet

When available, Digital Subscriber Lines are expected to be provided in more than one form:

ADSL, or rather xDSL, will come in several flavors

- ADSL, which is expected to transmit over twisted-pair lines at 1.5 Mbps to 10 Mbps downstream, 16 Kbps to 640 Kbps upstream.
- HDSL, High [Data Rate] Digital Subscriber Line, which is expected to transmit at T1 speeds over twisted-pair lines. A variation of this, SDSL, Single [Line] Digital Subscriber Line, has been defined for single lines and presumably would be appropriate for individual subscribers.

- VDSL, Very [High Data Rate] Digital Subscriber Line, which is expected to transmit—but only over short distances—over twisted-pair lines at up to 52.8 Mbps.

Advanced Networking Services

Finally, to round out your tour of technologies related to LANs and WANs, take a quick look at some "comers" in the world of communications services. Some of these technologies are already available but are at the beginning of their potential growth. Their value is easily seen from descriptions of what they do. If you are looking to the future, these names will probably crop up in discussions of faster ways to move data, sound, and video.

Frame relay is fast data transfer designed for reliable, secure, point-to-point lines

Frame Relay Frame relay is an advanced relative of packet switching that, because it operates at a low (data-link) level of the OSI model, can work with a number of different protocols. Best suited to a "clean" environment such as fiber-optic cable, frame relay transmits data only, but in variable-length packets rather than the fixed-size units required by packet switching. Frame relay is fast and transmits at rates as high as 2 Mbps. Part of the reason for such speeds is that frame relay can adjust transmissions to take advantage of available bandwidth. In addition, because transmissions over fiber-optic lines are remarkably error-free and safe from eavesdropping (because they are encoded onto light, not sound), frame relay eliminates some of the time-consuming error-checking and transmission-control procedures required by X.25 and packet switching. If packets go astray during transmission, frame relay relies on higher-level protocols to take care of resending the information.

Frame relay relies on permanent virtual circuits

In transmitting messages, frame relay establishes a point-to-point connection between the sender and the receiver. This connection, however, is not a physical circuit that requires a permanent cable between the two participants. It is, instead, a *virtual circuit,* which sets aside a portion of available bandwidth to establish a link—a transmission route—between two computers after they establish contact and agree on the method and routing to be used. Unlike a physical circuit, which costs the same whether a lot or a little traffic flows, a virtual circuit costs only for the time it is used.

BISDN *BISDN (Broadband ISDN)* is not yet widely available, but it is another significant contender for the role of WAN standard. BISDN is an extension of the same specification that defined ATM in the late 1980s and is intended to support not only data but also sound, video, and graphics. BISDN can therefore support such up-and-coming uses as interactive videoconferencing and broadcast services that deliver select information, such as news reports, to validated recipients. The BISDN standard calls for transmission in the multimegabit to gigabit range. Very fast.

BISDN is faster than ISDN

ATM Outside the banking community, *ATM* does not stand for Automatic Teller Machine. It stands for *Asynchronous Transfer Mode,* which is an advanced, high-speed, packet-switching system that is growing in popularity, although it has been somewhat handicapped by the expense required to install ATM-compatible hardware. Unlike a system such as FDDI (described on the next page), which is limited to a range of about 100 km (62 miles), ATM can be used for both LANs and widely distributed WANs.

ATM is fast but expensive

A broadband technology that supports voice, data, fax, real-time video, CD-quality audio, and graphics images, ATM supports transmission rates over high-bandwidth material such as fiber-optic cable that range from a "slow" 155 Mbps to a high of 622 Mbps and possibly up to 1+ Gbps (gigabits

This broadband technology is suited to high-speed lines such as fiber-optic cable

per second). This is not exactly shabby performance when you consider that WANs are generally not as fast as LANs. Fast WANs, for instance, typically transmit at a maximum of 1 Mbps or 2 Mbps, whereas Ethernet, which is popular on LANs, runs at about 10 Mbps. Given such a consideration, you can put ATM in perspective by figuring that even 155 Mbps is about 15 times Ethernet speed, 100 times ISDN speed, and 5500 times the speed of a modem transmitting at 28,800 bps.

With ATM, fixed-size packets and multiple computers talk at the same time

On an ATM network, messages are sent on their way in fixed-size cells of 53 bytes apiece. To create these packets, ATM relies on a set of services comprising what's known as the *AAL (ATM Adaptation Layer)*. Essentially, the AAL takes in whatever type of information—data, voice, video—needs transmission and breaks it into neat little 53-byte bundles. These bundles *(cells)* then go to routers or switches that launch them onto the network carrier. Unlike other network architectures (Ethernet and Token Ring), ATM is not limited to listening to one computer sending one message at a time. It can pay attention to, and transmit for, several computers at the same time by multiplexing cells from different messages into the traffic stream, interleaving the cells in much the same way that cars merge onto the freeway.

FDDI is for high-speed but relatively small (geographically speaking) networks

FDDI *FDDI (Fiber Distributed Data Interface)* conforms to an *ANSI* standard—that is, a standard set out by the American National Standards Institute—that describes high-speed fiber-optic networks that can connect up to 1000 nodes within a relatively limited area of 100 km (62 miles). FDDI, sometimes pronounced "fiddy," is based on a token-passing architecture and operates at speeds of up to 100 Mbps.

FDDI is characterized by token passing over two rings

The basis of an FDDI network is a pair of rings on which traffic flows in opposite directions. One, called the *primary* ring, normally handles all of the network traffic; the other, the *secondary* ring, is primarily a backup resource that is automatically brought into play when the primary ring "goes down," or fails. FDDI can be used in several ways:

- For *backbone networks* to which multiple LANs are connected
- For linking high-volume, high-performance equipment, such as mainframes, minicomputers, and their peripherals
- For graphics, engineering, or scientific workstations to enable rapid transfer of information that would clog a normal network

SMDS *SMDS (Switched Multimegabit Data Service)* is a high-bandwidth, packet-switched service that operates at speeds of 1 Mbps to 34 Mbps and transmits fixed-length cells as ATM does. SMDS is available from local carriers and works over public lines. It is a *connectionless service,* meaning that it does not rely on virtual circuits. Instead, each network node is assigned its own address. Network switches use these addresses to forward transmissions to their destinations by the best available route at the time the messages are received. In other words, routes between the sending and receiving computers are not preset, so information can be sent by any of a number of possible paths, depending on available routes and the destination address.

SMDS is a cost-effective way to link multiple LANs

SMDS requires an SMDS CSU/DSU and router. It is an effective technology for linking networks with large numbers of separate locations. It can, for instance, be used to link university locations or to connect local-government LANs throughout a city to form a WAN-like configuration often referred to as a *MAN (Metropolitan Area Network).* Because SMDS is provided by local telephone companies, however, it is not especially suitable for networks that cross boundaries between carriers or for transnational or global corporate networks.

SMDS is good for large networks, but it has some potential geographic limitations

SONET offers
blazing speed and
supports ATM
or BISDN

SONET *SONET (Synchronous Optical Network)* is an optical carrier in which transmissions are converted from electrical to optical signals and back again. As you would expect from the way it works, SONET is designed for fiber-optic networks. It is new and viewed as the likely transport service for networks based on ATM packet switching. An extremely high-speed means of transmission, SONET comes with a correspondingly high price tag that can run into six figures or more if the cost includes laying fiber-optic cable. It does, however, move information at breathtaking speeds from 51.84 Mbps to a potential high of 622 Mbps.

It's fast and robust
and best suited
to high-volume
networks

SONET is a standard of the American National Standards Institute. It is reliable and can handle data, voice, and video. In its most often used form, known as a *self-healing ring,* SONET is capable of recovering from breaks in transmission by switching traffic to an alternate route. Because of its high bandwidth, SONET is especially suited to networks that must move quantities of information that would swamp a typical network—medical images, for example, or large amounts of video.

Where to Next?

This is where you end your tour of the present and future components of a functional network. The pieces you've read about here form the corporate and communications infrastructure that is needed to support the operating and applications software that, in turn, forms the foundation of an easy-to-use, intuitive, truly collaborative environment. The next chapter explores the software that creates the underpinnings of a collaborative environment. Beginning with the operating system that maintains harmony in an invisible world where cacophony could easily become an unwelcome visitor, you'll see that a number of critical pieces known as *servers* work together to create an electronic universe where Bill Gates's vision of "Information At Your Fingertips" becomes more of a reality every day.

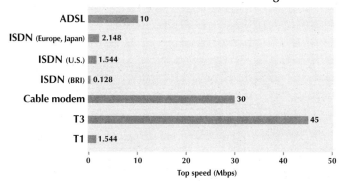

Communication Technologies

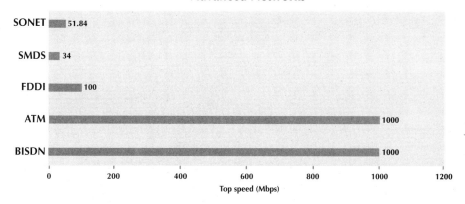

Advanced Networks

Chapter Four

The Collaborative Environment

Information At Your Fingertips starts with a lot of high-performance software layered onto the network. The actual software varies, depending on both the network environment and, of course, the software provider. Software in the minicomputer and mainframe world is not the same as software in the client-server world, and client-server software from Microsoft differs from client-server software from Netscape, Sun Microsystems, and other providers, not to mention from programs created by in-house developers who work on business-specific or task-specific applications.

Pretty much everything you've read up to this point is applicable to client-server environments in general. That is, TCP/IP and Ethernet are what they are, whether the software that runs on the network is UNIX or Microsoft Windows NT. Likewise, ATM is ATM, and T1 lines are oblivious to the lineage of your mail program or Internet browser.

However, this exploration of the group computing environment will now become more specific and, in so doing, will turn its focus to Microsoft. This chapter looks at the Windows NT operating system and some of the Microsoft BackOffice servers, including Microsoft Exchange, that support e-mail, conferencing, scheduling, resource sharing, and other activities that contribute to interaction in a collaborative environment. The next chapter will move on to Internet-related technologies and products that are bringing global information to the fingertips of end users everywhere.

You'll get a general overview in this chapter and the next

This chapter will not teach you how to use the products it describes; that's for other books to do. Nor will it probe far into the innards of the products; that's mostly fodder for programmers. You will, however, find out what the products are and what they're designed to do, and through this begin to understand their underlying precision, complexity, and sophistication. Along the way, you'll decipher many "buzzwords" that crop up frequently. In the end, you should be able to see how the software parts contribute to the networking whole, and you should come away with appreciation for the depth of the environment needed to enhance and support the growing corporate enthusiasm for the Internet, intranets, and the newly discovered possibilities of extranets.

An explanatory note

Because this chapter focuses on Microsoft products, you might wonder whether the book shortchanges you by ignoring other client-server and Internet software providers. To some extent it does, but then this is a Microsoft Press book. However, you can expect other books from other sources to cover products such as Netscape's SuiteSpot and Communicator and Sun's Java programming language. For now, it's a far, far better thing for you to make friends with new technologies one at a time. Wading through product comparisons while simultaneously attempting to sort the trees from the forest would cause not only confusion but some truly stinking headaches.

That said, on to some fascinating examples of mind over matter.

Network Software

Your network is in place, ready and able to send digital data representing crucial information across the country or around the world. But the network is nothing without the software that enables Jane to send her budget to John, Tom to collaborate with Harry on their report, Dick to check inventory and pricing from the field, and everyone to send messages to everyone else.

A network is nothing without software

Like the earth's crust, network software is composed of layers. Some layers are "thicker" than others, but all contribute to the whole. And, like the layers in the OSI model, each stratum in the network software environment focuses on a particular task. Of course, all layered structures also rest on something. The earth's crust floats on magma; the OSI model sits on hardware. And the layers of software that make up a collaborative, interactive network rest on an operating system foundation.

The software comes in layers

Operating Systems

Operating systems, whether they run on mainframes and minicomputers or network servers and desktop PCs, whether they are Windows, Macintosh, or Java-based, are all essential to the most basic activities of the computer. To the person using the machine, the operating system's most visible and essential role is that of providing (through the keyboard, mouse, and interface) the only way a human can communicate with applications and hardware. To the hardware and software, the operating system is the overseer responsible for opening and closing files, interacting with the network, moving information to and from disk, displaying and updating the screen, keeping track of mouse clicks, watching and using communications ports, and so on.

The operating system is the basis for everything

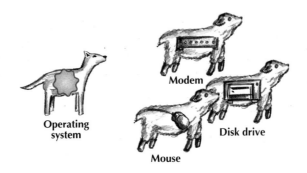

Operating system

Modem

Disk drive

Mouse

It's the mediator, interpreter, drill sergeant...and sheepdog

Without an operating system, each piece of hardware and software in the computer would have to be responsible not only for doing its own job but for interacting smoothly with every other component and program. Your word processor, mail program, disk drive, video card, modem, network adapter, printer port, and every other bit of code and circuitry would need to be much smarter—and more expensive—than it is. Without an operating system to protect programs from one another, monitor and service requests for processor time, and regulate memory use, chaos would be the normal machine state.

Two Paths to the Same Goal

Networking can be built in or added on

When networking becomes part of an operating system's job description, you find two paths to enabling computers to communicate with one another. One is by adding networking software to a stand-alone operating system, such as MS-DOS, that is designed to function in solitary splendor. The second, newer path is to incorporate networking capability within the operating system to provide an all-in-one solution. This is the path taken by Microsoft Windows 95, Windows NT, OS/2, Novell NetWare, UNIX, the AppleTalk protocols on the Mac, and other current operating systems.

A third, somewhat hybrid alternative is provided by the diskless or semidiskless workstations being developed by Oracle, IBM, and others as network computers (NCs). These also rely on operating systems, but not in quite the same sense as described in this chapter, which focuses on Windows/Intel (Wintel) computers in the server–PC-client model. NCs are described in more detail in Chapter 7.

Network computers march to a different drummer

Servers and Clients Again Operating systems with networking capability also come in two not always distinct varieties, *server* and *client,* which are optimized to match the differing capabilities and functions of the server and client machines on a PC-based network. Whereas a server operating system must concentrate on volume and resource management, a client operating system must concentrate on keeping its owner happy—on doing the work it's given as quickly and efficiently as possible. Although this description could actually apply to both the server and the client, the server's work involves keeping large numbers of client machines (and therefore their owners) happy, whereas the client's work is much more likely to involve an application such as a word processor, mail program, or spreadsheet over which the computer's owner is likely to go ballistic if spell-checking, opening a message, or recalculating figures takes an inordinate amount of time.

Just as there are servers and clients, there are server and client operating systems

Typical business networks have a variety of PC-based server operating systems to choose from, among them Windows NT, OS/2, Novell NetWare, UNIX, and the Macintosh OS (1997 incarnation) with its AppleShare and AppleTalk networking capabilities. Generally, these operating systems can function as either client or server, and they might very well come with desktop siblings; Windows NT Workstation, OS/2 Warp, and NetWare's workstation software are all smaller, less capable variations of their larger, server-based counterparts.

These are some well-known server operating systems

Platforms Discussions of operating systems, client or server, invariably touch on the issue of *platforms.* Just as in everyday life, a platform is a support—in this case, either the hardware "stage" on which the operating system performs or the combination of hardware and hardware-dependent operating system. Some operating systems, such as the Macintosh OS and OS/2, run on only one type of processor, OS/2 being designed for Intel-based processors, although it originally was also intended to support the PowerPC chip. Other operating systems, such as UNIX and Windows NT, are *portable,* meaning that they can be used on hardware based on different processors. Various forms of UNIX and Windows NT, for instance, run on both *CISC (complex instruction set)* and *RISC (reduced instruction set)* chips. CISC chips, which predominate on PCs, include the well-known Intel x86, Pentium, and Pentium Pro chips. RISC chips, which rely on fewer and simpler instructions for performing very low-level tasks such as addition, include DEC's Alpha, Sun's SPARC, and the Apple/IBM/Motorola PowerPC. (RISC architecture is generally believed to be faster than CISC; performance tests, however, do not always turn theory into practice.)

A Touch of History

Tradition and history have made UNIX the number-one operating system on networks...to date. Pronounced "you-nicks," UNIX is an acronym of sorts that stands for

Uniplexed Information and Computing System. The rather weird name is a playful dig at MULTICS (Multiplexed Information and Computing System), a failed earlier operating system for which UNIX was supposedly a "simplified" replacement. A longtime Internet staple and a fixture in academia, UNIX comes from the minicomputer world rather than the PC world. Even so, it has made its mark on the growth and development of PC-based client-server networks and the growing intranet movement in one crucial respect: protocols. TCP/IP, discussed in Chapter 3, was originally a staple of the Internet dominated by UNIX, even though today it has become the most widely supported set of protocols on client-server networks.

The original UNIX was—and still is—a powerful, text-based operating system reminiscent of a gargantuan MS-DOS but with even more cryptic commands. UNIX comes replete with utilities that, even to non-UNIX users, invoke a certain fondness partly because they have intriguing names, such as *grep* (pronounced the way it looks) and *vi* (rhymes with "high"). UNIX itself is available in a number of variants known by different names, depending on the type of machine they run on and/or the organizations that developed them.

UNIX is powerful and is either text-based or graphical

Widely known granddaddy versions of UNIX were developed by AT&T and at the University of California, Berkeley. These are known as the BSD releases. Another form of UNIX, known as X Windows, was developed at the Massachusetts Institute of Technology and provides support for a graphical user interface (similar but not related to Microsoft Windows) that makes UNIX easier to use. Because UNIX is still a significant network operating system, some names you're likely to hear include the following: A/UX for the Macintosh; AIX for the IBM RS/6000 RISC computers; LINUX, Xenix, and UnixWare for Intel processors; and Solaris for Sun SPARC (RISC) and Intel machines.

UNIX, from AIX to Solaris

The Server's Job

Network operating systems have more to deal with than clients do

Network operating systems are designed to concentrate on the "big picture"—tasks related to managing and servicing very large numbers of client requests, often simultaneously. For instance, a network operating system must provide strictly controlled access to large numbers of files, whereas a desktop operating system normally has to worry only about those on its local drives. Similarly, a network operating system must take responsibility for verifying user accounts, passwords, and user privileges (who can and who cannot view or change which files). The network operating system must also be held to higher standards of fault tolerance to ensure both continuous performance and the integrity of the potential gigabytes or even terabytes of information entrusted to it, and it must manage resource sharing, remote access, network administration, mail services, and all the other details needed to create the foundation for a smoothly functioning collaborative environment. All these server tasks can be divided into three categories:

It's about management

- Managing resources. This category includes such tasks as managing files, controlling access privileges (read-only, read-write, and so on), and coordinating activity so that multiple requests do not "attack" the same file, printer, or other resource at the same time.

- Managing users. This work includes maintaining permissions and lists of valid user accounts. Without the ability to separate valid users from intruders, network operating systems would open the door to a near anarchic, opportunistic free-for-all.

- Managing the network. Some of this work is related to performance, as in monitoring activity, pinpointing bottlenecks, and troubleshooting the network. Some of it is administrative, as in maintaining inventories of clients and of licensed software from other companies and centralizing software distribution and updates. Not all network operating systems have this capability built in.

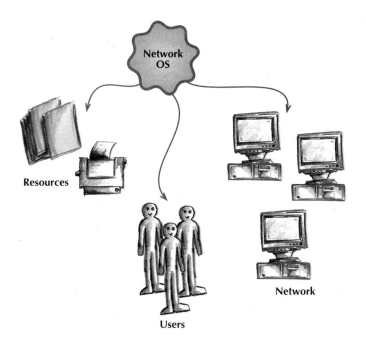

Network OS

Resources

Users

Network

In Pursuit of Efficiency

Because a network operating system has so much to handle, it needs to perform as quickly as possible. Three ways of building anywhere from a little to a lot of overdrive into the system are through the three M's: *multithreading, multitasking,* and *multiprocessing.*

Multithreading Multithreading is a star feature of Windows NT. A means of optimizing performance by utilizing processor time as efficiently as possible, multithreading is a marvel of complexity that takes advantage of the fact that the microprocessor, which is ultimately responsible for getting all the work done in a computer, runs at an incredible speed measured in minuscule units of time known as *cycles.* These cycles happen whether or not the processor is actually working on a task, and as fast as a computer is, it often happens that many cycles go by in which the processor is idle—for example, when a program is waiting for a relatively slow device, such as a disk drive, to retrieve data needed for "crunching."

The three M's

Multithreading is performance art starring the microprocessor and the operating system

With multithreading, the requirements and work of a *process* (an application such as a word processor) are broken out into separate tasks, or *threads,* and each of these threads is *executed* separately by the microprocessor. The threading itself—the breakdown into separate tasks—is controlled by the program that owns the tasks (the word processor or whatever). The *scheduling* of those threads—the order in which they are given processor time—is controlled by the operating system. Or at least it is when the system, like Windows NT or OS/2, supports *preemptive multitasking.* Multiple threads also help enable multiprocessing, which is discussed on the next page.

Multithreading

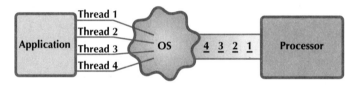

Multitasking One of the features of modern operating systems ranging from Windows 95 to Windows NT, OS/2, and UNIX is their seeming ability to handle more than one process (sometimes but not always synonymous with thread) at the same time. This ability, known as *multitasking,* makes it appear as though the computer is doing the equivalent of patting its head while rubbing its belly. It might, for instance, be downloading a file while it's formatting a document.

...by interweaving
tasks into the
processor's time

In actuality, multitasking is closer to a magician's sleight of hand in that no two tasks happen truly simultaneously on a single-processor computer. Instead, the processor's time is given over to each task or thread separately. Because the processor works so quickly, however, and because it can interleave time periods (known as *time slices*) devoted to different tasks rather than finish one task before starting on another, the jobs appear, to a human, to be handled at the same time. The trick, if you want to think of it that way, is in the fact that time, to a computer and its operating system, runs vastly faster than it does for people. To the machine, humans are somewhere between slo-mo and practically immobile.

Multitasking

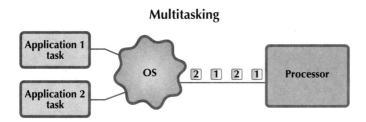

Multitasking can be implemented in either of two forms, *preemptive* or *nonpreemptive* (also called *cooperative*). In the former, the operating system controls who does what and when. It is able to override a task/thread, when necessary, to allow another, higher-priority task to run. In a non-preemptive operating system, tasks must essentially live by an honor code, determining for themselves when they are willing to turn the processor over to another task—a problematic situation, as you can imagine, if a greedy task takes over. Multitasking in either form, but especially when preemptive, has great benefits for a network operating system in terms of efficiency. On a busy server, for example, the advantages are obvious. When combined with multitasking capability on the client system, the gain is, again obviously, even greater because interactions between the server and the client system can be coordinated and controlled more effectively than if both, or either, were required to concentrate on, or give control to, only a single task at a time.

Multitasking benefits both the server and the client

Multiprocessing In situations in which very large amounts of traffic are relatively constant on a network, a network operating system can go multitasking one better by also supporting multiprocessing. A multiprocessing operating

In more demanding environments, multiprocessing can spell relief

system supports anywhere from several to many processors and can distribute the server's workload among them so that multiple tasks are truly being handled at the same time, one task per processor.

The two forms of multiprocessing: asymmetric and symmetric

Like multitasking, multiprocessing comes in two forms, in this case *asymmetric,* abbreviated as *ASMP,* and *symmetric,* abbreviated as *SMP.* In asymmetric multiprocessing, work is divided among the processors, with one or more handling operating system tasks only and the others handling applications only. In symmetric multiprocessing, any available processor can be assigned any process that needs doing. Because of the greater flexibility of symmetric multiprocessing, an SMP operating system offers two significant advantages on a network: First, greater *fault tolerance* because any processor can handle any task and so the failure of a single processor does not bring down the system; and second, better *load balancing* because the operating system can distribute the workload evenly across all processors and thus avoid bottlenecks caused by heavier demands on some processors than on others.

Symmetric Multiprocessing

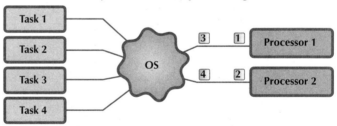

Windows NT Server

Windows NT is a growing force in client-server networking

Microsoft's entry in the network server category is Windows NT Server, which is rapidly becoming a network staple, especially in its new, improved version 4.0 form, which includes built-in *Active Server* support tailored specifically for intranet development and management (more about this in the next chapter). Version 5.0, due in 1997, will take network management further with Microsoft's *Zero Administration initiative* (described at the end of this chapter), which will reduce the cost and complexity of maintaining client PCs by centralizing control of the clients and their software.

Windows NT is a multithreaded, multitasking 32-bit operating system that comes in two versions: Server and Workstation. In its Server form, Windows NT is the backbone of the BackOffice suite of network tools, applications, and Internet services. In its Workstation form, it is a high-performance operating system that is essentially the same as Windows NT Server but optimized for the desktop.

It comes in two versions, Server and Workstation

Windows NT is happiest on a computer with considerable memory and disk space. The memory requirement is a minimum of 16 MB of RAM, but performance is much faster and smoother with 32 MB or more. In this respect, Windows NT is just like games, Windows 95, and applications such as Microsoft Office 97, all of which run better with more than the minimum required memory. Disk space depends on the type of system Windows NT runs on: On Intel-based servers, Windows NT settles into 125 MB or more of hard disk space; on RISC-based systems, 160 MB or more is more like it. In terms of server types, Windows NT works with anything from single-processor computers that are like more powerful versions of the one on your desktop to brainy SMP wonders that contain anywhere from 2 to 32 processors working in tandem.

Windows NT likes memory and disk space; it can work with up to 32 processors…

In addition, given that most networks are not "pure" PC or "pure" Windows but rather a conglomerate of platforms and even network architectures, Windows NT, like other server operating systems, is well aware of alternate lifestyles. It can, therefore, work alone or with other networks, including Novell NetWare, DEC Pathworks, and the venerable UNIX. It can connect to IBM SNA mainframes, Macintosh networks running AppleShare and AppleTalk, and any TCP/IP-based

…and with a variety of networks

networks, including, of course, the Internet. It also provides support for client computers running the Macintosh OS, OS/2, UNIX, MS-DOS, and the various flavors of Windows, including version 3.1.

It's elegant | **A Quick Tour of Windows NT Architecture** Although there is little, if anything, that a lay individual needs to know about the way Windows NT is constructed, its architecture, to those who appreciate such matters, approximates the cleanliness and functionality of a building designed by Frank Lloyd Wright. (Perhaps that's a slight exaggeration, but Windows NT is certainly put together at least as nicely as the average movie star.)

And layered | Like everything else in the network environment, Windows NT is built of layers. The layering comes from separate, task-specific components that, much like the layers in the ISO/OSI model, sit on top of the hardware foundation, like this:

Windows NT Structure

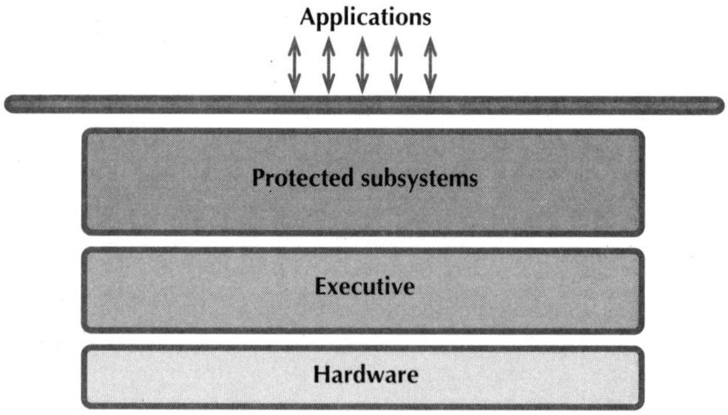

Applications

↑ ↑ ↑ ↑ ↑
↓ ↓ ↓ ↓ ↓

Protected subsystems

Executive

Hardware

And modular | In addition to being layered, however, Windows NT is also *modular*—that is, these layers are, themselves, divided into different components built into the two main segments of the operating system, the *executive* and the *protected subsystems* illustrated above.

The Executive and the Redirector The executive contains a number of components that are completely separate from one another but can communicate through tightly controlled methods. These components handle jobs such as memory management, operating system resource management, security enforcement, input/output both on the local machine and the network, and process (very roughly, task) management.

Executive components are separate but integrated

In terms of network functionality, one of the most important—though small in the scheme of things—pieces of the executive is a portion known as the *redirector*. When you have a network operating system running on a server and a client operating system running on a client, you need one other key ingredient: a pipeline between the two so that the client can send input/output requests to the server. That something is the redirector. Input/output requests can be generated either by the user (as in a request to move files from server A to server B) or by an application (as in a request to save document Y on server Z). In either case, because the request involves information that is not available on the local machine, the redirector is responsible for checking requests and, when appropriate, sending—redirecting—them to the server for processing. The Windows NT redirector is capable of routing requests not only to servers running the same or highly compatible operating systems but, with the help of additional system components, to other widely used network systems.

The redirector is part of the executive

The Protected Subsystems Windows NT's protected subsystems are divided into two groups, *integral* and *environment*. The integral subsystem carries out operating system tasks that apply to all of Windows NT. For example, the security subsystem, which is part of the integral subsystem and is described on page 97, verifies the person who logs on to the network as a valid user. The environment subsystems,

Two types of protected subsystems

on the other hand, provide support for application programs. Currently Windows NT supports not only its own environment, known as the Win32 subsystem, but two others: OS/2 and a widely used IEEE standard known as *POSIX,* which is supported by other operating systems ranging from UNIX to MS-DOS. In essence, the earlier diagram can be refined as follows to show the modular components of Windows NT.

Windows NT Components

Applications

Integral subsystems	Environment: Win32	Environment: POSIX	Environment: OS/2

Memory		Security Ref. Monitor	I/O	
	Resources			Etc.

Hardware

Two modes of work

When Windows NT is at work, the executive runs in a special mode known as *kernel* mode, which gives it ready access to system resources and the hardware. The executive handles tasks that, because they are critical to keeping the system functioning correctly, cannot be preempted by any lesser process. The protected subsystems, in contrast, run in a less privileged mode known as *user mode,* wherein they are limited to the use of clearly defined programming tools known as *APIs,* or *application program interfaces,* to access data and resources. These APIs define routines that perform very small, very specific tasks for the applications they service—the equivalent of one routine being responsible only for writing the letter *a,* another being responsible only for the letter *b,* and so on. APIs are the only way programs are allowed to interact with the operating system when they require attention.

Of Special Interest: Security Security on any network necessarily involves validating users and ensuring that people cannot either willfully or inadvertently access information or resources that they are not allowed to use. When a network becomes available to a wider audience, as over the Internet, security becomes a larger issue that involves protecting the network and its data from what, for want of better terms, must be called invasion, theft, and vandalism by unauthorized individuals. To contend with these issues, Windows NT supports a level of security known as *C2/E3* that conforms to the C2 security guidelines established by the United States Department of Defense and to the E3 assurance level defined by ITSEC (Information Technology Security Evaluation Criteria) of the United Kingdom and Germany.

Windows NT security is based on Defense Department guidelines

Level C security is one of four major grades ranging from A, the highest, to D, the lowest. Levels A and B require mathematical verification to ensure that security measures conform to strict guidelines, and even to be granted Level B classification a system must be proactive in searching and maintaining security. Level C, which applies to network operating systems such as Windows NT and UNIX, is divided into two classes, 1 and 2. Class 1, which is the less secure, requires a system that relies on password protection, is able to restrict access to documents and resources, and is able to prevent damage to the system. Class 2 includes these requirements as well as the following:

C2 is stricter than C1

- Discretionary access
- Authentication and identification
- Auditing
- Object (program code) protection

The Value of Modularity Although the structure of Windows NT seldom intrudes on anyone other than program developers, it's valuable to know at least something of its essential

Modularity means that Windows NT can be easily upgraded or added to

form because this executive/subsystem modularity means that Windows NT can easily be modified without worrying about how one change will affect some presumably unrelated portion of the operating system. Thus, it's possible for Microsoft to improve or add new technologies to one component without affecting the performance or integrity of the whole operating system. Because each component is so neatly self-contained, there is no need to worry that changes to one will cause unwelcome surprises in another—any more than there is reason to worry that changing a light bulb in the living room will blow out the one in the kitchen or make it turn blue. For network administrators, modularity means easier installation, maintenance, and upgrades. For everyone who uses Windows NT, the same modularity means a very stable operating system. And the benefits are noticeable too, at least to people who have worked closely with different operating systems. Windows NT *feels* good—and yes, one operating system absolutely can feel better than another.

Resource Sharing

Networks rely on shared files and printers (among other things)

Intriguing as structure can be, a network operating system is expected to function well, period. And in a collaborative environment, there are two highly visible ways in which its performance can be judged by all users: *file sharing* and *printer sharing*, both of which are strongly supported by servers (of the software kind) built into Windows NT Server and dedicated to each of these tasks. If someone cannot gain access to a needed file stored on the network server, that person is not likely to sing the praises of the operating system or the network. If that same someone cannot send a document to a network printer, that person will most likely be a thoroughly unhappy camper. Resource sharing, more than perhaps any other network feature besides e-mail, must function well and as reliably as possible. Ensuring that this happens is, of course, within the purview of the network operating system.

An aside of sorts: In dealing with networks, particularly when you become immersed in the many types of software used to create and maintain Internet and intranet web sites, you'll come across a host of products lumped into a category called *servers.* You might be somewhat confused because you've become used to the idea of hardware servers handing out files, access to printers, and so on, but you can think of each such additional software server as one more piece of a modular whole—a piece that exists to literally "serve up" a particular service or product. Though the services and products in the overarching "server" category can differ radically, each is based on the same essential job description: making something, from e-mail to news to databases, available to clients over a distributed, client-server network.

Servers can be hardware or software

Communication

Operating systems, dear to the heart as they are, are but one piece of the environment puzzle. In order to collaborate in any way (to send or receive information), you must have software that enables communication—task-specific software that is wedded to but separate from the network protocols, modem standards, routers, switching services, and other low-level ISO/OSI technologies described in earlier chapters. For program developers working with Microsoft tools, the communications intermediaries that bridge the gap between applications and service providers are the euphoniously named siblings known as *MAPI* and *TAPI* (pronounced "mappy" and "tappy") that deal with messaging and telephone requests. MAPI's goal in life is covered, briefly, in the description of Microsoft Exchange later in this chapter. We'll discuss TAPI here because it's part of Windows.

Communication is also crucial

TAPI

TAPI, which stands for Telephony Application Programming Interface, is a set of programming functions that allow computer applications, including word processors and spreadsheets, to use a telephone to support such desirable collaborative tools as:

- Conference calls
- Data transmission, including faxes and e-mail
- Remote access
- Interactive computing
- Information retrieval from bulletin boards, news groups, and so on

TAPI is strictly for program developers, but despite its complexity it is remarkably easy to understand in theory. Essentially, TAPI is a set of services that sits between the application that uses the telephone and the program— provided by the telephone service and known as a tele- phony *service provider*—that handles the actual hardware: phone, fax, modem, and so on. TAPI is bundled neatly into Windows and is the way, the only way, that a Windows- based application can manipulate a telephone.

TAPI can be used either between a desktop computer and a desktop telephone or through a LAN. It comes in two basic flavors, *Assisted Telephony* and *(Full) Telephony*. Assisted telephony enables application programs, such as spread- sheets, to make simple telephone calls without having to bother with the myriad details underlying the connection. A program developer can, for example, use the Assisted Telephony function *tapiRequestMakeCall* to enable an application to dial a telephone number previously stored by the user.

Full Telephony, which is not recommended for use in combi- nation with Assisted Telephony, supports more complex actions, including both inbound and outbound calling. It consists of three increasingly sophisticated levels known as *Basic Telephony, Supplementary Telephony,* and *Extended Telephony.* Basic Telephony supports good old POTS (Plain Old Telephone Service) and is compatible with all TAPI service providers. Supplementary Telephony increases an application's flexibility by supporting additional services such as call transfer and conferencing. In order to work, however, these features must be supported by the service provider as well as by TAPI. The highest level, Extended Telephony, pops the ball into the service provider's court by supporting device-specific features defined by individual service providers. This is the part that extends TAPI to meet the needs of service providers with unique or additional features not supported by Basic or Supplementary Telephony.

Forms of TAPI

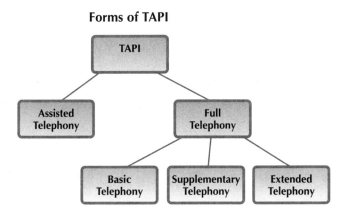

Exchange

Beyond the telephone, of course, there's *e-mail,* blessing and sometime bane of everyone in the enterprise, from the newest trainee to the most senior employee, right on up to the president and CEO. Where would many companies be without e-mail? Stuck with paper memos, trips down the hall, telephone tag, and sticky notes on doors, desks, and chair backs. How is a body supposed to "do lunch," anyway?

E-mail—'nuff said

In the Windows NT and BackOffice world, e-mail is practically a given and is provided by Microsoft Exchange Server. Exchange Server is, in fact, the BackOffice component that provides not only e-mail but also the assortment of built-in capabilities that most people clump together under the umbrella term *groupware*—programs for scheduling, tracking, and information-sharing. In addition to e-mail and groupware, Exchange Server also supports Internet access, a capability that is growing increasingly valuable as more businesses, wishfully or otherwise, come to see this standards-based global network as *the* information superhighway not only for communicating but for marketing, "over-the-counter" sales, real-time collaboration, and, eventually, tightly monitored, secure, time-critical transactions of the sort now handled by banks and other financial institutions. Exchange Server, of course, doesn't handle all these tasks, but it *is* the messaging piece of the Windows NT and BackOffice pie, and it *does* enable easy e-mail communication via the Web.

Exchange Server is scalable and thus can be used in situations ranging from small offices with a few dozen network clients to large, enterprise-wide networks with many thousands of users. In any such incarnation, it supports four different capabilities required for effective communication and group computing:

- Mail, which includes both e-mail and faxing
- Scheduling by time or task
- Public information sharing via bulletin boards and databases
- Information management in the form of filters, electronic forms, and application-development tools that give users and developers control of everything from sorting messages by topic to automatically deleting "junk" mail to automating tasks and creating reporting forms

Exchange, like Windows NT and (it sometimes seems) everything else in the networked world, comes in two forms: client and server. Unlike Windows NT Server and Windows NT Workstation, however, which are similar, Exchange Server is clearly delineated and separate from Exchange Client: The Server delivers the mail, the Client writes the love notes.

Exchange Server Exchange Server, rather obviously, resides on network servers. It has as its main job the storing, routing, and delivering of mail. The task sounds simple enough, but as with most computing there's much more to this than meets the eye. For example, consider that many people regularly communicate over the Internet with Exchange. Their messages, however, are not always plain-text variations on "Hi, how are you?" Often, the text is dolled up with color or italics. And often it is supplemented with attachments, such as word-processed documents, graphic images, and even sound or video to create a single *multimedia* document. That type of creativity is fine for the sender and the receiver, but all these types of information differ not only in appearance but in the way they are built up out of bits and bytes, and in the way they must be handled, especially when transmitted to a different platform or environment.

To enable such messages to pass freely and reliably over the Internet, Exchange supports two well-known mail standards known as UUENCODE (pronounced "you you encode") and MIME (as in a street performer). Both represent complex processes. UUENCODE converts files of all kinds, including programs, into ASCII, the *lingua franca* of computers. The files are transmitted in ASCII form and are then reconstituted at the receiving end by companion software called UUDECODE. The transformation, though technically dissimilar, is comparable to the digital-to-analog conversions practiced by modems. In a somewhat similar way, MIME,

Exchange also has client and server forms

Exchange Server is simple on the surface, but…

…the closer you look, the more you see

which stands for Multipurpose Internet Mail Extensions, provides a means for a mail program to define and convert into "traveling" form the types of information—such as plain text, rich (formatted) text, audio, and video—that make up a multimedia, or mixed media, message. Because MIME handles the conversion, the documents can travel safely to different platforms and, when "read" by a receiving program that also supports MIME, can be returned to viewable form.

Without support for standards like these, e-mail containing anything other than plain text would end up looking like missives from the planet Babel. And Internet mail is but one of the technicalities involved in the seemingly simple process of sending a message from here to there. Exchange, like most aspects of computer technology, takes on a considerable amount of complexity when seen close up. Indeed, when you look at the details it becomes easy to see that the content of the message is often far outweighed by the sophistication of the messenger.

Exchange supports connections to both Windows NT and other systems

Exchange Server is tightly integrated with Windows NT Server but not dependent on it. Thus, for example:

- Its support for commonly used transport protocols, including IPX/SPX and TCP/IP, allows Exchange to work with networks running such widely used networking software as Novell Netware, UNIX, and AppleTalk.
- Its support for industrywide standards such as SMTP (the TCP/IP mail transport), MIME, several Web-related protocols, and the CCITT's X.400 message-handling standard gives Exchange the ability to transfer mail over the Internet and to work with any X.400 messaging applications.

At the same time, however, the relationship between Exchange and Windows NT remains a close one. Exchange components mesh with Windows NT like pieces of a jigsaw puzzle so that, for instance:

It also has a symbiotic relationship with Windows NT

- Exchange components run as Windows NT *services,* acting like extensions of Windows NT itself.

- Exchange takes advantage of Windows NT capabilities—for example, its load-balancing ability on symmetric multiprocessing systems and its disk mirroring, which duplicates information on multiple disks to prevent data loss.

- Exchange, like Windows NT, provides centralized administrative tools, and both can work from the same basic "phone book" listing of users and resources to make life easier for the network administrator.

Two big buzzwords: digital signatures and encryption

- Exchange takes advantage of and extends Windows NT's security. On the e-mail front, this partnership means that user access to the Windows NT network also means access to Exchange without the bother of separate logons and the increased potential for lost or forgotten passwords. On a more public scale, this security provides a level of support for consumer safety and privacy on the free-for-all Internet. Exchange and Windows NT, for example, support coded identifiers that can be attached to a transmitted message or piece of software to verify for the recipient that the contents have not been altered during transmission. Another feature, *encryption,* uses binary strings known as *keys* to encode and decode messages. Encoded messages are unintelligible unless they are decrypted with the same keys. The length, in bits, of encryption keys and the right of law enforcement officials to gain access to these keys have been topics of discussion (or, to put it bluntly, debate) between the White House and industry leaders regarding the export of United States software to other countries.

Exchange across the enterprise

A bird's-eye view of Exchange as it is deployed throughout a corporation would show you one or more servers on which Exchange Server works to collect, transmit, route, and organize e-mail and other information. These servers would be grouped into one or more Exchange *sites,* usually based on geography, and each site would include numbers of *clients* who used Exchange for e-mail, scheduling, and information-sharing.

And on the desktop

Exchange Server and its clients, such as Exchange Client and the new Microsoft Outlook desktop information manager, work hand in virtual hand. To the person using Exchange, the connection is utterly invisible. To understand how Exchange works, at least from a practical point of view, you need only understand the Exchange Server and two concepts: *mailbox* and *public folder,* both of which are close analogs of the noncomputer items they are named after.

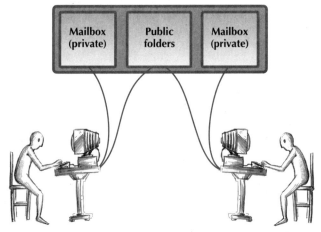

Exchange Server

Exchange Server is set up and run by the network or mail administrator and is the central repository for Exchange users. Only the administrator handles the server, but without it, Exchange doesn't work and people cannot send or receive mail through the client software on their computers. In addition to a post office address or account, however, each user must also have a mailbox, which is a private, secure portion of server space dedicated to that individual's message deliveries and storage. The post office and the mailbox are the key pieces required for sending and receiving e-mail. The user receives new messages in the *inbox* portion of his or her mailbox and sends new messages to other users via the server.

Exchange Server and mailbox

To enable groupware activities, Exchange also supports the concept of public folders, which are shown in the preceding illustration. Like mailboxes, public folders are portions of server space. In this case, however, the space is open to everyone or to a group of interested individuals, depending on how its creator, the folder's owner, chooses to share its contents. Inside this public folder, the owner can include items such as messages, pointers to the locations of documents either shared by individuals or stored on a network server, and faxes. To facilitate group discussions, invite opinions, and ease reporting requirements (as with time cards), the owner of a public folder can also create electronic forms with a Forms Designer to provide participants with an easy-to-use "template" on which to respond.

Public folders and forms design

Like Windows NT, Exchange Server is a piece of software made up of a number of components, some essential and some optional. The core components are the *Directory,* the *Information Store,* the *Message Transfer Agent,* and the *System Attendant.*

Core components and optional components of Exchange Server

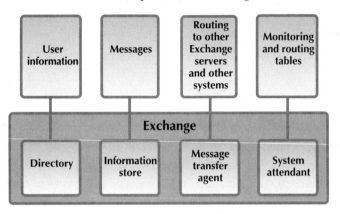

Core Components of Exchange

- The Directory is the master list used by Exchange Server to keep track of, find, and validate users who have been given access to the system by the administrator. The Directory is actually a database, and although its name brings telephone directories to mind, it is actually much more, for two reasons. First, it can be *replicated* and *synchronized* so that multiple identical copies can be maintained by widely separated servers and even client machines throughout a large enterprise. Second, it contains far more than names and "phone numbers." It also includes data on routing, addressing, shared resources, public folders, and even distribution lists that enable Exchange users to "broadcast" a single message to multiple individuals at once—for example, users can send revenue data to all people on the "finance" list or inform the entire "R&D" list of a groundbreaking achievement in molecular biology.

- The Information Store is similar to the Directory in that it's a database, but instead of containing information *about* users, it contains information *created by* users. This is essentially a message warehouse located on a server and is used to hold not only e-mail but attached documents, forms, and public folders.

- The Message Transfer Agent, or MTA, is the part of Exchange Server that actually routes mail to other Exchange servers. This is also the part that relies on X.400 and protocols such as IPX and TCP/IP to route mail to and from "foreign" networks and messaging systems. The MTA supports different *connectors* that are used to transfer mail between Exchange servers, allow remote access, and connect with the Internet and with other networks.

  The MTA is for going outside the neighborhood

- The System Attendant is the janitorial portion of Exchange Server. It is responsible for such tasks as monitoring server activity, logging mail activity, and building the databases known as *routing tables* that the MTA uses to transfer messages to other servers and networks.

  The System Attendant keeps things running smoothly

In addition to these core components, Exchange Server also works with a number of optional components that extend its flexibility and usefulness. These include:

Options you can add to the base model of Exchange Server

- The *Schedule+ Free/Busy Connector,* which allows individuals to view each others' free and busy schedule periods while setting up appointments, tasks, and other engagements across multiple sites in an enterprise.

- The *Internet Mail Service,* which enables people to send and receive mail over the Internet. This is where UUENCODE and MIME are involved.

- The *X.400 Connector,* which can be used either to connect Exchange sites or to route messages to systems based on the X.400 standard.

- The *Microsoft Mail Connector,* which is used to enable Exchange users to communicate with people on Microsoft Mail for PC and Microsoft Mail for AppleTalk networks.
- cc:mail Connector, which lets Exchange users send and receive messages from cc:mail users.

Outlook is a new
1997-vintage
Exchange client

Outlook No doubt you've heard of a new desktop tool known as Outlook, which comes alone or as part of the Office 97 application suite. Outlook looks like this:

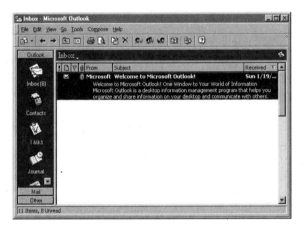

Outlook is a powerful addition to the Windows set of productivity software. Known as a *desktop* (or *personal*) *information manager,* Outlook works with Exchange but can supplant Exchange Client on the desktop if the user chooses. It offers much the same functionality as the more established Exchange Client, but it includes a number of enhancements that can make its window a kind of one-stop shopping center. Click an icon in the lefthand pane, and its contents immediately appear in the righthand pane. From the Outlook window, the user can access any of the following items.

- E-mail
- Public folders

- A number of built-in groupware and productivity applications, including a contact list, task manager, scheduler, personal journal, and an electronic notebook

- The My Computer icon in Windows 95 and Windows NT Workstation that represents the desktop machine and all its attached resources

- Any personal folders, including icons representing often-used network servers, that the individual cares to add to the lefthand pane of the Outlook window

Because Outlook is attuned to the Internet and does much more than handle mail and scheduling, it is covered in Chapter 6. For now, take a closer look at a more "traditional" mail client.

Exchange Client Connecting to Exchange Server is Exchange Client, which runs on the user's desktop and provides a single collection point called the *universal inbox* for all incoming messages, from e-mail to documents, faxes, and voicemail. Exchange Client consists of three main components:

There's a universal inbox on the desktop

- The client messaging portion, Exchange, which is responsible for all messaging-related tasks, including providing different, and customizable, *views* of message lists, public folders, and so on.

- *Schedule+,* which is the time-scheduling and task-scheduling component used to maintain contact lists, view schedules, and request and confirm group meetings.

- The *Electronic Forms Designer,* which is used for creating task-specific forms, such as time sheets or expense reports, that users can simply fill in and return electronically to the appropriate department or individual. Forms design ranges from easy to complex and can require programming skills. This is by far the most demanding of the three components, primarily because the others are so intuitive that even newcomers quickly become comfortable with at least the basics of using e-mail and scheduling meetings.

Under the hood of Exchange: remote procedure calls and MAPI

Although Exchange is easy to understand on the surface, it is also made up of a multitude of building blocks whose names can crop up in detailed discussions. Most are far more relevant to developers than to administrators or end users, but two in particular make their presence known in relation to Exchange: RPC and MAPI.

RPCs transfer information between the client and the server

RPC, which stands for *remote procedure call,* is basically the way that Exchange Server and Exchange Client communicate over the network. Acting something like a telegram (although that is not a technically accurate description), an RPC is a *routine*—a piece of program—that takes care of transferring information between the client and the server, independent of the network on which the client and server are running. In a sense, using RPCs for communication is like sending international mail. The contents of the message are meaningful to, and understood by, sender and receiver; the rest of the world doesn't matter, nor does the fact that delivery uses North American, African, or Far Eastern roadways.

MAPI provides a set of rules that allow messaging between different applications

While RPCs enable the client and the server to communicate handily, MAPI is an industry standard that enables messaging programs to pass information to each other. It is kind of a common language that can enable different programs to understand and work with one another easily. On the server side, MAPI enables Exchange to work with many different types of mail clients and services, such as online providers. On the client side, it enables Windows-based applications such as Exchange Client to send and receive mail with any MAPI server without having to fuss with details such as interpreting the recipient's e-mail address or working with the message server to contact the recipient's computer.

Like other APIs, MAPI works at a very low level, far from the view of the user, even though it is essential to even the simplest activities, including reading and deleting mail messages. Developed in collaboration with numerous software vendors, MAPI was created to describe and standardize features needed by modern-day messaging applications. Exchange, because it is built on a MAPI foundation, can (and does) work with any *message provider* (program) that is MAPI-compliant. MAPI is, essentially, the "post office and delivery" portion of a MAPI-compliant application—up to and including applications such as word processors and spreadsheets.

MAPI brings order to potential chaos

Groupware Components Aside from intranet *browsers* (more about these in Chapter 5) and custom software designed for specific purposes, such as searching a corporate database, Exchange is the most visible part—to the user—of the BackOffice collaborative environment. E-mail is familiar enough that it needs no extended coverage, but Exchange's other groupware components are likely to be harder to picture by those who are not familiar with it.

Group computing means other things besides e-mail

Scheduling, as already mentioned, is handled by Schedule+, an application that runs on Windows NT Workstation, Windows 95, earlier versions of Windows, and the Mac. Schedule+ is separate from Exchange Client but closely tied to it. Schedule+ includes the following capabilities, some of which (as assumed here) require user access to a network running Exchange Server.

Schedule+ offers individual and group scheduling as well as task management

- Views of the user's schedule by day, week, or month
- To-do lists that can group tasks by project; can include start and end dates, durations, and percent completed; and allow tasks to be electronically "checked off" when finished
- Contact lists that allow for business information, personal information, and notes; can automatically dial a phone number; and can both import contact

information from and export it to other systems and application programs

- Group scheduling in which individuals can, on a network, check participants' free and busy times before sending a single meeting request to all

Public folders are for getting the word out

Public folders are part of Exchange Server's Information Store and are used to hold messages, documents, forms, and other information that the folder's owner wants to make accessible to all or part of the organization. Behind the scenes, public folders, like most other parts of Exchange, are created and manipulated with MAPI functions. On the desktop, public folders appear as icons in the Exchange window and can be opened to display collections of shared information, usually relating to a single topic. Owners of public folders can create and delete them at will and, in situations in which the "public" represents a limited list of people, can use Exchange to determine the names of those who can access the folder(s). Public folders can be duplicated on additional servers to improve accessibility across a geographically far-flung enterprise. In addition, users can easily copy public folder contents onto their local hard drives for work off line—a considerable benefit for people using remote access and telephone lines to communicate.

The Forms Designer allows for custom solutions

The "groupware" part of Exchange is largely bundled into the Exchange Forms Designer, sometimes referred to as the *EFD*. The Forms Designer facilitates information sharing throughout a workgroup or even the entire enterprise in a number of ways, all based on electronic "forms" that can be designed either to request or to share needed information. The Forms Designer essentially provides the person creating a new form with a blank "sheet" on which to place a number of components, such as To, From, and Subject fields; list boxes; labels; and various buttons for printing, saving, sending, and so on.

Although the Forms Designer can be used by someone with no programming experience, it is frankly better suited to someone who is at least somewhat familiar with programming, especially because the Forms Designer does include advanced capabilities, such as support for menus and Help screens. The Forms Designer also supports MAPI and the form of programmability known as *OLE Automation* that enables applications to work together to share data, and it can be used with the Visual Basic programming language if developers need a richer environment for creating custom or enterprise-specific applications. (One example of such an application comes in a sample Exchange "form" that uses OLE and Visual Basic to create a chess game.)

But programming experience helps

The Forms Designer can be used in one of two ways: to create either *stand-alone* or *folder-based* applications. The former are not specific to any particular folder—telephone message slips, for instance—and are simply sent from one user to another. The latter, more focused applications are stored in public folders and are used for such purposes as tracking sales calls or creating *bulletin boards* where interested participants can post comments on specific topics which, depending on the latitude given to employees, can range from an electronic suggestion box to recommendations on good restaurants or the latest hit movies.

Forms can be wide-ranging or on a leash

Here are some common types of group-computing applications supported by Exchange and the Forms Designer:

And they can be used for many purposes

- Bulletin boards
- Individual reporting forms, such as time sheets or vacation schedules
- Information request forms, such as employee surveys
- Information distribution, such as the employee handbook (As described in the next chapter, this type of information is also easily posted on an intranet.)

- Tracking forms, such as customer contacts or project schedules
- Special-purpose forms that rely on Visual Basic to automatically gather information from databases

Tomorrow and tomorrow and tomorrow…

A Note About Coming Attractions Exchange, like other pieces of the BackOffice suite, is constantly undergoing enhancement and improvement. By the time this book is in print, a new version of Exchange Server, version 5.0, should be available or nearly so. Version 5.0 strengthens group and collaborative computing by supporting Web access and more Internet standards to open up wider communication paths both inside and outside the enterprise.

Database Management

Databases are essential

Related to, but not the same as, forms design is the whole area of database management in a collaborative environment. Databases might appear to be boring, technical aggregations of factoids, and database programs are, in fact, among the more difficult applications to master, but these applications are essential in an information-sharing environment.

Welcome to the information age

In the corporation, databases store both personal and nonpersonal information, ranging from employee records and payroll to customer lists and inventories. In the wider world, databases hold an amazing (some think chilling) amount of information on everything from automobiles to zoology, not to mention information on birth records, auto loans, stock sales, bank transactions, real estate listings, market surveys, and everyone's favorite: tax records. Databases are, in fact, so important that in late 1996 the United Nations considered databases one of the forms of intellectual property potentially worthy of international copyright protection.

How Databases Are Organized

Given that databases are omnipresent, it helps to know how they're organized—the better to understand how they're used. Whether the actual data in the database deals with personnel or payroll, invoices or inventories, cabbages or kings, is immaterial. The structure is the key.

At its heart, a database is simply a collection of information, just like a phone book, a world atlas, or grandma's recipe box. The difference is that a database is electronic, and its contents are clearly organized into a spreadsheet-like grid of columns called *fields* and rows called *records*. Each field contains a particular type of information about an entry, and each record contains all the fields for that entry. For example, your birthdate might be one of numerous fields in a personnel database; the aggregate of fields—including those for name, department, employee ID, and so on—would comprise a single database record about you.

In a database, data is arranged into fields and records

Fields	Emp ID	Dept	Name	SSN	Hire date	Etc.
Record 1	XXX	XXX	John Doe	XXX	XXX	XXX
Record 2	XXX	XXX	Jane Doe	XXX	XXX	XXX
:	:	:	:	:	:	:
:	:	:	:	:	:	:

This field-record structure is typical of both simple and complex databases, and it forms the basis for all the information retrieval that makes databases so valuable. Want to know if anyone in your building speaks French and reads Russian? Assuming that the appropriate fields for location and language proficiency are already in the database, all you need do is put together a *query* telling your database program what you want. The program will then put its *search engine* to work, sifting through the fields to retrieve only those records that match your specified criteria.

All databases have the same basic structure

For all but the most elementary needs, the type of database
program required for serious searching is known as a *relational database.* It is far more powerful, flexible, efficient,
and extensible than the much simpler type, known as a *flat-
file database,* which is often used for address books, contact
lists, and so on. Whereas a flat-file database is essentially a
single container into which a collection of data is poured,
a relational database is a deeper, richer construct of multiple
tables, each of which is a complete "mini-database" in its
own right, as well as a contributor to the much larger picture painted by itself and other tables containing related
information. To make flexible information retrieval possible,
a database designer can specify *relations,* or *joins,* based on
keys contained in fields common to two tables. These act as
a means of tying one table to another so that a single query
can search both to find needed information. Tables and
relations are difficult concepts to visualize and far more
difficult to implement properly, but the following illustration
shows a simple model that should help matters:

Fields	Emp ID	Dept	Name	SSN	Hire date	Etc.
Record 1	123	XXX	John Doe	XXX	XXX	XXX
Record 2	456	XXX	Jane Doe	XXX	XXX	XXX
:	:	:	:	:	:	:
:	:	:	:	:	:	:

Order #	Order date	Emp ID	Customer acct #
1011	XXX	123	XXX
1012	XXX	456	XXX

Although at first glance it might seem that breaking information out into multiple tables rather than keeping it all in one
place would be inefficient, in fact the reverse is true. Think,
for instance, whether the preceding type of structure would
work poorly or well for a music critic. Would this person be
more or less productive relying on a single massive database

with a zillion fields, or relying on one that separated the information into more manageable tables that dealt separately with, say, recordings, biographical data, bibliographic references, and previously published articles? (Assume, of course, that the database tables are linked effectively so that, for instance, the critic can use a single query to search both the biographical table for data on Bobby McFerrin and the recordings table for Mr. McFerrin's music.)

Within the enterprise, databases are often entrusted with, literally, the wealth of the kingdom, and they are, or should be, pampered, petted, and groomed accordingly. Depending on the data it contains, the database is almost certainly not open to creation, modification, or updating by just anyone. In some instances, as with data accessed via an intranet, anyone is free to view and download the information. In other cases, strict rules determine who is allowed to access the contents. In the BackOffice environment, the role of groom, guardian, and handler is assumed by a sophisticated *RDBMS (relational database management system)* named SQL Server—pronounced "sequel" or, sometimes, "ess-cue-ell," and standing for *Structured Query Language.*

SQL Server is a relational database management system for the enterprise

SQL and SQL Server

Databases—the collections of tables, fields, and records that make up a stored body of information—are created with database applications. This is all fine and good, except that one of the regrettable aspects of computing, on big machines as well as small, has been the development and sometimes proliferation of multiple, incompatible ways of doing the same thing. Everyone who grew up with PCs in the 1980s can remember the frustrations of dealing with word processors that could not use each others' files, spreadsheets that could not exchange numbers, and databases that were oblivious to all but their own records. Woe, in fact, to the person who used a PC in the office and a Mac or an Apple II at home.

Ease of access is required

As happened in many branches of computing, forward-thinking people looked around, saw chaos or potential chaos, and decided that across-the-board standards would be good. And so it happened that standards were created and adopted. From ASCII to ANSI, modems to monitors, the industry gradually moved—and is still moving—toward standardization. In the context of BackOffice and databases, two standards have emerged: SQL and ODBC ("oh-dee-bee-see", not "oddbuck").

SQL and ODBC are the solutions

SQL is a language of commands and keywords that is used to work with the records in databases: to read tables, insert new records, delete old records, update modified records, and even to access information in "foreign" databases created with different applications. Adopted as a standard by the ISO in 1986, SQL support is now built into most, if not all, widely used database management systems. In the beginning, however, there were variants of SQL. In an attempt to smooth out the differences between them, industry leaders from both the hardware and software communities developed what is called *CLI (Common Language Interface)* to act as a common denominator that would enable different SQL products to interact. In a further refinement, Microsoft developed an API known as *ODBC (Open Database Connectivity)* to serve as a standard for databases running on the Windows operating system.

SQL Server is integrated with Windows NT

As for SQL Server, it is part of the BackOffice suite and is Microsoft's SQL-based database platform designed specifically for use in a distributed client-server (as opposed to a stand-alone desktop or mainframe) environment. Tightly integrated with Windows NT, SQL Server is a scalable RDBMS that has built-in C2 security for safeguarding transactions, centralized management features, and the ability to replicate databases on different servers automatically to maintain uniformity across all copies of a database—such as an inventory—throughout the enterprise.

Microsoft's alternative to another respected database, Oracle, SQL Server is used by organizations as diverse as NASDAQ, General Electric, Federated Department Stores, Windermere Real Estate, and the Texas Department of Public Safety and is used in a variety of situations ranging from standard database access to intranets, real-time online searches, and time-critical applications.

It's widely used for some very large databases

To see how actual organizations are using SQL Server—and other BackOffice products—go to the Microsoft web site at *www.microsoft.com*. Look for Solutions pages. SQL Server solutions, for example, are at *www.microsoft.com/SQL/ websites.htm*.

Database Considerations The mechanics of getting and keeping a large database functional are many, subtle, and technical. For users, it's probably enough to know that someone, somewhere, created a front end—preferably user-friendly—through which you can query, search, and update the database. From a management or decision-maker's point of view, however, evaluating a large-scale, client-server database platform involves a number of important considerations, among them:

Points to consider

- Speed, or cost per transaction
- Connectivity to existing mainframe systems
- Security of both data and user transactions
- Replication and synchronization on multiple servers
- Usefulness as a development tool—for example, in integrating with off-the-shelf applications as well as in creating client applications and value-added products and, of course, in building interactive Internet and intranet web pages

SQL Server handles these tasks and more. Designed and optimized for the Windows NT environment, it is integrated with the other BackOffice servers, such as Exchange and the Internet Information Server (described in the next chapter) to make development across applications easier. It is scalable, handling databases as small as 4 GB to those as large as 100 GB, and can support from a few to thousands of users. To increase performance, SQL Server runs on SMP systems and can also distribute workload by taking advantage of *clustering,* a process in which a single large database is distributed over multiple servers, each of which carries part of the total load. In its latest version, 6.5, SQL Server also includes a feature called the *Distributed Transaction Coordinator* that eases the process of creating distributed applications by automating transaction management on multiple servers.

Replication From a moderately geekish standpoint, one of the most fascinating aspects of an enterprise-wide RDBMS is its ability to *replicate* databases on multiple servers, maintaining and updating the data in each copy so that everyone has access to current information. Without such consistency across servers, collaboration and information sharing can easily become more confused than helpful and can lead to costly mistakes.

To handle replication, SQL Server relies on three different mechanisms: a *publication server,* a *distribution server,* and a *subscription server.* As these names indicate, SQL Server's solution to database replication is based on, of all things, a print-based metaphor. Thus, the server providing the source database is known as a *publisher* or publication server, and the server that receives replicated content is known as a *subscriber* or subscription server. The material itself, if coming from a single database table, is known as an *article,* and a collection of articles is known as a *publication.* Sometimes the same physical server can act as both a publisher and a subscriber, handing out data from one publication and receiving data from another. Carrying the journalistic metaphor a little further, SQL Server also uses an intermediary, a *distributor,* or distribution server, which takes the content to be replicated from the publication server and sends it to each subscription server (there can be more than one) that expects to receive the information. In this way, the distribution server acts very much like the newspaper or magazine "middleman" who moves the printed media from the publisher to newsstands, stores, and other distribution outlets. The process can be diagrammed as shown below, but it's important to remember that three *physical* (separate) hardware servers are not necessarily involved in moving information from the publisher to the end user because the same server can function in more than one capacity.

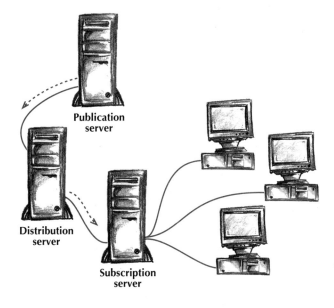

Publication server

Distribution server

Subscription server

In the SQL Server world, subscriptions themselves come in two varieties, labeled with names you'll hear frequently in the Internet and intranet world: *push* subscriptions are those in which the publisher controls events by sending information to one or more subscribers in a broadcast kind of activity; *pull* subscriptions are those in which the subscriber controls events by choosing when (and whether) to gather

Push information out or let people pull it in

information from the publisher. Push and pull mechanisms, especially with regard to advertising and broadcasts customized to user preferences, are a very big topic in the Internet world right now, primarily because the push approach (a) can help people find information quickly and (b) allows advertisers to target selected markets. On the intranet front, push techniques can enable intranet administrators to easily update lists and tables of data stored and made available as HTML-based Web documents.

A lot happens in distributing data

The actual process of distributing information, whether push or pull, is accomplished in SQL Server through a mechanism known as a *transaction log.* This log is created and maintained by the publisher of a database destined for replication, but it does not itself represent either a source or destination database. It is, rather, a collection point for transactions—records—that need to be added, updated, or deleted from a copy of the source. In moving transactions from the publisher to the subscriber, SQL Server relies on a *log reader* that moves *committed* (all-done) transactions to the distribution database, and on an initial *synchronization* process that ensures that both the source and destination databases start out as a matched pair before any updates are made to the copy.

Consistency and data integrity must be maintained

Even with synchronization, however, one large potential problem raises its head when you think about replicating an important database on multiple servers: Who maintains control? Suppose, for instance, that you have a database residing on an East Coast server, but you want to make it accessible on the West Coast and in Europe, Africa, and Asia. Because of time zones, modems, and local speed of access, the easiest solution is to replicate the database on regional servers. But how do you ensure that everyone, everywhere, sees the same consistent, accurate information and that your poor database isn't deluged with electronic versions of "change it this way"… "no, change it *this* way" and "I need this record"… "no, *I* need it"?

SQL Server helps maintain data integrity and consistency in a number of ways, some of which are listed below:

- *Automatic synchronization.* Briefly described in the preceding section, automatic synchronization ensures that publication and subscription databases are identical *before* any or all of the source data is replicated on other servers. Such synchronization is essential if accurate and consistent copies of your data are to be maintained across multiple servers in a distributed environment.

  SQL Server relies on synchronization and other tools

- *Constraints to replication.* These constraints, which can be applied by the database developer, can ensure that changes can be made *only* to the original (source) database. Replicated versions consisting of all or part of the source are *copies* that reflect the source information, and SQL Server can automatically reject attempts to change or update source data.

  Constraints keep changes under control

- *Record locking.* Locking means that records being worked on—updated, added, or deleted—are temporarily blocked to other users so that one operation does not interfere with another. This locking occurs rapidly, in nanoseconds. Under the control of SQL Server, locking is both automatic and invisible to the user.

  Locking blocks multiple access to the same record

- *Programmable server.* If SQL is a database programming language, it stands to reason that SQL Server is programmable. True, but in this case server programmability has a direct impact on data integrity, because SQL Server allows developers to store business-wide policies and rules on the server, *with* the data. So what? So when rules change, they can be changed once—on the server—and shared among client applications. There's no need to build complex sets of rules into each and every client database distributed throughout the enterprise, and

  Programmability makes wide-scale updates easier

so this programmable server provides not only consistency and integrity but savings in time and development costs as well.

Redundancy prevents loss of data

- *Data redundancy.* To ensure that critical information is not lost, even temporarily, because a server "goes down," SQL Server includes built-in replication that allows such databases to be maintained on multiple servers. These redundant copies can even be held in readiness as *warm* backups that can be brought on line quickly if disaster strikes the main server.

Security Data security is always a prime concern. Within the enterprise, SQL Server provides for expected types of security by allowing database owners to restrict access, both in terms of what users can do (read-only, for instance) and in terms of who can view, use, or change a database. In addition, since SQL Server is tightly integrated with Windows NT, the usual network logon process ensures that only valid users of the network can gain access to information on any of its servers. This single logon procedure also reduces administrative headaches by, if nothing else, reducing the number of "Help, I forgot my password" calls.

Three types of security

All told, SQL Server supports three types of security:

- *Integrated,* in which SQL Server security joins forces with Windows NT security so that users log on to both the Windows NT network and gain access to SQL Server with a single network ID and password. This type of security is based on a single type of network connection known as a *trusted* connection—that is, one in which the workstation connecting to the network server is running a protocol that supports *authenticated* connections. Clients with this capability include those running Windows NT, Windows for Workgroups, and Microsoft LAN Manager with Windows or MS-DOS, as well as those using the Novell NetWare IPX/SPX protocols from Microsoft Windows 3.1.

- *Standard,* in which SQL Server validates the connection. Standard security requires the user to type in a SQL Server ID and password.
- *Mixed,* in which SQL Server bases validation on either integrated or standard security, depending on the type of connection, trusted or *nontrusted.*

SQL Server also supports encryption of passwords and data to increase security between linked networks, and it enables encryption of stored procedures for safety as well as to maintain the integrity of programs stored on a server.

ADC Even though the Internet and intranets are not discussed until the next chapter, brief mention of a new Microsoft technology known as *Advanced Data Connector (ADC)* fits nicely here to close out the description of SQL Server. ADC is a web-based technology that is closely integrated with SQL Server. Primarily a developer's tool, ADC is based on the ActiveX programming technology (also described in the next chapter). It's importance from a managerial or supervisory viewpoint, however, is easily explained: ADC marries the power of the Internet to the power of SQL Server. With ADC, it's possible to create easy-to-find, easy-to-navigate applications that provide users with both the intuitive, page-based metaphor of the Internet and the power of a client-server corporate database—a healthy partnership for distributing and gathering needed information.

ADC joins databases and the Web

Mainframe Connectivity

Not all networks
are homogeneous

Enterprise networks, although somewhat tangential to
"pure" LANs and WANs, are an important part of any large
corporation. What are they exactly? Probably the norm
rather than the exception. The blending of traditional minicomputer and mainframe technology with the newer world
of PC-based and distributed client-server technology, enterprise networks are those in which PCs connect to large host
computers to share information and resources.

Computers are
choosy about
communicating

In theory, you would think that since most computers are
binary devices, a simple cable would be all that's needed
to connect a PC, Windows-based or otherwise, to an IBM
mainframe computer. Well, not so. As you saw in earlier
chapters, computers are very picky not only about who they
talk to but about how they communicate with one another.
And so it is with the PC-mainframe connection.

Terminal Emulation

Mainframes expect a
certain world order

In its traditional universe, a mainframe computer expects to
find an unthinking, utterly obedient dumb terminal tied like
a worker bee, a drone, to the end of any communications
line. PCs, being both more egalitarian and far more intelligent, don't fit this picture. Yet more often than not, the
computing facilities in large organizations are built on a mix
of systems: Wintel PCs, Macs, UNIX workstations, and
mainframes.

PCs usually must
emulate dumb
terminals

Traditionally, stand-alone PCs entering the mainframe environment communicated with their larger cousins through
terminal emulation hardware or software. Terminal emulation, despite sounding like a hopeless case of "I wanna be
just like you," is actually a process that enables a PC to
pretend it is a dumb terminal of the specific make and
model expected by a mainframe. In the newer PC–client-
server environment, however, Windows NT and BackOffice

provide two additional means of opening up communications: a protocol known as *DLC (Data Link Control)* and a complex but invisible-to-the-user solution known as *SNA Server.* First, though…

SNA

SNA, pronounced "ess-en-ay," is short for *Systems Network Architecture.* Designed by IBM to enable any of its computers or peripherals to communicate with any other, SNA is a proprietary and intriguing multilayered architecture that runs the gamut from the physical (hardware) layer through a top layer called *transaction services.* Although the names are different, the various SNA layers are roughly comparable to those in the seven-layer ISO/OSI network model.

SNA is a network architecture

SNA	ISO/OSI network model
Transaction services	Application layer
Presentation services	Presentation layer
Data-flow control	Session layer
Transmission control	Transport layer
Path control	Network layer
Data-link control	Data-link layer
Physical control	Physical layer

SNA is essentially a complex set of specifications that defines different types of protocols to enable communication between an SNA mainframe and various devices, including printers and terminals. Originally designed for a network in which mainframes sat at the top of a hardware hierarchy, SNA now also covers peer-to-peer communications and PCs on networks through an extension known as *APPC (Advanced Program to Program Communications).*

It now covers peer-to-peer communications and network PCs

APPC specifies the types of communication links that are used between different devices, such as printers and PCs. The devices themselves are categorized as *physical units* (or *PUs*) and *logical units* (or *LUs*). The difference between the

APPC deals with both physical and logical devices

two categories is somewhat blurry, because the same device can be both a physical unit, meaning an actual device on the network, and a logical unit, meaning a virtual "device" that corresponds to a single network session (an instance of a specific application program). But all that anyone other than a network guru needs to know is that a PC can represent both a PU, meaning a node on the network, as well as one or more LUs, each representing a different application session—for example, e-mail and access to a SQL database—on the PC.

DLC

DLC enables a Windows NT computer to connect to a mainframe

DLC—the protocol, not the SNA layer—is built into Windows NT Workstation and Windows NT Server. Any computer running either form of Windows NT and connected to an Ethernet or Token Ring network can use this protocol to communicate with an IBM mainframe and/or with certain peripherals (such as printers that hook directly into the network via an adapter rather than being connected to a computer that, in turn, connects to the network and acts as a server for the printer.)

For other situations, there's SNA Server

DLC is a fine solution for Windows NT clients, but in the real world not all PC clients run Windows NT. Many run Windows 95, Windows 3.1, MS-DOS, or OS/2, and Macintosh computers obviously run the Macintosh operating system. In addition, large organizations have large LANs and need considerable amounts of both flexibility and connectivity to integrate these LANs with their host computers. In such environments, the solution—Microsoft's, anyway—is SNA Server.

SNA Server

It's something like a gateway

SNA Server links mainframes and client-server networks by sitting between the mainframe and the LAN on a separate server computer that essentially filters the view seen by the machines on either side of the protocol fence.

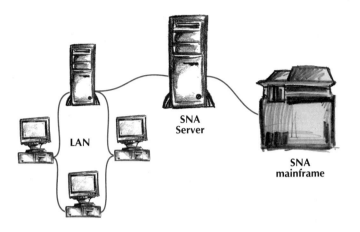

LAN

SNA
Server

SNA
mainframe

To the mainframe, SNA Server represents the LAN as a group of PUs and LUs. To the clients on the LAN, SNA Server represents the mainframe as just another server that they can communicate with freely.

Although the SNA server computer must run the SNA protocols required to communicate with the mainframe, the client computers not only can be running Windows, MS-DOS, OS/2, or the Macintosh operating system, they can also use their normal network protocols, such as TCP/IP or IPX/SPX, to communicate with the server and, through it, with the mainframe. The result, to those who use the network, is a clean, invisible means of accessing either Windows NT servers or the mainframe whenever and however they want. (Application development, however, as your programming staff will tell you, is another story and is not necessarily a trivial job for this or any other environment.)

SNA Server mediates between the network and the mainframe

Because speed and ease of access are essential on a smoothly running network, SNA Server also performs a number of jobs behind the scenes. For instance, because it is integrated with Windows NT, it uses the same security and thus avoids the multiple-password hassle. In addition, SNA Server moves the communications burden from the network client to the server and so allows the client machine to use its own resources more effectively. In terms of user demand, SNA

And it makes life easier for client computers

Server itself can support up to 250 connections and up to 10,000 individual sessions per server, while automatically balancing the workload across connections and servers for peak performance.

Controlling the Cost Beast

Of course, cost is a factor

This chapter has covered many, though not all, of the bits and pieces of networked computers, operating systems, and applications. However interesting you might have found these components, if you are in a managerial, IS, or supervisory role, one very important question has probably crossed your mind: How much does this cost in time and money? The exact figures obviously depend on the size and complexity of your organization and, of course, on whether some, most, or all employees have computers on their desktops. Then, too, there's the issue of whether you have a well-seasoned, mature network in place or are at some stage of the deployment cycle. Many organizations are also actively planning Internet and intranet development efforts so they can establish a presence in the "global village," and these not insignificant costs must also be factored in. Finally, in addition to all this, there are ongoing considerations such as:

There are many enterprise-specific considerations

- The frequency with which you update capital equipment and software
- The amount of custom development you require (personnel or contractor expenses)
- The ease with which individuals in the organization learn, adapt to, and use computer hardware and software (training costs)
- The amount of non–work-related activity that occurs on the Internet (if you provide access) or with such, uh, stress relievers as Solitaire, Hearts, and other computer games (productivity costs)

These critical but highly individual factors aside, however, BackOffice and Windows offer two administrative aids to help manage the network and control costs. One, already available, is known as *SMS (Systems Management Server).* The other, to be supported in future versions of Windows, is called the *Zero Administration initiative.*

SMS and the Zero Administration initiative can help

SMS

SMS has two goals in life: to centralize network management and to ease the distribution of software and software updates to client systems. A Windows-based network management tool that relies on both built-in and Windows NT security features, SMS works with both small and large networks. It is also designed to support a growing and changing network without requiring reinstallation. SMS allows the network administrator to do all of the following from a central location:

SMS centralizes management

- Observe each PC connected to the network
- Account for installed software as well as update and install operating systems and applications at times chosen to avoid lost productivity and traffic overloads
- Install software on specified servers for shared use by specified groups of individuals
- Inventory hardware and keep track of machine configurations
- Monitor machine performance
- With the user's permission, control a Windows NT, Windows, or MS-DOS computer remotely when needed for troubleshooting or training
- Store important hardware and software information in a central and expandable database
- Define desktop setups for individuals that they can use from any machine connection to the network
- Monitor network traffic—that is, "sniff" the network

Zero Administration Initiative

It's still to come, but it promises increased efficiency...

Building on and extending the philosophy embodied in SMS is Microsoft's Zero Administration initiative, which is designed to allow organizations to build on their investments in Windows while continuing to minimize the administrative tangle for network administrators by providing control over PC management and application installation. As Bill Gates stated in an October 28, 1996, Microsoft press release, "Customers want to be able to update software without touching every machine and allow users to seamlessly move from one machine to another. And they want to gain these benefits without introducing the unnecessary complexity of new, incompatible hardware and operating systems."

...and improved centralized control

In all, the Zero Administration initiative outlines the following four features:

- The Automatic Desktop, which will automate both operating system updates and application installation.
- Server-based information on the status of users' applications and desktop setups, plus the ability to "reflect" data to a server to provide easy access to a familiar computing environment and needed information regardless of the individual's location.
- Centralized administration and control to enable network administrators to monitor client systems and maintain secure, compatible configurations that work in harmony for groups of users.
- Implementation of client-server technologies in Microsoft's Active Platform for application development. The Active Platform is focused on Internet and intranet application development (described in the next chapter). Its inclusion in the Zero Administration initiative essentially provides network developers and administrators with the ability to rely on easy-to-use, "thin client" Internet capabilities as well as traditional desktop applications.

Support for the Zero Administration initiative will be built into the next major release of Windows NT Server (version 5.0), and some or all capabilities will appear in future versions of Windows 95 and Windows NT Workstation.

Chapter Five

Internet/Intranet Technologies

"**W**e have met the Internet, and it is us."

Tens of millions of people would probably use some form of that twist on Pogo Possum's famous "We have met the enemy" line to describe the Internet, the cyberphenomenon of the 1990s. Sometimes rollicking, sometimes scurrilous, often thoughtful, and occasionally profound, the content of the Internet mirrors "the enemy" quite well. In case you haven't seen it, this is the "us" we're talking about:

The Internet is everywhere

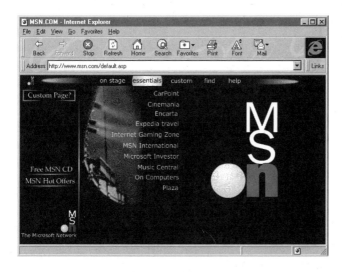

From home to business, from sea to shining C, people use the Web to communicate and to tour millions of sites as if they were visitors to a high-tech supermall. Currently an estimated 10 to 15 percent of end users are at least marginally involved in Web surfing, and their numbers are expected to grow as explosively as the dandelions in your lawn, especially if Web TVs and President Clinton's ambitions succeed, bandwidth improves, and a lot of hype is to be believed.

Some people claim to be addicted to the Internet. They probably are. After all, the world is also populated by compulsive joggers, shoppers, and string collectors. What is it that so intrigues these Internauts? Information. Entertainment. Both. Sometimes neither.

The Internet, or rather the multimedia-based part of the Internet known as the World Wide Web, is a virtual universe (*virtual* as in virtual reality) populated by people and places ranging from Wall Street to government, schools, universities, Fortune 500 corporations, baseball teams, auto dealers, movie studios, cooks, programmers, writers, booksellers, environmental activists, and fans of hot pepper sauce. If you want to buy a horse, sell a horse, or trade a horse, chances are that you can do so on the Web.

Part of the Web's capabilities are used for interactive pastimes, such as telephony, videoconferencing, and newsgroups, as well as for live (real-time) chats in which all manner of topics from business to technology to games to…stuff…are discussed in private or semiprivate electronic "rooms." Most of today's Web, however, is still primarily distributive. Individuals and organizations typically create web sites telling about themselves and offering information, services and merchandise, software, or other products. E-mail addresses and predesigned response forms are common on such sites, as are plain old telephone numbers, but as hardware and software development continue, these types of interactivity will no doubt become just part of a richer, more fully collaborative World Wide Web.

As interesting as the Web happens to be, and as easy as it can be to cruise it, there's an enormous amount of technology supporting this global network. This technology not only runs the *hosts,* or servers, and the communications facilities that make up the Web, but as it evolves it will determine how people use the Web to fulfill personal and business needs.

Creating this new, improved Web is obviously not a trivial task. (Neither, assume most people, is achieving its promises of glory and riches.) As a result of the former, if not the latter, the task of bringing this still-evolving world into being has primarily fallen to telecommunications companies and to hardware and software companies of all sizes, from the giants Microsoft, Netscape, IBM/Lotus, and Sun Microsystems to smaller organizations involved in every aspect of Internet growth and management from the technical to the artistic.

Origin of the Species

The World Wide Web, often abbreviated as W3 and sometimes wryly known as the World Wide Wait, is part of the massive network of servers spread out over the globe that make up the Internet. Physically, the Internet is the widest of wide area networks. Culturally, it ranges from lawful to anarchic. These days, the Web in particular is becoming increasingly business-oriented and transaction-oriented.

An earlier chapter described the World Wide Web as the graphical, or multimedia, part of the Internet. That's true, but brief definitions, though often easy to remember, are not always as accurate as they could be. By looking deeper into the Web, you can come to see it in its Internet context,

Ease of use does not mean simple

The Web is the Internet with sound and pictures

where it is not only a place of sorts (as most people think of it), but also a concept, a tool, and most of all a new computing paradigm.

The Internet

Thank the DOD for the Internet…

The Internet, where it all started, began as a U.S. Department of Defense project to link computers at universities and research and defense labs around the country. The precursor of today's Internet was created in 1969 as a packet-switched network known as *ARPANET* (after *ARPA,* the government's Advanced Research Projects Agency). ARPANET at first linked only a few computers—big ones— but it gained in popularity with academics and researchers over the following years, and by the early 1970s new sites (nodes) were connecting to the network at the rate of about one a month.

…which actually started out as several networks

In 1975, ARPA brought the growing network under its wing but also limited access to institutions with ARPA-related interests. In response, academics and researchers formed non-ARPANET networks of their own, chief among them *CSNET (Computer + Science Network),* the whimsically named *BITNET (Because It's Time Network),* and *NSFnet (National Science Foundation Network).*

TCP/IP arose to standardize communications

With the creation of multiple networks, however, the bugaboo that still dogs computing raised its head in the form of incompatible communications protocols. In response, the networking community, sponsored by ARPA, developed a brand-new set of "universal" protocols—those you now know as TCP/IP. With the development of TCP/IP, the Internet was truly born. It is now a massive structure consisting of several network levels known as *backbone networks* (of which NSFnet is one), *mid-level networks,* and *stub networks,* as shown on the next page.

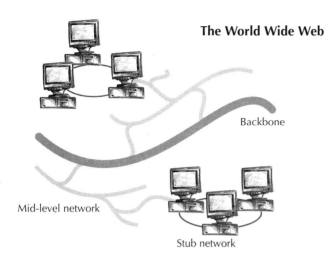

The World Wide Web

Backbone

Mid-level network

Stub network

The World Wide Web

Although most people think of the World Wide Web as the Internet, it is not. True, the Web is part of the Internet and it cannot be peeled away from the Internet's non-Web portions; but in actuality, it's better to think of the Web more as a highly graphical collection of multimedia documents than as some physical entity making up part or all of the Internet.

Like the larger Internet, the Web has a global presence and the same freewheeling spirit, but it is also dolled up with a kaleidoscope of color and sound. The Web is flash, dash, and pizzazz, and soon it will be video and 3-D environments too. But attractive as these adornments are, the Web is more than a pretty face. It is, and has been since its inception, a new computing paradigm. At its core, the Web is a tool based on a once-radical concept originally known as *hypertext* but now more often referred to as *hypermedia* because of the variety of information types combined in web documents.

Hypertext is the foundation of the Web

This concept, which has truly changed not only the way people view the Internet but the way they navigate from one document to another, began at the CERN particle physics laboratory in Switzerland in 1989. At a time when the Internet had already hit its stride in its (academic) home community, the World Wide Web was designed to allow scientists in different countries to collaborate and share their work easily through the use of hypermedia *links* embedded in documents. These links would enable the viewer to jump from document to document, or document to picture, or picture to picture, or whatever.

Links allow you
to go wherever
you want...

Links might not seem like such a big deal, but the beauty of hypermedia linking is that jumps can go anywhere. They can be as *nonlinear* as anyone's individual thought patterns can be. Thus, a person wanting to get from document A to document Z can go straight there, without having to wade sequentially through B, C, D...and all the way through X and Y. With hypermedia, you can move forward, backward, sideways—the Web doesn't care. Meander from idea to idea, document to document and, these days, from web site to web site in whatever order you want, following the way you think or the mood you're in. This ability to browse with a computer the way you browse in a library is, above all, what makes the Web so special.

Think of each web document as a *page* (which is the actual term used) and each link on a page as a live cross-reference to another page, and you have the concept of the World Wide Web in a nutshell, as shown on the next page.

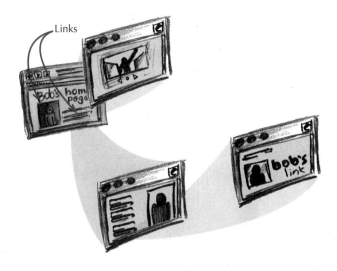

Links

Mosaic: The Graphical Ancestor

The Web, as created at CERN, soon attracted a following, but it did not really begin its climb into the stratosphere until 1993, when an easy-to-use mouse-and-multimedia-oriented program named Mosaic was released by the National Center for Supercomputing Applications (NCSA) at the University of Illinois in Urbana-Champaign. Developed by a group including then-computer-science-student Marc Andreessen (now of Netscape fame), Mosaic became the product that launched a million sites and more.

Mosaic was born at the University of Illinois

The first of a group of programs known as *browsers,* Mosaic integrated the many different types of data on the Internet, doing so seamlessly in the background and thus making this information in all its variety easily available to ordinary mortals unfamiliar with, and perhaps intimidated by, the ftp'ing, telnet'ing, and gopher'ing that were (and still are) the norm on the nonmultimedia part of the Internet. Through Mosaic, the mouse became the surfboard of the Web, and the Internet gained sound, color, and movement.

It was the browser that popularized the Web

Although originally developed for UNIX, Mosaic was later released in versions for Microsoft Windows and for the Macintosh, and in its latest (version 3) release it is a sophisticated browser with built-in real-time capability. Mosaic is still available at no charge for personal use at a number of sites on the Web, among them, of course, the NCSA, which is accessible at *http://www.ncsa.uiuc.edu.* (More about this type of address, known as a URL, a little later.) The NCSA has, however, recently announced that it is reducing its development efforts on Mosaic, so the browser field now largely belongs to the commercially produced Netscape Navigator and Microsoft's Internet Explorer.

Mosaic's Successors

Internet Explorer and Netscape Navigator, Mosaic's current successors, are both highly graphical, easy to use, readily available, and very attractive. Internet Explorer is free, and Navigator is available for a nominal price. Both are solid products, and both—more to the point here—are based on the same intuitive page-and-link metaphor illustrated in the earlier diagram.

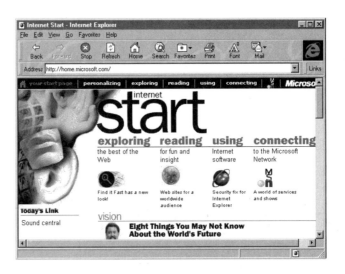

Navigator was first to arrive on the desktop, and according to a survey of 200-plus enterprise sites in early 1997 it held pride of place with about 70 percent of the sites reporting it as the primary desktop browser. But the same census showed Internet Explorer rising rapidly in the same environment, with 28 percent of sites reporting it as the primary browser. Increases in the use of Internet Explorer are expected as more sites turn to Windows 95. (The survey was conducted by Zona Research, Inc., and reported by Business Wire on January 28, 1997.)

The "Browser Wars"

Yes, indeed. Internet Explorer and Netscape Navigator are the products that set off the "browser wars" reported in and sometimes seemingly fomented by the press. Navigator vs. Internet Explorer. Netscape vs. Microsoft. Version *x.x* of Navigator vs. version *y.y* of Internet Explorer. Whose version will be out sooner? Whose will be better? Whose bug, overlooked in the race to release the product, will prove more embarrassing?

Does any of this matter? To Netscape and to Microsoft it does. In the end, however, this is what the tempest boils down to: Both are fine products; both are available. Decide for yourself which you prefer.

Web Hosts and Web Browsers

Underneath the point-and-click accessibility of the Web is a client-server–type network model of amazing scope. Web hosts (servers), like the servers on a corporate network, store published information and wait for browsers (clients) to come and request specific documents. Hosts can be dedicated to handing out Web content, or they can be multifaceted and also handle e-mail, files, and other server chores.

Browsers unlock
the Web

Where Web hosts are passive in the sense that they respond but don't initiate, browsers such as Internet Explorer actively locate and display Web content for the user. They are tools for viewing the Web's hyperlinked, hypermedia documents. You can think of them as software analogs of those colored glasses that brought 3-D movies into focus or, to use a more current comparison, the virtual-reality goggles that turn computer signals into a house, a world, or a molecule that you can "see" and "walk" in.

On the surface, a browser just looks like a cool graphical interface. Underneath, however, it is a much more complex entity that handles the work of finding web sites and of making all the different types of information on a web page visible. To the end user, the appeal of a browser is its ability to do all this without requiring help or technical sophistication. When things are working right, the magic simply happens.

They also do more
than show pages

Although cruising the Internet and making its contents visible would seem important enough, in their most recent forms browsers even go beyond this basic duty. Internet Explorer, for instance, supports Java and ActiveX programming (described later), and it also supports internal and external security features, including:

- Authentication of users and of servers to ensure (to try to ensure) that everyone stays honest.

- Compatibility with *firewalls* that enable companies to filter access to their internal networks and thus keep intruders out.

- Protocols known as the *Secure Sockets Layer (SSL)* and *Private Communication Technology (PCT)* that use encryption based on either 128 bits (United States and Canada) or 40 bits (elsewhere) to ensure that communication over the Internet remains private and safe from eavesdropping.

- The right to refuse *cookies.* Delectable though they sound, these cookies are actually small bits of information that a web site downloads to a visitor's computer to help it find out when the individual last visited and what the person did while at the site. Just saying no to a cookie lets a person maintain a certain amount of anonymity.

Between them, Web hosts and Web browsers define the World Wide Web. As in any client-server network, however, they need a common language to communicate, and this is where you begin to encounter some often used but nonintuitive terms: HTTP, URL, domain, and so on. To dig into this soup, the best place to start is at the top, with the web site.

Beneath the Web lies a host of acronyms

About Web Sites

Everybody talks about web sites. "Suchandso is a really great site." Or "I just created a site of my own." Or "You can find what you need at site X." So what's a site?

A web site is not so much a place as it is a collection of pages—documents—made accessible on a host server. Together, these pages present whatever information a person, group, company, school, or other organization has decided to make available, literally to the world. Sometimes only a few documents comprise a web site; other times, as at the sites for Microsoft, IBM, and the federal government, you can encounter encyclopedia-length collections of thousands of pages that take you deeper and deeper into myriad areas of interest.

Web sites can be small or very, very large

Although visitors can jump to and through the pages at a web site in any order they choose, they must have a place to start, and that is with the document known as the site's *home page.* Like the trunk of a tree, the home page is your first stop and the place from which all linking (branching) to other pages takes place, either directly or indirectly through other pages. Very often, the actual name of this home page is *home.*

The starting point is a place called "home"

Sites and Their Names

What defines a web site, other than its content? Its name, and in the TCP/IP-based Internet and intranet world, what's in a name is very important. Web names—any Internet names, in fact—are known as *domain names* and look like this:

In the kingdom of the Web, domain names represent "addresses"

microsoft.com

and this:

ncsa.uiuc.edu

Simple enough on the surface, easy to remember, and easy to type, the parts of these names actually have names of their own:

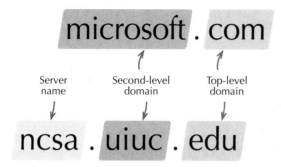

All Internet names come in parts separated by dots. Somewhat confusingly, however, more than one part refers to a domain (roughly equivalent in human terms to a little kingdom). The difference between one domain and the other is that the *second-level domain* name, *microsoft* in one example and *uiuc* in the other, refers to a smaller, more specific "kingdom" than does the *top-level domain* name, or *TLD*. As to what, exactly, these names refer to, well, you know how computer people love abbreviations....

Domains also come in different levels

DNS
An Internet site's domain name follows conventions set out by the *DNS,* or *domain name system* (sometimes *domain name service*). The DNS is a set of services designed to maintain order in a diverse virtual world and to allow for continued growth as the population of that world grows. On one level, the DNS is a classification scheme that groups Internet sites in different categories, or domains. On a whole 'nother level, the DNS is also the foundation of a distributed database that enables computers using it to locate Internet sites anywhere in the world. Let's take the classification first; it's easier to understand.

Taxonomy is the, er, domain of the DNS

The DNS groups sites either by type or by country, as shown in the following illustration:

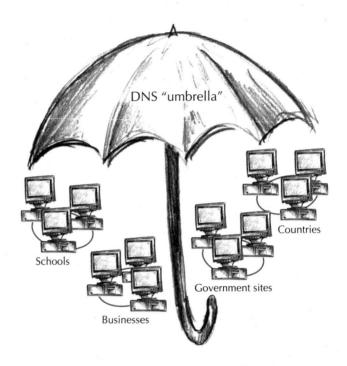

The nature of this scheme is hierarchical, allowing for increasingly specific naming that falls under the control of different authorities. At the highest level are the organizational and geographic top-level domains, which are under the authority of an organization called the *Internet Assigned Numbers Authority,* or *IANA.* IANA currently recognizes seven international organizational TLDs (*com* and *edu* being two of them) and more than 200 two-letter geographic TLDs corresponding to different countries. The seven organizational TLDs, plus a sampling of geographic domain names, are listed in the accompanying tables.

Organizational domain	Used for
com	Commercial enterprises
edu	Educational organizations
gov	U.S. government
int	International organizations
mil	U.S. military
net	Networking organizations
org	Noncommercial organizations

A Sampling of Geographic Domains

Ar	Argentina	Fr	France	Nz	New Zealand
At	Austria	Gr	Greece	Pl	Poland
Au	Australia	Il	Israel	Pt	Portugal
Be	Belgium	In	India	Se	Sweden
Br	Brazil	Is	Iceland	Sg	Singapore
Ca	Canada	It	Italy	Tw	Taiwan
Cn	China	Jp	Japan	Uk	United Kingdom
De	Germany	Kr	South Korea	Us	United States
Dk	Denmark	Mx	Mexico	Ve	Venezuela
Eg	Egypt	My	Malaysia	Za	South Africa
Es	Spain	Nl	Netherlands		
Fi	Finland	No	Norway		

Obviously, the TLD alone is not enough to identify an Internet site uniquely. For that reason, you need the next level in the naming hierarchy, the second-level domain name. This is, simply enough, the unique name under which an Internet site is registered. (Yes, each site must be registered; it's not enough to set up a host and then expect the world to beat a path to your server door.) Registration of second-level domains is handled by a number of authorities, the most frequently mentioned being the *Internet Network Information Center,* or *InterNIC,* which assigns new sites to appropriate organizational domains. The combined second-level and top-level domain names are what you see more and more often on television and in publications, where giving out the name of your web site is becoming as commonplace as handing out your business card.

To complicate the situation somewhat, a second-level domain can also be divided into a number of *subdomains,* each of which can contain multiple hosts. In addition, a domain and its subdomains can be grouped into different *zones* reflecting different divisions of authority or responsibility. Whereas a subdomain is defined by its hosts, a zone is defined by an actual file on disk that contains records for the domain and subdomains within the zone. This fragmentation gets a little confusing, but you can see the descending treelike structure by taking a look at a hypothetical company named Microsoft Cats. (Notice, by the way, that the name is read, or *resolved,* from right to left, with the highest-level domain at the far right.)

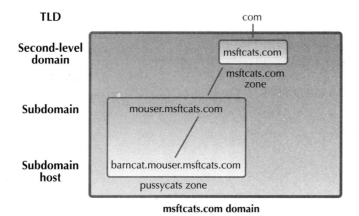

msftcats.com domain

Now for the database part of DNS.

The DNS Database and IP Addresses

Because people are the way they are, all but math geniuses
vastly prefer to specify an Internet site by typing or choosing
a host's "friendly," readable Internet name. Computers,
however, being linguistically challenged but mathematically
agile, consider these friendly names unfriendly but have no
problem with something like this:

Computers prefer
numbers to names

198.105.232.4

This collection of numbers and dots, known as an *IP
(Internet Protocol) address,* is the way computers refer to
themselves and to each other on the Internet. The format of
an IP address is strictly defined, literally byte by byte, with
the sections separated by dots. (The whole is technically

These numbers are
called IP addresses

known as *dotted octet* format.) At any rate, each IP address is unique and must be assigned to an Internet site—sometimes by an Internet authority, other times (depending on how the computer connects to the Internet) by an Internet Service Provider, or ISP. Regardless, all Internet and Web sites must have IP addresses, even though only the computers need actually know what they are.

Roots and Servers, or How They Find Each Other

Domain names are
kept in databases

Given the millions of Internet and Web sites in the world, you have to wonder how the PC on your desktop can find, much less connect to, a web server it's never heard of. After all, the "knowledge" isn't built into the machine. Aha, but that knowledge *is* stored on other computers, in a series of DNS databases stored on a number of dedicated servers known as *DNS name servers.* These name servers mirror the naming hierarchy of the DNS itself and work together, consulting the information in their respective databases, to resolve address queries and pinpoint Web locations.

These databases pair
friendly names
and IP addresses

Far from representing simply a naming convention and list of registered Internet sites, DNS databases exist to match friendly names to IP addresses much as a phone book matches names to telephone numbers. To allow humans to use friendly names, yet allow computers to hail one another numerically, DNS databases cross-reference the two so that their combined stores of information can be used either to translate a friendly name into an IP address (as when a computer searches out a web site) or do the reverse (as when a web administrator has the host resolve the IP addresses of visitors to find which domains they connect from). This mix-and-match capability, however, doesn't explain how your computer can both find and connect to a stranger on the other side of the world. For that, computers rely on one another.

As mentioned, DNS databases are hierarchical and distributed among many computers, each responsible for maintaining information about some portion of the hierarchy from the TLD on down. Because different servers "know" about different levels of the hierarchy and each knows how to contact a server one level up, they can refer requests for IP addresses to higher-level servers as appropriate.

Domain name servers can pass the buck to other servers

For example, suppose that you, inside your corporation, want to connect to an external web site. Although the actual process can involve multiple servers and zones, the process of connecting takes roughly the following path:

- First your computer sends your request for the site to whichever corporate DNS name server it is set up to contact. This type of request, known as a *recursive query*, moves only between your computer and its DNS name server and results in either a connection or a "can't find the location" message.

A request to connect goes first to the corporate DNS server

- Because your request in this example is for a site outside the corporation, the DNS name server probably sends it on to a second type of server called a *forwarder*. Forwarders represent your corporation to the outside world and are the only ones able to communicate with other name servers on the Internet. At this point, your request becomes an *iterative query*, meaning that it is sent repeatedly to a succession of DNS servers containing more and more specific information.

The corporate server sends the request to a forwarder

- Starting from the top, the query first goes to a *root server* containing information about top-level domains. This root server won't have the specific address of the site you want, but it will be able to refer your query to another server with references to computers in the domain that interests you.

Once outside the corporation, the request goes to a root server

The root server
returns the address
of another server

- The root server returns an IP address for, say, "com server," which contains the actual address.
- The query then goes to "com server," which returns the actual address you need.

And you finally
connect—actually, it
all happens quickly

- Finally your computer makes the connection, probably through a *proxy* server that acts as a security buffer between internal computers and the Internet.

Considering how distant some servers are, it's difficult not to feel at least a little awed to have such technology literally at your fingertips, to be used for anything from scientific research to checking the traffic report.

Web Pages and Hyperlinks

Everything described so far in this chapter, aside from site names, is to some extent distant from your desktop. Now, however, you have the background to put some commonplace acronyms in context. They are the often-mentioned *HTTP, URL,* and *HTML.* These are the tools that not only take you to a web site but that locate a particular document and make it visible on screen.

HTTP and URLs

HTTP is the
spaceship of
the Internet; a URL
gives the destination

HTTP is short for *hypertext transfer protocol,* and it is the underlying transport mechanism of the Web. URL is short for *universal resource locator.* Usually pronounced "you-are-ell" but increasingly pronounced "earl," a URL specifies the exact location of a document stored on a web server. Similar in function but not in form to a typical MS-DOS filename, such as C:\windows\desktop\my work\letter.doc, a URL includes not only the name of the document but also a full description of it, beginning with the protocol used (*http* for Web documents) followed by the top-level domain, second-level domain, possibly a subdomain and subdomain server, and the name of the actual document. A typical URL thus looks like this:

http://www.microsoft.com/cio/industry.htm

The forward slashes, following longtime Internet and UNIX conventions, always separate the major parts of a URL.

Who Finds Them and How

Even though the DNS can explain how one computer can find another anywhere in the world, that doesn't explain how *you* can find the computer you want to hook up with. How do you figure out where to go in the first place? There are a number of ways:

There are different ways to find a URL in the first place

- Someone gives you the domain name or URL. This is a nice solution, especially if the reference comes to you in e-mail or in a document that automatically turns such references into actual links. Click the link, and you're on your way.
- You type what you think is the domain name—for example, *microsoft.com* is a pretty logical assumption if you want to connect to Microsoft. This approach actually works quite often with commercial organizations and with large, well-known entities such as *whitehouse.gov* and *nasdaq.com*.
- You use a *search engine,* such as Alta Vista (a personal favorite), Yahoo, or Lycos. This is the most effective method when you know what you want but not where to find it. Search engines are what the remainder of this section is about.

Many sites, such as The Microsoft Network (MSN), include a choice of search engines you can use. The actual process of using one is a simple matter of pointing, clicking, and typing one or more words describing the information you seek. In addition, large sites such as Microsoft's allow their own site-specific searches to help visitors find documents within the welter of pages available.

Search engines help when you're clueless

They can also
respond to some
fairly refined queries

When you give a query to a search engine, whether the query is Web-wide or site-specific, it consults its own *index* and returns a list of sites or documents that match your query. Even though different search engines index different numbers of documents, a generalized query such as "sailboats" can net you tens of thousands of documents about sailboats. You can narrow the search by including Boolean (logical) operators in a query—operators that specify "find apples *and* oranges," "find apples *or* oranges," "find fruit [but] *not* apples," and even "find apples [if the word is] *near* oranges [in the document]." Concocting these so-called advanced searches takes practice and can still result in tens of thousands of *hits,* but tens of thousands is better than a million (a definite possibility), and practice not only makes relatively perfect, it also exercises your logic muscles, which can come in handy when time is short and you need information immediately.

From an observer's point of view, perhaps the most fascinating aspect of search engines is *how* they create their indexes in the first place. Sometimes, the indexing is done by humans and thus offers a certain amount of thoughtful filtering that computer indexing cannot match. Other times, however, the indexing is done by some clever programs variously known as *Web crawlers, spiders,* or *robots.* These programs actively roam the Web, searching out and indexing new sites. One especially appealing member of this clan is, in fact, a *super spider* created by Digital Equipment Corporation for its Alta Vista search service. Digital's super spider, announced in 1996, is known as "Scooter" and (not to give it animate characteristics or anything) is not only fast enough to look at 3 million-plus sites in a day but also well-mannered enough to avoid intruding on private sites.

Push and Pull Technology

Search engines are invaluable for finding information, and sites, once found, are easy to return to as long as you remember to save the location—for example, with a command such as Add To Favorites in Internet Explorer. Currently the entire Web is primarily a *pull* environment in which people seek out and either consult or *download* (save to disk) the information they want.

Searching out information, however, is not the only way to use the resources of the Internet, and currently one of the "hot" technologies involves using *push* techniques, also known as *multicasting,* to provide Internet users with rapidly changing or frequently updated information, such as stock reports, news articles, and, yes, advertising. Support for delivering this type of information is built into the Java and ActiveX programming platforms described later in this chapter.

Push technology is bringing customization to users

More visibly to the end user, push technology is also incorporated in both the Microsoft and Netscape browsers, and it shows up as a significant feature in services such as MSN. While push technology is rapidly becoming commonplace in banner advertising and other Web displays, the best-known provider is a California-based company called PointCast. PointCast has built its renown by providing news, weather, stock reports, company overviews, and other information free to subscribers via "channels" of information displayed as screen savers. (The service is currently supported by advertisers and so costs the user nothing more than the connect time needed to download its software.)

PointCast is a well-known purveyor of push technology

HTML

On screen, web documents—at least those with an aesthetic sense—are a fine mixture of text, graphics, headings, and other elements. Your browser has the ability to *render* the document, deciphering which element is which and displaying each appropriately. But how does it do that? The answer is *HTML,* which stands for *hypertext markup language.*

HTML tells the browser what a page looks like

Essentially a coding scheme that relies on *tags* embedded in angle brackets <>, HTML literally describes each element of a web document. At first glance, HTML codes look almost like a foreign language, especially because HTML includes abbreviations, numbers both arabic and hexadecimal (the base-16 numbering beloved by computers), links to other documents, and special characters such as & and /. Some HTML codes are easily readable. <TITLE>, for instance, specifies a document title. Others are a little less easily understood. The HTML code for a paragraph, for instance, is <P>, and the code indicating a break to a new line is <BR>. HTML is not as alien as most programming languages, probably because the tags are sprinkled through a document and thus give you some context for understanding what they do.

HTML is standardized by an organization called the *Internet Engineering Task Force (IETF)* and lies primarily in the province of web designers. Some software, such as Microsoft FrontPage, is dedicated to helping users create HTML documents. Given the increasing importance of the Web, some newer application software, such as Microsoft Office 97, even contains built-in support for HTML. Both FrontPage and Office 97 can even help novices publish web documents without learning the actual codes. Given such user-friendly tools, only programmers and web professionals really need to understand HTML, but the term itself does crop up frequently in discussions of Web technology.

HTML normally doesn't show up on screen via your browser, but it is still the underlying support structure that makes all the flash and dash happen. The illustration on the next page, for example, shows a typical web document on screen:

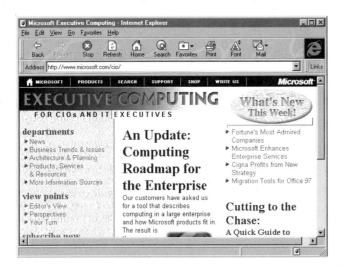

Shown below are some of the HTML tags for the page that your browser sees.

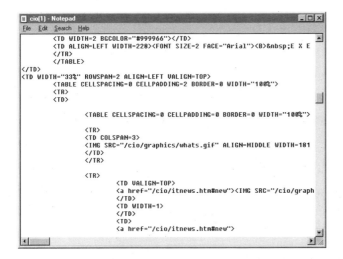

(You can see this for yourself, by the way. With Internet Explorer running, just place the mouse pointer somewhere on the page, click the right mouse button, and choose View Source from the menu that appears.)

HTML is a
scripting language

HTML is, of course, supported for viewing by Internet Explorer and other browsers. For web *authoring,* i.e., document creation, HTML doesn't require any special tools simply because it consists of plain ASCII text even though it is a sophisticated *scripting language*—a set of commands that tell a program what to do—in the way it functions.

From the Internet to Intranets

Once you've grown to appreciate the Internet, either through personal use or through corporate access, the leap to an intranet seems natural and, as many enterprises are discovering, even inevitable.

Intranets are Internet
technology applied
to the corporate
network

The intranet, an offshoot of client-server networking that is based on the client-server technologies described in earlier chapters, can justifiably be called an Enterprise Wide Web because it applies the open TCP/IP protocols and intuitive metaphor of the Internet to the service of private or semi-private corporate webs. Relatively easy (for experts) to establish, an intranet has few requirements other than a functioning internal network. On the plus side, an intranet offers:

- Rapid access for employees. Network connections are far faster than modem-based Internet connections.
- Wide dissemination of information. Intranet speed of access combined with computer-savvy employees turns all kinds of information into useful, legitimate fodder for the web. Intranet documents can range from the CEO's vision statement to HR policies, employee training programs, "who we are"

162   Chapter Five

department overviews, and even individual stabs at creativity.

- Privacy. Although documents created for public (employee) consumption on an intranet are visible to all who connect, network security safeguards these documents from unauthorized access by individuals outside the corporation.

- Ease of use. A well-designed intranet with easy-to-find links to logically organized areas containing information on topics such as personnel, products, and sales beats the heck out of searching for old memos, archives, and corporate handbooks. It can also significantly reduce requests of the "do you have," "can you get," or "would you copy" genres.

- Timeliness and accuracy. Because a single document is the source of information for all users that have access to it, updated information becomes available to everyone at the same time. Distribution lists are not needed, nor are numbered releases of a frequently modified document.

Negatives. Are there negatives? Not really. But intranets do require the following:

- Planning.
- Some type of centralized administration and support for *webmasters,* who are the individuals responsible for separate sites—subdomains or zones—within the main site.
- Intranet specialists who know and can apply Internet technologies. These specialists come with two separate and distinct sets of talents. Technical people, such as network administrators and webmasters, understand and maintain the intranet hardware and software; content producers, such as writers, artists, and designers, create the substance of the intranet.

While an intranet demands new sets of skills and a willingness to keep pace with technological development, the truth is that planning, management, and expertise are basic requirements of any operation in a well-run organization.

Maintaining Secured Access

On the desktop, the browser's eye view seamlessly blends the internal and external worlds. Intranet or World Wide Web, it all looks the same to the end user. About the only difference anyone ever notices is the domain name listed in the URL. Well…actually, that plus the occasional frustrating "site not found" or "connection timed out" messages that appear when a web site is unavailable or repeated attempts to connect are unsuccessful.

Security becomes a concern when intranet and Internet mingle

Given this inside/outside blurring of boundaries, however, any corporation must wonder not only how to keep the home team from wandering too far afield but how to keep visitors from wandering inside and snooping around. The trick, if you can call it that, is to provide controlled access to the Internet and, essentially, keep the internal network completely separate from the big world outside. Microsoft and many other enterprises set up a corporate *firewall* to keep intruders out and rely on a *proxy server* to provide controlled access to external sites.

Firewalls are standard barriers to access

Firewalls Firewalls, as you would assume, create firm and hopefully impenetrable barriers between internal networks and external computers, including those on other networks and on the Internet. Standard security features of large corporations, firewalls are conceptual in the sense that they are based on an organization's approach to security, and they are physical in the sense that they are deployed in various combinations of hardware and software. The idea of a firewall is illustrated in the diagram on the next page.

Firewall

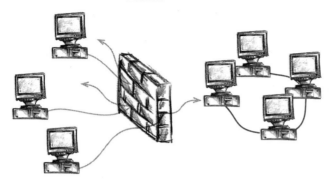

Although components and configurations differ, all firewalls filter electronic traffic passing in both directions through the communications doorway, and they are critically important in protecting an organization, its computers, and its proprietary information from unauthorized intrusion. While such intrusions are not necessarily hostile, they are nevertheless described with words such as *attack* and *invasion,* which clearly denote the intent to harm. Similarly, firewalls are most often described by words such as *defense* and *protection,* which just as clearly denote their mission.

They work by filtering traffic

Like most aspects of networking, firewalls are marvels of engineering complexity that involve a number of technically challenging concepts. But essentially they must do the following:

Firewalls must distinguish between "good" and "bad" traffic

- Allow authorized messages to reach their destinations while refusing entry to all unauthorized transmissions.
- Serve as electronic watchdogs that stop all attempts by hackers and others to penetrate the home network, known as a *trusted* network, from external, *untrusted* computers.

Although firewalls can range from a single component to a combination of computers, routers, and network access points, they generally rely on *packet sniffing* and *proxying* to

They do this through "sniffing" and proxying

maintain security. All firewalls use the former; some also rely on the greater control provided by adding the latter.

Packet filtering can sort the good, the bad, and the ugly

Packet Filtering When traffic moves between an internal and an external network, its baggage includes a number of usually unseen add-ons, such as the sender's and receiver's IP addresses and identification of the type of service being used—such as the Internet's SMTP e-mail protocol or its FTP file transfer protocol. This type of information can be used by a packet-filtering computer called a *packet-filtering router* to determine which packets can pass through to the internal (or external) network and which cannot.

Such a router examines the IP addresses or the type of transport service used in transmission and accepts only those packets it is allowed to forward into or out of the home network. Because some types of services are always routed to the same *port,* just as national television stations are always associated with particular channels, a packet filter can also be used to screen services selectively, either barring unwanted ones completely or (as shown by the SMTP routing in the illustration on the next page) forwarding their contents to dedicated—usually segregated—host computers within the organization. Internet (SMTP) e-mail and FTP file transfers are commonly routed in this way to provide convenience to users without opening the entire internal network to connections with foreign sites.

It's a first line of defense

All forms of packet filtering provide trusted networks with a first level of defense based on screening transmissions. On the outgoing front, the same type of filtering can be used to control access to the Internet and to other networks by blocking certain types of transmissions or connections to unapproved sites. A simplified illustration of packet filtering is shown on the next page.

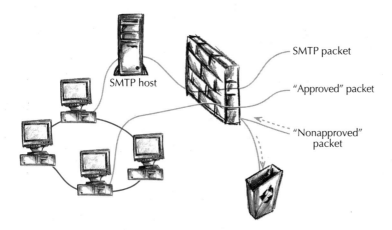

SMTP host

SMTP packet

"Approved" packet

"Nonapproved" packet

Proxy Servers The Internet is all about making connections. Client to host, person to person, place to place. Without such connections, the Internet and the World Wide Web could not thrive and grow, and collaboration via Internet and Web standards could not evolve. But in the closed environment of any corporation, such direct *point-to-point* connections raise the dual specters of uncontrolled, unproductive roaming from within and possibly unfriendly, potentially disastrous unauthorized snooping from without. To permit access to the Web and yet maintain network security, many large organizations rely on proxy servers.

Proxy servers take defense to a higher level

Just as proxies stand in for people at shareholders' meetings and other events, a proxy server stands in for people when they connect to an external computer. In the former case, the proxy is human and represents people only. In the latter case, the proxy is a machine and represents people and the corporate network to the outside world. Thus, when people inside the corporation want to connect to an external site, their requests in the form of URLs go to and through the proxy server, which makes the actual connections with outside hosts and routes the desired information back to the requesters.

A proxy presents a single corporate face to the world

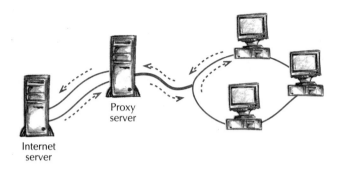

Internet
server

Proxy
server

In doing its job, a proxy server actually performs a number of services:

- It completely separates the internal network from external computers, but it provides quick, *controlled* access to Internet and other sites.
- It can secure internal DNS hosts by presenting a single DNS address (its own) to the world.
- It can *cache* frequently accessed web pages to speed the flow of information and reduce the number of individual connections required.
- It can filter requests to prevent connection to unapproved sites—the most obvious being collections of X-rated (or X-ratable) junk.

Proxies and filters complement one another

Sometimes known as *application gateways,* proxy servers deal directly with client and host applications and thus function at a higher level than do the hardware-and-protocol–based packet filters. Together, proxy servers and packet filters can complement one another to provide the corporation with two levels of security based on all manner of rules and preferences implemented through the hardware and software. Even though the capability is there, however, it's important to remember that security is only as good as the planning and maintenance that go into it. After all, a Doberman without teeth is just a big dog.

For More Information There's obviously a great deal more to be learned about network security, not only in relation to Internet connections but also in terms of protecting the network while providing dial-up access. If you need to study firewalls in detail, a short booklet by Stephen Cobb titled "NCSA Firewall Policy Guide" provides a good starting point. The publication is available from the National Computer Security Association. Information about the NCSA (not to be confused with the National Center for Supercomputing Applications) and a link to this publication are on line at *http://www.ncsa.com/ncsamain.html.*

There's a policy guide available on line

A Store of Internet/Intranet Acronyms

The preceding sections described the genesis and foundation of the Internet, the World Wide Web, and intranets. As you might expect, there is far more to be known about them all, not only technically but in terms of economics, profitability, and end-user software. Because this book focuses on the technology, most of what remains to be covered in this chapter involves, naturally, acronyms and abbreviations that want nothing more than to find a home in your working vocabulary—or at least in your store of "I kind of know what that means" words.

More acronyms; tired of them yet?

True, these acronyms and abbreviations are so abundant it's a pity they can't be deposited in the bank. And true, they make comprehending a new area of technology a little difficult. But their existence can be justified to a great extent by a number of common-sense factors: the rapid emergence of new technologies, the fact that these new technologies demand names of their own, and the fact that computer experts, like even the least sophisticated Internauts, prefer 50 repetitions of "TCP/IP" to 50 repetitions of "Transmission Control Protocol/Internet Protocol."

They're necessary— and useful

The alphabetic stew becomes especially confusing when these terms crop up in news releases, quarterly reports, product descriptions, and, especially, reports from your information technology group. Although only specialized technical documents and communications-centered dictionaries can help you with most of them, the following brief sections provide a sampling of the most common or most current acronyms you're likely to encounter in Internet-related discussions. The terms are grouped by the type of function they represent.

The Retrievers

Although the World Wide Web and HTTP are creating their own special niche, it's important to remember that there was an Internet before there was a Web. And even before hot links and pages, there was a need to locate and transfer information. On the Internet, two widely used text-based players involved in the finding and fetching game are named FTP and Gopher.

FTP is a trusted
moving van for
Internet files

FTP *FTP,* briefly described in Chapter 2 as a TCP/IP protocol, stands for *file transfer protocol* and is a longtime staple for moving files between Internet sites. Although FTP isn't needed for cruising the Web, this venerable protocol is something of a rapid transit delivery system, especially for large files such as graphics and binary files (software).

Archie helps you
find what you need

Sites with large amounts of information available for download often set aside an FTP server that visitors can search and use. Accessing such a server is similar to accessing a web page, except that *ftp* takes the place of *http* in the URL (for example, *ftp://ftp.microsoft.com*). To find information, FTP users can turn to a service named Archie (after the comic strip), which searches for files by name or descriptive keyword. Conceptually, Archie works like a DNS server in passing a request from place to place until the search is complete.

Gopher   *Gopher* is the name given to a search service distributed on various servers across the Internet. These servers tidily categorize masses of documents and provide access to them through a series of menus that take the user to successively more specific levels. The information resources available through Gopher are known collectively by the comically imaginative term *gopherspace.*

To make searching easier, Gopher provides two search tools named Veronica and Jughead (again, named after characters in the comic strip). Veronica allows refined searches—for example, with Boolean operators—but searches all of gopherspace. Jughead allows the user to specify which Gopher servers to search.

The Supporting Cast

You might think that assigning acronyms to a group called "support" is (a) vague and (b) applicable to everything related to the Internet. You're right, but two terms belong here more than anywhere else in this section. If you prefer, think of this category as "important miscellany," but do pay attention to both. They are strong supporting players, indeed essential ones, in creating an Internet/intranet environment.

DHCP   Pronounced "dee aitch see pea," *DHCP* is short for *Dynamic Host Configuration Protocol.* (Yes, yet another protocol.) This one is an industry standard that enables computers known as *DHCP servers* to maintain a network's TCP/IP configuration and, more important from an administrative point of view, assign IP addresses to network and remote workstations dynamically—on the fly. Thus, instead of having to manually configure each workstation, network/ Internet/intranet administrators can configure the server and leave the job of assigning IP addresses and associated DNS servers to the machine. DHCP is a term often encountered in reference to Internet Service Providers and web servers such as Microsoft Internet Information Server, which is built into Windows NT.

Winsock connects Windows and the TCP/IP stack

Winsock A friendly term perhaps reminiscent of airports or Chelsea Clinton's cat, *Winsock* is short for the more mechanical-sounding *Windows socket* and refers to an API (another one) that provides the connection between Windows and the TCP/IP protocol stack. Essentially, Winsock is the conduit that enables information to flow to and from a Windows-based application and the Internet.

The Enhancers

Extensions give programmers more power

The term *server extension* refers to any of a group of tools that extend the scope of a web server's activities by enabling programmers and high-end users (with permission) to create scripts or programs that customize a web site—for example, by returning stock quotes or by extracting requested information from a database. Some of the best-known server extensions, not including ActiveX, which is described later in this chapter, are described below.

CGI allows information exchange

CGI *CGI,* pronounced "see gee eye," stands for *Common Gateway Interface* and is a standard, maintained by the NCSA at the University of Illinois, that controls how information is passed between a non-Web application and a web server.

In this context, it's important to understand that *gateway* refers to a program and not to a piece of hardware mediating between two different network environments (the way "gateway" is defined earlier in this book). Both gateways are mediators of some sort, but the *Gateway* in CGI definitely refers to either a program or to a script written to pass information to or from an otherwise *static* "what I got is what you get" web server. CGI supports HTTP documents only, although CGI programs can be written in a variety of languages, including C, the UNIX Bourne and C shell scripts, and PERL (Practical Extraction and Report Language). CGI programs are commonplace on the Web but are being supplanted by newer techniques, such as ActiveX.

IDC *IDC* ("eye dee see") stands for *Internet Database Connector* and is a means of creating scripts that can access any ODBC database, including Microsoft SQL Server. IDC can thus bring a SQL database into the Web both by pumping selected information from a database and collecting information for it. The possibilities, in terms of making financial, product, productivity, and other information widely available, are easy to see.

IDC is for ODBC databases

ISAPI A mouthful in its own right, *ISAPI* ("eye-sappy") is short for *Internet Server Applications Programming Interface.* Like CGI, ISAPI is a means of enabling programmers to develop applications that do anything from generating HTML pages that return user-specified information to updating server-based databases. ISAPI applications require less processing overhead than CGI applications do and so tend to run faster. IDC and ActiveX are both based on an ISAPI foundation.

ISAPI is like CGI but newer

The Conduits

This section describes both old and new protocols that enable transmission across the Internet. The acronyms are listed in chronological order, from oldest to newest.

SLIP Short for *Serial Line Internet Protocol, SLIP* (pronounced "slip") is an older protocol. Designed to enable *point-to-point*—that is, direct—connections between

SLIP is an older protocol that is used to connect computers directly computer A and computer B over the Internet, SLIP is not designed for routing through multiple nodes and thus does not provide for the Internet addressing supported by more sophisticated protocols. SLIP has been widely used and is still supported because of that, but it has largely been replaced by *PPP,* the *Point-to-Point Protocol* described next.

PPP is the current standard for point-to-point connections

PPP An industry standard, PPP is newer than SLIP and is a term that crops up often. Like SLIP, PPP is concerned with transmitting data packets over a serial (telephone) line. It is generally considered to be "smarter" than SLIP, however, because it "negotiates" a number of connection and configuration parameters that aid in transmitting the data. To help with making, maintaining, and ending the connection, PPP relies on *LCP* or *Link Control Protocol.* To deal with network-layer protocols, PPP includes a set of *NCPs,* or *Network Control Protocols.* Like SLIP, PPP is widely supported by Internet software because of its longstanding use. More recently, to support private connections through public Internet bandwidth, an enhanced form of PPP, known as *PPTP,* has appeared.

And PPTP is an enhancement of PPP that is used to enable virtual network connections

PPTP *PPTP,* short for *Point-to-Point Tunneling Protocol,* enables secure remote access across the Internet, essentially turning a public phone call into the equivalent of a secure connection between two computers on a private network. PPTP is the basis for creating a *VPN,* or *virtual private network,* in which the calling computers, even if they are off site, become virtual nodes on the network. PPTP can be used to connect remote users or remote office sites to the corporate network.

PPTP wraps nonstandard data formats in an IP "envelope"

As mentioned, PPTP is grounded in the PPP standard, as well as the ever-present TCP/IP environment that, more than any other technology, defines the Internet. Like other transmission protocols, PPTP works by *encapsulating* data in packets. PPTP, however, combines the ability to transmit data packets in non–Internet-standard form with the ability to transmit these nonstandard packets over the public TCP/IP bandwidth of the Internet. In this way, PPTP allows for security measures including data compression, encryption, and authentication, while treating the transmission as a standard PPP connection—in essence blending the accessibility of a public telephone line with the security of a private network connection.

The method by which PPTP transmits data packets is known as *tunneling,* a conceptual misnomer that has nothing to do with digging. Instead, tunneling involves "wrapping" a nonstandard data packet in an Internet-standard IP envelope "stamped" with Internet addressing and routing information. In this way, a non-IP transmission, such as one encoded for security or one using a non-IP protocol, can still travel over the Internet. The process is comparable to using a standard shipping box to wrap anything from a T-shirt to Aunt Molly's homemade jam for delivery via the post office. The "tunneled" message, like the box contents, remains wrapped in the IP packet only until arrival. At that time, the receiving (private) network strips off the wrapper and sends the transmission on to its destination.

The Mail Carriers

E-mail, although not as sexy as talkative and animated web pages, nevertheless is and has been one of the mainstays of the Internet. In terms of e-mail, there are three protocols you're likely to hear about: SMTP and POP3, which work as two halves of an e-mail whole, and IMAP, which is gaining recognition as a means of creating mail delivery systems that do more than simply move messages around.

SMTP is a mail protocol widely used in schools and the government

SMTP *SMTP,* or *Simple Mail Transport Protocol,* is a long-time Internet standard that does one thing: routes and delivers mail over a TCP/IP network to an SMTP server and, once there, to the recipient's e-mail address. Efficient, effective, and reliable, SMTP runs at the application layer of the ISO/OSI network model. It is widely used in schools, government, and business and is a standard protocol in server software, such as Microsoft Exchange, that sends and receives Internet e-mail.

POP3 adds storage options to basic mail delivery service

POP3 *POP3,* short for *Post Office Protocol version 3,* furthers the job done by SMTP in handling delivery of e-mail from the server to the client. While you can think of SMTP as comparable to the mail carrier who delivers letters to people's mailboxes, POP3 is closer to the recipient in actually retrieving the mail from the box. In other words, POP3 is the protocol that enables the downloading of mail from temporary storage in the user's mailbox on the mail server to the desktop PC, where the mail is read and processed. The type of service provided by POP3 is often referred to as *store and forward* because mail is temporarily stored on the server before being forwarded to the client for handling.

IMAP extends storage and mail handling options even further

IMAP Newer than POP3, *IMAP,* or *Internet Mail Access Protocol,* is a mail retrieval protocol that appeared in 1994 and is gaining support from developers of e-mail server software. Unlike POP3, which essentially holds mail, delivers it, and then "forgets" it ever existed, IMAP is designed to provide considerably more control over the status and handling of e-mail while it is on the server. Depending on how the server software itself is designed, IMAP can, for instance, be used to:

- Enable users to check their mail from any location, rather than from a single PC, without losing access to any messages they've already seen. This capability might not sound like such a big deal, but it is when you consider that e-mail downloaded to a PC generally becomes accessible only from that location—a problematic situation for travelers or telecommuters.
- "Flag" messages to indicate their status, for example "read" or "deleted." In the latter instance, server software can be designed to keep deleted mail until it is explicitly thrown out.
- Store e-mail either on the server or on the client.

The Expediters

This category includes protocols that deal with *directory services.* So what are directory services and why are they important? Think about how group computing happens—not the hardware, not the software, but the type of information required to make it work. E-mail, shared files, and printer locations are all essential, of course, but even more essential is the basic information required to find people and resources within the distributed environment. From user accounts and workgroup names to file directories, print queues, and the locations of shared software components, this information is kept in *data stores.* These data stores, together with the software services that access them, are directory services. Like the phone-based folk at directory assistance, the software-based functions in directory services look up and provide essential information when it is needed.

Directory services help make information accessible

DAP *DAP,* short for *Directory Access Protocol,* is part of the CCITT X.500 specification. X.500 sets out the rules and

DAP is the X.500 set of rules for programs that use directories

regulations for programs needing to use directories, whether they need to store information in them or garner information from them. DAP is the protocol within the X.500 specification that sets out guidelines for the way end users, via client applications known in the specification as DUAs (Directory User Agents), retrieve information from a DSA (Directory System Agent).

LDAP *LDAP,* short for *Lightweight Directory Access Protocol,* is the functional offspring of DAP. Whereas the more full-featured DAP supports sophisticated features such as browsing, internationalization, administration, and authentication, the lighter LDAP is an open, standard-based protocol designed expressly for providing directory access to Internet clients, applications, and servers via a TCP connection. A newcomer to the enterprise/Internet scene, LDAP is expected to gain support as a standard means of providing directory access and is or soon will be supported in versions of Microsoft products, such as Exchange and Microsoft Windows NT. Support for LDAP should provide benefits in several areas:

- Improved communication between organizations
- Continued expansion of Internet technologies to corporate intranets
- An environment in which software from different vendors can communicate through the same protocol using a single set of interfaces

Active Directory Descriptions of Microsoft's "active everything" initiative are coming up shortly, but here's a peek at a small piece of the action. *Active Directory* is an API designed to provide applications with a single set of directory-service interfaces they can use regardless of the operating system running a particular network or the way a particular

LDAP is the Internet-specific "son of DAP"

Active Directory is designed to standardize directory access across platforms and applications

directory is organized and stored. Active Directory will be part of the next release of Windows NT and as such represents a step beyond LDAP.

(Prepare for abbreviation overload here.)

Active Directory is part of *ODSI (Open Directory Services Interface),* which is itself part of a larger interface called *WOSA (Windows Open Services Architecture).* WOSA includes the ODBC API, mentioned in Chapter 4, which helps applications widen their horizons and access any relational database that complies with ODBC standards. Active Directory, ODBC, and other WOSA APIs are all designed to help give programmers standardized tools for accessing information across multiple applications and even multiple platforms in the ever more complex environment of networked and group computing. Active Directory, LDAP, and other directory services are all supported by Microsoft's *ADSI (Active Directory Service Interfaces)* specification.

Enough already? Turn, then, from the environment and its standards to the tools that turn ideas into reality and, in the process, give everyone the chance to become a software critic. ;-)

Hammering out the Code

If you've been around computers and programmers for the last few years, you've probably heard more than your fill about objects, OOP, properties, OLE, COM, and, recently, Java and ActiveX. If you're not quite sure what these terms refer to, enter here for object kindergarten. The concepts are sometimes relatively easy to understand—in theory—but of course putting theory into practice is not a trivial matter. That's why, in fact, even way back in the 1980s (long ago on the microcomputer time scale), *wizard* became an accepted designation for a gifted programmer.

Among programmers, objects are hot properties

Objects and OOP

So in the programmer's world, everything's coming up objects

Object-oriented programming, often called *OOP* (as in "oops"), is the bedrock of current software development. Developed in the mid-to-late 1980s, OOP is the method of programming—the paradigm—that underlies C++, Java, ActiveX, COM, OLE, and all the other technological tools in the current development toolkit. OOP has, in fact, displaced *structured* or *procedural* programming as the way to go in software design.

Unless you are a part-time or full-time programmer, you probably have little desire and less need to learn about OOP. If you want to hold your own technologically in a computer environment, however, it behooves you to know what OOP is and why it's considered so great. If nothing else, knowing the terminology and a few very elementary basics can prevent some embarrassing conversational missteps or, worse, keep you from having to nod sagely when the conversation zings over your head. Even though Robert Browning decreed that "a man's reach should exceed his grasp," in some cases a little grasp is needed to extend the reach.

Two Styles of Programming

Before, programming was procedural and sequential

In the days before OOP, a program was written as a set of sequential instructions that followed an outline, an *algorithm,* that defined the steps required to accomplish what the program was supposed to do. The program instructions were grouped into tasks and subtasks *(procedures)* for easier creation and more efficient running and debugging, but the program was essentially created from scratch, line by line, and various procedures were called into action as needed to process the *data,* which formed a separate bundle of information for the instructions to act on. There was no firm link between instruction and data, although the two definitely had to match—for example, an instruction that expected to work with numbers had to be passed data in numeric form. A *very* simple set of instructions that requires numeric input is shown below:

A simple example in Basic that prints "You chose 1" or "You chose 2" on the screen in response to user input:

```
INPUT "Please choose 1 or 2: ", num%
IF NUM% = 1 THEN
    PRINT "You chose 1."
ELSE
    PRINT "You chose 2."
END IF
```

Although the preceding example is simple in the extreme, creating structured programs that actually did something was not easy. This description is thus not meant to belittle structured programming in any way. After all, structured programming was the method of creating the software that ignited the PC explosion. In terms of OOP, however, it's important to remember that structured programming was comparable to building a house by creating each individual piece of it—walls, roof peaks, window frames, the whole thing. Although structured programming resulted in some seriously impressive software, the components of program X ended up being pretty much limited to use in program X, even if program Y could use similar code to accomplish basic tasks, such as file transfers or list management.

Structured programming involved a lot of custom coding

In the late 1980s and early 1990s, a new paradigm came along—object-oriented programming. OOP treated programs as collections of self-contained software modules called *objects* that programmers could save and *reuse* in other programs that needed the same functionality. Now the focus was turned toward using "off-the-shelf" components wherever possible, both to save time and effort and to create sturdier programs that could be based on modules that had already proven themselves on the job and often had been created by programming experts for that particular type of

With OOP, the focus has turned to reusable code and component software task. In contrast to structured programming, object-oriented programming offered developers the equivalent of a builder's precision-made window frames, doors, and roof trusses. This emphasis on objects as the building blocks of larger programs lies at the heart of object-oriented programming. It's a simple concept, at least on the surface, and it is elegant in its simplicity.

Class libraries have evolved to provide developers with often-used objects

By the way, creating objects was—and is—a lot of work. Over time, however, objects that handle all kinds of routine tasks have become available in collections of code called *class libraries,* one of which is the *Microsoft Foundation Class (MFC)* library for Windows programming. These libraries are enormously useful because with them, programmers can concentrate on building the house rather than on making all the pieces first.)

Although object-oriented programming is easy to understand as a concept, it is not at all easy to understand as a technology. The reasons are many, among them:

- Programming languages, like any other languages, are mystifying to the uninitiated.
- Computers are coldly logical and currently unthinking, and so their programs must break tasks down into simple actions that brook no machine misunderstanding. These actions, and the code that describes them, can be incredibly detailed—to the point that nonprogrammers attempting to decipher even simple code literally cannot see the forest for the trees. (Think, for instance, how difficult it would be to tell a robot with your computer's IQ how to start your car.)
- Most object-oriented programming is done in C++, the object-based version of the C language which, itself, is not an easy beast to master.

- Programming immerses the newcomer in a welter of new ideas, and object-oriented programming is no exception.

A small book like this can do little to help with most of these technological stumbling blocks, but it *can* introduce you to the basic concepts underlying object-oriented programming. This is interesting stuff, so here goes.

The Elements of OOP

The core concepts of OOP are also its greatest strengths. These concepts are:

- Classes and objects
- Encapsulation
- Abstraction
- Inheritance

In turn, these strengths give object-oriented software its greatest benefits:

- Flexibility
- Reliability
- Reusability

"Reduce, reuse, and recycle" applies to program objects too

Classes and Objects At the highest level in object-oriented programming is the concept of a *class*. Think of a class as a *blueprint* for creating an object. To define the object-to-be, the class describes two complementary sets of features: the object's *properties* and its *procedures* or *methods*. Yuk. Let's try that again with something real.

The basis of object-oriented programming is the class

Consider cars. There are two ways you can define a car: by what it is (its properties, or data) and what it does (its procedures). Color, type of engine, transmission, brakes, battery,

Classes have properties, and they have procedures

and so forth all define what a car is, but they don't actually *do* anything by themselves. On the other hand, the car's procedures—burns gasoline, speeds up, slows down, carries small numbers of people—define the car in terms of its behavior. Together, the properties and procedures define the class of transportation known as a car. In fact, the procedures need the properties in order to perform.

Abstraction Now think about a blueprint of any kind. Does it represent something real? No, it is an *abstraction* of something real. No actual example of "car," for example, travels the roads anywhere in the world. Fords, Mercedeses, and Porsches do, but not "car." Every car, from the orange VW in front of you to the Ferrari that just blew past you, is an *instance* of the abstraction known as "car."

> Abstraction allows a class to be applied to more than one specific object

The same is true of OOP classes and objects. Objects are instances of the class they belong to, and the process of creating objects is known as *instantiation*—just as the process of creating a Taurus is the process of creating an instance of the Taurus object in the car class.

> Creating a living, breathing object is called instantiation

Encapsulation In object programming, *encapsulation* refers partly to the fact that objects are self-contained. Between their properties and their procedures, objects contain both the data and the instructions required to perform the task for which they are created. More important, encapsulation enables objects to take self-reliance—and self-protection—to rarefied heights by allowing them to keep private the way they get things done, thus keeping their important workings safe from tampering. Objects are, in a sense, *black boxes* that produce a desired result without anyone or anything knowing or caring how that result happens.

> Encapsulation allows objects to protect their data and procedures

Such encapsulation, however, also means that, in order to function as part of a program, objects must be able to interact with other objects. And so they do. In the way they are formed and the way they behave, objects act like workers that say, "Here I am; if you need this task done, let me know." Like people, objects communicate through *messages;* unlike people, however, they rely on clearly defined *interfaces*—methods of getting them to respond—to do so.

Encapsulated objects communicate via interfaces

Moving from cars to people, you can think of encapsulation and communication as comparable to a group of individuals collaborating on a project. Each person relies on his or her expertise (encapsulation) and the project members communicate by using e-mail or other application software and the same language (their "interfaces").

Inheritance Finally, although you've really just scratched the surface of object-oriented programming, you come to the matter of *inheritance*. To return to the car analogy, think about how you can *derive* classes from the car class. You can, for example, derive the Ford class, the BMW class, the Toyota class, and so on. Similarly, you can derive object classes. And because these classes come from a defined class, they *inherit* the characteristics of the class they come from, while adding new features of their own.

"Child" objects can—and do— inherit their characteristics from "parent" objects

A Simple Example Understanding object-oriented concepts can be difficult, so this section concludes with a much-simplified example to help clarify matters. To make the "program" easier to follow, a real-world counterpart keeps pace alongside in the diagram on the next page.

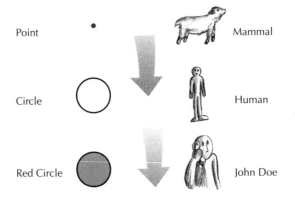

Point

Circle

Red Circle

Mammal

Human

John Doe

As you can see, this example draws a red circle on the screen. That's not exactly one of the world's great applications, but here's one way to go about creating the result you want:

- Start with a class defining one of the simplest possible shapes in the universe—a point. This class boils down to one property, the position of the point on the screen (given as X,Y coordinates marking X pixels from the left and Y pixels from the top), and one procedure, drawing the point. If you actually ran this "code" to draw a point, you would be running an *instance* of the Point object.

- Now derive a class called Circle, which inherits the property and procedure of Point but adds a second property, the radius of the circle, and a procedure that uses the point and the radius to actually draw the circle. If you ran *this* "code" to draw a circle, you would be running an instance of the Circle object.

- Finally, derive a class called Red Circle, which inherits the properties and procedures of Point and Circle but adds color and fills the circle with red. Of course, running this "code" would mean running an instance of the Red Circle object.

Now that you know roughly what the fuss is about object-oriented programming, you're in a better position to understand where some commonly used terms fit in. These terms usually appear in relation to the Internet and intranets, but they are not limited to the TCP/IP environment. You'll also see them used in descriptions of desktop and other software.

OLE and ActiveX

OLE, pronounced "olay," originally came into being as a Microsoft technology known as *object linking and embedding* and was a means of allowing people to create *compound documents*—documents containing elements created by different programs. For example, a word-processed document with a graphic or a spreadsheet embedded in it would be a compound document. Like raisins in a cookie, each element was a self-contained object the user could manipulate (copy, delete, or edit) as an entity separate from the remainder of the document. The whole point of supporting OLE objects was to provide people with a means of focusing on the document they were creating rather than on the application being used to create it.

> OLE started out as a means of creating blended, or compound, documents

Eventually, the OLE concept spilled out and away from compound documents and came to be identified with any object that could be manipulated by other software, from operating systems to applications. To put it another way, OLE came to represent an approach to enabling software to interact. Developing in parallel to the increasing emphasis on networking, OLE became less about creating compound documents and more about giving programs the freedom and the means to communicate and make use of one another's capabilities.

> But OLE eventually grew to represent a better way of enabling software to communicate

With this expanded definition, OLE became part of a larger Microsoft strategy that, in 1996, was renamed *ActiveX* and was extended to embrace the Internet. These days, OLE remains a legitimate term. It no longer refers to "object linking and embedding," but to some extent it has returned to its old, *document-centric* focus.

COM

COM is the blueprint for creating component software

COM is short for *Component Object Model,* a standard developed by Microsoft that provides the programming foundation for creating *component* software—task-specific software built of objects that can interact with other objects within the same or different programs and whose services can be called upon where and when they are needed. Through component software comes the promise of *distributed computing,* in which end users can transparently access needed software no matter where it is located on a network.

It defines the way objects communicate with one another

The foundation on which OLE and ActiveX are based, COM is a (pardon the expression) COMplex mass of technical detail. Neither a language nor a programming paradigm, COM is a model for enabling *interprocess communication,* itself a fancy term for the methods by which *client* and *provider* objects interact by requesting and providing needed services. For example:

- Suppose that Object 1 provides the world's best sorting of lists.
- Suppose that Object 2 needs to sort a list but doesn't have the ability to do so on its own.
- The solution is for Object 2 to become a client of Object 1, requesting and receiving Object 1's services.

As you saw in the general description of object-oriented programming, Object 2 has no need to understand how

Object 1 handles the sort. That's fine with Object 1, of course, because it is encapsulated to prevent inexperienced clients like Object 2 from monkeying around with its procedures. To satisfy the needs of both, all that's required is a means of communicating and passing the desired information. That's where COM steps in by defining a single, standardized means for all COM objects to use in establishing communication. In a way, implementing COM is a little like reducing government services to a single procurement process. (There's a thought for you.)

COM, then, defines the way in which Objects 1 and 2 make contact. It doesn't prescribe *how* the objects are to do their work, nor does it even specify which language they are to be written in. In this respect, COM resembles standards like the CCITT recommendations. Actual creation is up to the developer; the standard simply describes how to handle a particular technological issue.

Although COM does not stipulate how to build programs and objects, it does define the characteristics of the object and, by extension, the methods used to communicate with other COM objects. At this level of detail, COM objects are similar to, but not exactly the same as, objects in the more generic programming sense. They *are* object-oriented, but they are distinguished by two main features:

COM objects are characterized by interfaces and pointers

- *Interfaces,* which are the procedures—known as *methods*—through which other objects access their services
- *Pointers,* which are the only means by which *client* objects can request their services (A pointer is a reference, rather like an address, to the location of some desired item—in this case, the "address" of the interface that gives the client access to a particular service provided by a COM object.)

The following illustration should help you visualize the relationship between COM objects, interfaces, and pointers.

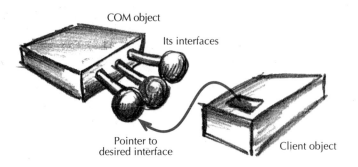

COM object

Its interfaces

Pointer to
desired interface

Client object

COM is not
dependent on a
particular language

To appreciate the value of COM, it's also important to understand that it is a *binary* standard. The benefits of using COM technologies don't come into play until *after* a program has been converted to binary form for running. As a result, software written to the COM standard can be written in any of several languages, including C++ and Java. COM is, in essence, a key to creating *polymorphic* software in which clients can interact with multiple providers without having to be concerned with the providers' locations or structure, or even the language they are written in.

Although COM itself needs the expertise of skilled developers, its value to corporations and end users is both visible and measurable. By defining a single way in which objects in any COM-based application can interact, COM does the following:

- Streamlines the development process.
- Makes objects easier to access, more readily available, and reusable.
- Supports distributed computing. Note, however, that here distributed computing does not mean supporting components across a network. That job belongs to DCOM (described on the next page). COM's support for distributed computing is more along the

lines of enabling distributed *access* to services by creating a single communications channel through which software from multiple vendors can interact without having to deal with multiple intermediaries in the form of system-specific and application-specific programming interfaces.

DCOM

While COM eliminates the distinction between objects in one process vs. objects in another, a related standard known as *DCOM,* or *Distributed COM,* promises to blur the distinction between local and remote computing to bring about a truer version of distributed computing. Like COM, DCOM is a Microsoft invention and a standard for handling and accessing objects. DCOM, however, extends the COM standard to cover networks.

DCOM extends COM to the vision of truly distributed computing

Supported in Windows NT version 4.0, DCOM supports components that can either stand on their own or be part of either an application or an operating system. At one time known as *Network OLE,* DCOM is the means by which developers will be able to create objects that work across multiple:

With DCOM, the world opens up across platforms, applications, and protocols

- Operating system platforms
- Network transport protocols
- Applications

With COM, DCOM, OLE, and ActiveX, the future becomes, well, not exactly easier for developers, but more standardized and more supportive of software evolution—the latter because objects, being self-contained, can be changed and improved without harming any greater whole to which they belong. For end users, the future of networking and the Internet becomes exciting, interactive, and a place where Information [will be] At Your Fingertips without requiring a degree in computer science.

ActiveX

ActiveX succeeds OLE but has a larger, Web-oriented vision

ActiveX is Microsoft's strategy for making COM, components, reusability, and interaction available across languages, platforms, and geography in the sense of integrating local and remote computing, especially over the Internet. Descended from an earlier specification for objects known as *OLE controls,* ActiveX is essentially a Web-oriented specification for creating faster, mix-and-match, interactive, component software (sometimes called *componentware*) unencumbered by some of the overhead that could make OLE controls larger than they need to be. The elimination of this overhead is deliberate and is intended not only to make ActiveX more flexible but to cater to the very real speed limitations of downloading objects over the phone-based Internet. At the moment, ActiveX is a Windows-based technology in the process of being extended to the Macintosh and UNIX platforms.

Controls are the basic components of ActiveX

At the heart of ActiveX are special-purpose components known as *controls* that programmers create to add new functionality to an existing piece of software. These controls are based on a programming language such as Microsoft Visual Basic. Like actors in a play, controls are highly individual and form part of a larger whole—in this case, software (such as Internet Explorer) known as a *container.* Controls vary widely in form and function and unlike actors are seldom recognizable to the end user as anything other than elements in the container software. For example, the Microsoft browser features numerous controls, one of which is labeled in the illustration on the next page.

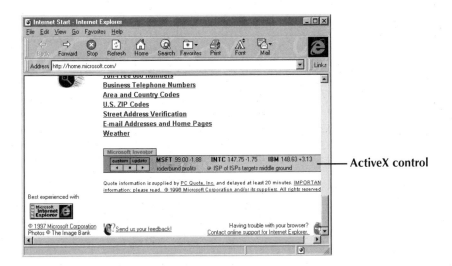

ActiveX control

As you can see, this control doesn't sit on the screen screaming, "I am a control!" It blends in, doing the job it was designed to do. (Although the illustration cannot show the action, the stock ticker actually streams across the screen from right to left and is frequently updated.)

Java

Ahh, Java. You've doubtless heard this word and variations on it so often by now that you automatically think of computers rather than coffee at the sound. What's so hot about Java, and why is it the *wunderkind* of computing and the Internet? Why are developers delighted by it? Why has Microsoft embraced a language developed by a competitor (Sun Microsystems)? Here you go.

Java is the darling of Web developers

It's machine-
independent,
so it can run
on any system

Java is a programming language. More specifically, it is a
machine-independent programming language that can run
on any system, regardless of make, model, or operating
system. Similar to but simpler than C++, Java was designed
from the ground up with the Web in mind, and unlike C++
(which developed from the non–object-oriented C language)
Java is fully object-oriented. Java's most common use at the
present time is in the development of small, downloadable
applets designed to add interest and interactivity to what
would otherwise be *static* web pages—that is, pages with no
more action to them than the average word-processed
document. In this respect, by the way, Java applets normally
are visually indistinguishable from ActiveX controls.

It's also small,
safe, and oriented
to networks and
the Web

Aside from being so Web-centric, what are some of Java's
main features? Here are the highlights:

- Java programs are small—a big advantage given the
  generally slow speeds attained via the usual Web
  connection based on telephone lines and modems.

- Java has built-in safeguards that prevent applets
  from tinkering with the computer to which they're
  downloaded. When you think about hackers, vi-
  ruses, and even the occasional buggy program that
  can inadvertently damage files, Java's safety is a
  welcome feature.

- Java is designed to work over networks. That is, it's
  a *distributed* language. For instance, because it is
  designed to work with URLs, the distinction between local and remote objects (files) becomes
  immaterial.

- Java programs are distributed in a form known as
  bytecode rather than in the more usual *executable*

format of traditional programs. This aspect of Java is described in a little more detail below but mainly is important because bytecode format is what makes Java machine-independent.

- Depending on how they are written and saved, Java programs can run either as small applets embedded in HTML web pages or as stand-alone applications.

Bytecode, Interpreters, and Virtual Machines When people say that Java programs are machine-independent or platform-independent, they don't mean that anyone, even the most experienced programmer, can sit down at a computer, type in a Java program, and expect it to run. Uh-uh. Computers accept input only when they have been taught to understand it via software. So to produce a working Java program, computers first need to "learn" the language through the tools available in a software development environment, such as Sun's Java Development Kit or Microsoft Visual J++. The actual process of creating a Java program (stripped of the creative part, that is) goes like this:

Java programs require a development environment and compiler for creation

1. The programmer creates the program within the chosen development environment.
2. The programmer *compiles* the finished program. This is the point at which the human-readable Java code becomes executable Java bytecode. This bytecode can run on any computer because it is one step removed from being refined into *native code,* which contains chip-specific instructions and is characteristic of platform-dependent programs written in C++ and other languages.
3. The programmer makes the program available for use, probably as an applet embedded in a web page.

Now suppose someone opens the web page and downloads the Java program to his or her computer. What happens next?

And they require
an interpreter for
execution

If the Java program is an applet, it runs within the user's Web browser. If the Java program is a stand-alone application (not very common as yet), it runs on the computer just like any other application does. Applet or application, however, the program cannot run without a piece of software known as an *interpreter.*

Java's machine-
independence is
provided by the
virtual machine
on which it runs

And what exactly does the interpreter do to run the program? In Java's case, the interpreter translates the bytecode into instructions tailored for a virtual computer known as the *Java virtual machine,* or *JVM.* Physically nonexistent though it is, this virtual computer provides the "hardware" environment in which the program runs. (Programs of any sort, remember, need to interact closely with hardware in order to do their work.) As long as the real computer has been provided with the Java interpreter and with the software that allows it to create, or emulate, the Java virtual machine, the Java program runs happily, neither knowing nor caring about its actual host.

Note: Microsoft's implementation of the Java virtual machine, usually known as the Microsoft VM for Java, is being developed as the Win32 Reference Implementation. The Microsoft VM for Java runs any Java program, as all Java virtual machines are supposed to do, and also supports COM and ActiveX to provide developers with the ability to use Windows-based features.

A Just-In-Time
compiler can
speed things up

Just-in-Time Compilers Although Java applets and applications normally run with the help of an interpreter, speed can become an issue because the interpreter translates and executes instructions line by line. To help increase speed, some virtual machines, including the Microsoft VM for Java, include a performance booster known as a *Just-In-Time* compiler, or *JIT* (rhymes with "mitt"). The JIT works by compiling bytecode into faster-running native code. In a nice display of juggling, the JIT earns its name by compiling code on the fly and executing it while continuing to compile the remainder of the Java program.

Chapter Six

Internet/Intranet Software

Understanding the Internet and the Web won't move anyone from solo computing to the global network. Aside from
the requisite hardware, one *does* need software. And luckily
for everyone, a profusion of Internet/intranet software is
either available or in the making—software from Microsoft,
Netscape, IBM, and numerous other companies.

This chapter will survey some of the Internet-related applications and tools available from Microsoft, to help you both
develop a feel for the size and scope of Web technology and
to see roughly what directions this technology is taking. As
in Chapter 4, bear in mind that these descriptions *are* bi-
ased, but as before, they are not intended to be interpreted
as advertising for Microsoft, nor are they meant to influence
any purchasing decisions. Just as the only practical way to
buy a car is to see it, feel it, and drive it, hands-on evaluation is the best way to buy software.

Your starting point for this tour is Microsoft's foundation for
both servers and clients: Active Platform.

Without software,
there is no Internet

This chapter covers
Microsoft software

Active Platform

Active Platform
is designed for
interactive software

In late 1996, Microsoft announced Active Platform, which was in large part (perhaps totally) developed in response to the company's incredible push into Internet/intranet technology. The underlying details of Active Platform are mostly of concern to software developers; for the end user, this announcement means that after getting used to the MS-DOS platform, the Microsoft Windows platform, the PC platform, and the Macintosh platform...you have the pleasure of learning about Active Platform. So what is it, and do you need it?

It's Microsoft's
route to the future

Take the second question first: Do you need it? Almost certainly, if any of the following holds true for your company:

- You are committed to client-server networking.
- You use Microsoft Windows NT servers.
- Your clients are Windows, Macintosh, or UNIX machines. (Kind of a no-brainer, this one.)
- You support Internet accessibility.
- You have, or soon will have, an intranet.
- You don't want to be left behind technologically. Sorry...science and invention do march onward, and these days even sheep serve the cause—at least where *reinvention* (cloning) is concerned.

Active Server +
Active Desktop =
Active Platform

As for what it is: Active Platform is a two-part invention, half of which is called *Active Server,* half of which is called *Active Desktop* (or *Active Client*). Together, these halves blend client-server, component, and Web technology with the goal of bringing the look, feel, and ease of the Internet to client-server networks and seamless distributed computing. On the development front, Active Platform actually gives programmers two valuable options:

Active Platform
allows for
cross-platform
development

- They can develop for cross-platform functionality to create software that is usable on the broadest possible computing base.

- They can develop for specific platforms, such as Windows.

And for Windows-specific programming

The difference between these two approaches is a topic of considerable interest right now and has gained importance with the growing acceptance of the multiplatform Java language. Some people feel that cross-platform development is essential in this Internet/intranet age. Others feel that traditional platform-specific software is still just as valid and, in fact, might be the only way to go in certain circumstances, such as on networks dominated by a single platform such as Windows. No doubt there is a "right" answer for everyone, and no doubt one person's right answer isn't necessarily correct for someone else. Certainly Windows is a well-nigh ubiquitous operating system, in both 16-bit (Windows 3.1) and 32-bit (Windows 95 and Windows NT) form. And certainly there is justification in taking advantage of its existing APIs and ActiveX, especially given the fact that aspects of its Internet-related functionality, including both Microsoft Internet Explorer and ActiveX, are being extended to other major platforms including Macintosh and major varieties of UNIX.

Both ways are valuable

So what exactly is the tradeoff between developing for multiple platforms (read Java here) vs. developing for a single, admittedly widespread platform? Essentially:

- Cross-platform software eases not only the costs of development but the costs associated with installing such software on the several system platforms usually found on large corporate networks. On the down side, creating software that can run on any system also means that such programs cannot include platform-specific enhancements and must necessarily exclude features supported by particular operating systems. As a result, these "lowest common denominator" programs might not perform as quickly or offer as much functionality as, say, Windows-only programs can.

Cross-platform development produces "universal" applications

Platform-specific
software can be
optimized for the
operating system

- Platform-specific software can be optimized for
  performance and features on a particular platform
  and can take advantage of existing class libraries
  and system-specific capabilities. Such software is
  obviously limited to one type of machine or operating system. On the other hand, these programs can
  offer greater functionality and performance than
  their cross-platform brethren.

Active Platform essentially offers the best of both worlds.
In addition, ActiveX and the component model on which
Active Platform is based lend themselves to a new and
increasingly significant form of programming known as
multitier application development.

Multitier application development (which, thankfully, is *not*
abbreviated as MAD) is entering mainstream development
efforts related to database access and transaction processing. As opposed to traditional *two-tier* client-server application development in which program logic is essentially
divided into front-end (client) and back-end (server) processing, multitier application development separates logic
into three layers: client, application server, and database.
In this model, the client, as usual, makes requests of the
server. The request, however, is not handled by a server
that combines application logic and database information.
Instead the server, acting as a middle layer, provides logic,
performance, directory services, and database connectivity.
The database represents a third layer that acts as information center and storage.

Two-tier application
development

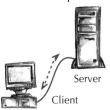

Multitier application
development

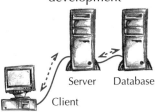

One of the important points to remember about multitier application development is that by concentrating application logic on the server, processing becomes available to multiple clients without the need for each to perform the work independently. Multitier application development is complex, as you would expect. Its benefits, however, include improved performance, security, and scalability within an Internet/intranet type of framework.

Multitier application development lets the server do the work for many clients

The Question of Security

As of early 1997, more and more software is blending Internet-related features with the traditional computing desktop of MS-DOS, Windows, Macintosh, and UNIX. Although this newly developed ability of individual computers to access the global network (and vice versa) is acclaimed as the next "good thing," the very fact that strangers no longer pass in the night but now meet, greet, exchange information, and gain access to one another's computers has given rise to significant questions about security beyond the corporate form that involves firewalls and proxies.

There is, for example, the issue of respecting individual privacy. This is evident in the international forum, where discussions and, indeed, national policy revolve around the question of allowing law-enforcement officials access to

In the Information Age, information security is a key issue

encrypted data. Another concern is whether and how much (if any) information a provider should be able to siphon off the files on a visitor's hard disk. And of course there are questions about who should be able to maintain and access databases containing information about individuals, how people should be allowed to use that information, and whether individuals have the right to know of their inclusion in these databases. Questions of this magnitude are as philosophical as they are practical and in some cases are almost cosmic in scope. All must obviously be answered in high places, but even the most casual Internet visitor and certainly all corporations that allow access to the Internet should be aware that such issues are being examined.

One of the security questions involves the safety of Java vs. ActiveX

Closer to home, there's the question of software security that, as of early 1997, has become the concern of businesses, the press, software developers (from individual programmers to organizations such as Microsoft), and numerous debaters on the Internet itself. Basically, the question boils down to whether cross-platform Java development or reliance on Microsoft's ActiveX technology is more secure in terms of keeping systems safe not only from marauding hackers and vandals but—equally importantly—from poorly designed applets and controls that inadvertently cause damage to the user's system.

Java applets generally run in a secure "sandbox"; ActiveX controls have more freedom

Here again, the issues are numerous, and so are the opinions. Java is built to prevent security lapses, in large part by keeping applets confined to a "sandbox" from which they cannot escape to tamper with sensitive portions of the system on which they are running. ActiveX, an alternative to Java, encases controls in "container" applications—primarily Microsoft Internet Explorer—but allows controls more freedom, including the ability to access files on the hard disk. (This is where the danger lies with respect to attacks on the system.) Java applets normally do not have such capabilities, although development of the Java language itself is tending to allow applets out of the sandbox and into the system playground too.

At least at present, ActiveX would seem to be less secure than Java, and to some extent this is true. To counter potential threats, however, Microsoft provides users with a security check known as *Authenticode*, which displays a certificate-like window on screen and asks the user whether to proceed before downloading Internet software. Authenticode, while not verifying the safety of the downloaded software, does identify the program's creator and also provides the user with assurance that the incoming code has not been changed since it was created.

Because Microsoft supports both Java and ActiveX, both roads to security—Java-only and Authenticode—are available to developers. Reassuringly, both are under constant scrutiny by professional organizations and by programming enthusiasts who use the Internet itself to publicize "holes" that they find in host programs such as Internet Explorer. All large software providers do their best to bulletproof their products and to fix flaws as quickly as possible, but it's important to remember that true security ultimately rests in the hands—and the skill—of each developer who sends an applet or control onto the Internet. To a great extent, the rest of the world must trust the integrity of these developers and hope that those driven by malice and immaturity remain a small, despised fraction of the population. Hackers are clever, but so are sewer rats.

Active Server

Because both Active Server and Active Client rely on the same component-object model, the most immediately visible advantage to Active Platform is its ability to allow easy (to developers) and seamless integration of software running on server and client. Distributed with Windows NT version 4.0, Active Server is based on the open standards of

Authenticode is designed to help tell users that downloadable software has not been changed

But integrity can't be legislated, and "bad guys" are always around

Active Server supports scalable component applications and, of course, HTML

the Internet and is designed to help developers create applications for network web servers. It's one step closer to the not-quite-realized goal of truly distributed computing in which the "where" of an object's storage no longer matters to applications or to users. Active Server is designed to simplify programming for networks and to provide Internet ease of use on the desktop. Through the Active Server model, developers can create scalable, component-based server software that can rely on—indeed, generate—HTML pages. These HTML pages can in turn distribute applications and customized sets of information, including data stored in SQL databases on UNIX and mainframe computers, to clients on the network.

It's built into Windows NT Server

Active Server is part of Windows NT Server version 4.0 and as such is (currently) a Windows-based technology. Because it is built into Windows NT, Active Server can take advantage of Windows NT's directory and security services to provide users with Windows NT's network accessibility and its ability to provide a common view of network resources. To promote interoperability, Active Server relies on DCOM to help components work together and thus disguise differences in platforms and applications from multiple vendors.

And sports several significant new technologies

Active Server is implemented in Microsoft Internet Information Server (described later in this chapter) and incorporates several technologies that you have heard about or will soon hear about:

- *Active Server Pages,* or *ASPs,* which combine scripting in multiple languages, ActiveX components, and HTML pages to create Active Platform applications that can deliver customized content to whole groups of users—for instance, sales or marketing staff, human resources departments, or even ski enthusiasts. Active Server Pages essentially combine the functionality of CGI with component software. Like Java, they compile to bytecode rather than platform-dependent or application-dependent instructions.

- Microsoft Transaction Server, which helps developers create component software for servers without having to concern themselves with low-level aspects of network programming. Transaction Server coordinates transactions and ensures their accuracy.

- Message queues, which will become available in 1997 and will enable *store-and-forward* queuing of network messages—not the e-mail kind but the kind that enable servers to work with one another—so that functionality remains and requests are not lost even if a server is temporarily off the network.

Active Desktop

Active Desktop, the desktop half of Active Platform, is intended to make the Web metaphor part and parcel of the user's computing environment. Standards-based and platform independent, Active Desktop is the set of technologies designed to enable developers to bring the Internet experience to the desktop. In addition, or in the process, Active Desktop is intended to make differences between network locations, the local hard drive, and the Internet a thing of the past.

Active Desktop aims to make the Internet part of everyday computing

Active Desktop is designed to provide developers with the means of delivering components and applications that can reach across, and run on, multiple operating systems and Web browsers. Still in the process of maturing, Active Desktop is meant to help developers improve on the speed, responsiveness, and interactivity of the Web metaphor. Because it is platform independent, Active Desktop will be able to run not only on Windows-based systems but also on Macintosh and UNIX systems. In fact, through its reliance on accepted standards, HTML, and ActiveX, Active Desktop should be able to allow compatible content to run on any system that hosts it.

Its goal is platform independence

In terms of specifics, the following list describes some of the features of Active Desktop:

- Cross-platform delivery of HTML pages as well as software components and network services
- Language independence that allows for client-side scripting in multiple languages, including JavaScript, Microsoft's VBScript, and JScript (Microsoft's implementation of JavaScript)
- ActiveX controls and Java applets delivered through the Microsoft JVM

Active Desktop will arrive in Internet Explorer 4.0

Active Desktop will be embodied in Microsoft's upcoming Internet Explorer version 4.0. Designed to make the Internet an integral part of the user's set of information resources, one of Internet Explorer 4.0's most significant goals is to eliminate the need to search for local, network, and Internet resources separately by providing "one-stop shopping" on the desktop.

Active Messaging

Active Messaging adds communication and collaboration to Active Platform

Cutting across the Active Server/Active Client dichotomy, but more closely tied to Active Server, is a third form of activity Microsoft has defined: *Active Messaging.* This technology is a component in Exchange Server version 5.0. Active Messaging is a component of Active Server and is designed to enable developers to use Exchange Server to provide both messaging and collaboration to any Active Platform application.

It works with Exchange Server

Through the use of Active Messaging, developers can enhance the power of an Internet or intranet site by enabling active applications to draw on Exchange Server's existing strengths: data storage, directory access, and (of course) messaging. By linking messaging to Web technology, Active Messaging is expected to help developers create more interactive web pages and, not incidentally, to enable any browser to act as a messaging client.

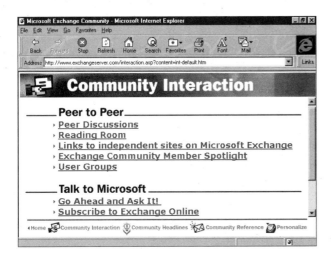

Active Messaging itself breaks down into two components:

- The *Messaging Object Library,* which supports standard messaging functions, including logon and access to messages and public folders, as well as sending, receiving, and managing messages, attached documents, and message folders.

- The *HTML Rendering Object Library,* which gives web pages the types of features that allow users to view messages and tasks in multiple ways and that are standard in mail clients such as Exchange Client and Microsoft Outlook. Through the HTML Rendering Object Library, for example, web pages gain the ability to sort and filter messages or to display calendar information by day, week, or month. Although such capabilities might not seem to break much new ground, just remember that these types of displays are being added to HTML pages, not messaging applications, but because of the object library, they require no HTML coding.

Essentially, Active Messaging is designed to help developers provide interactivity on the Web as painlessly as possible. And that's a good thing.

Through Active Messaging, HTML can become more interactive and personal

Windows NT and BackOffice Internet Servers

Windows NT Server is the solid ground beneath Active Platform

Although Active Platform provides the set of technologies that can bring Internet capability to enterprise computing, technologies alone don't to the job. So Microsoft provides a number of actual products that put Active Platform into play at all levels—server, client, and developer. At the core of all this service is, of course, the network operating system.

Windows NT Server

Beginning with version 4.0, Windows NT Server is an active partner in Internet accessibility

Windows NT Server version 4.0 is the platform supporting Microsoft's approach to marrying Internet technology with the enterprise network. As described in an earlier chapter, Windows NT Server provides the networking advantages of modularity, security, and an extremely close working relationship with Microsoft BackOffice products such as Exchange and SQL Server. As an Internet/intranet platform, Windows NT Server version 4.0 also includes a number of tightly integrated products specifically designed to provide or enhance both internal and external web accessibility:

- Microsoft Internet Information Server
- Microsoft Index Server
- Microsoft FrontPage
- Microsoft NetShow
- Microsoft NetMeeting

(If you read product descriptions, you might be somewhat perplexed to find that some of these products seem to be inseparable from one another. Index Server, NetShow, and FrontPage, for instance, are all built into Internet Information Server. Because all are designed to support different functions, however, they are described individually in the following sections.)

Internet Information Server

Internet Information Server, or *IIS,* is Microsoft and Windows NT's means of providing web services to the organization. Looking in the direction of the Web, IIS supports Internet/intranet site creation and management. Looking in the direction of traditional client-server networking, IIS also supports access to the range of back-end services made possible by its integration with BackOffice.

IIS is designed to simplify web-site creation and management and to make performance as fast and powerful as possible. For example:

- IIS is the piece of server software that provides Active Server Pages. As already mentioned, these pages support on-the-fly creation of HTML pages by the server, and they support scripting, through which HTML documents can be customized to deliver a certain amount of dynamism and "intelligence" to what would otherwise be static web presentations.

- IIS incorporates Index Server, which performs the unenviable but necessary task of indexing content on the site to provide users with better access to information, as well as the inherently more interesting job of handling queries and returning lists of matching documents.

- On the fun-and-desirable front, IIS, through Net-Show, enables use of a technique called *streaming media* that speeds the delivery of audio and video to the end user. Although streaming media at first sounds more entertainment-oriented than practical, the reverse is actually true when you consider the benefits of on-demand, companywide availability of training sessions, speeches, and announcements via the intranet.

(sidebar) Internet Information Server sounds sort of ho-hum, but it drives Windows NT's Internet support

(sidebar) It supports on-the-fly creation of HTML pages

(sidebar) It indexes content

(sidebar) It adds sound, video, and pictures to network broadcasting

Index Server

Index Server creates the intranet's store of key search words— just ask...

Index Server, the product that "reads" web documents and indexes key search words, is designed to make information of many types—in seven languages—accessible to Internet and intranet users through queries that look like this:

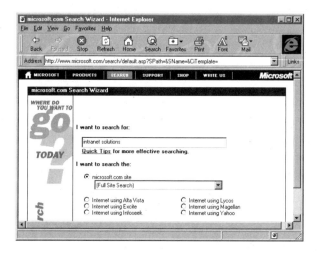

...and you shall receive

It is also designed to produce lists of matching documents like this:

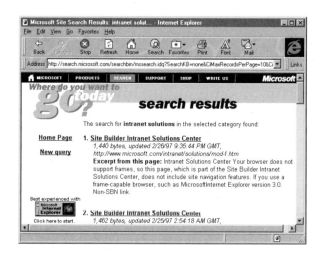

Index Server works with HTML, plain text, Microsoft Word and Microsoft Excel documents, and Microsoft PowerPoint slides. When it wears its indexing hat, it is also capable of working with embedded objects in compound documents—for example, with an Excel spreadsheet in a report created using Word.

Index Server "reads" all kinds of documents

Performing a two-part job, Index Server both indexes document content and handles queries from users requesting lists of documents that match certain search criteria. Index Server even performs searches with discretion so that someone searching for *cloud,* say, will also be presented with *cloud-burst,* and someone searching for *run* will also find *ran* and *running.*

And uses alternative word forms when searching

One of the most fascinating examples of Index Server's smarts, however, is the way it indexes documents. In brief, indexing happens in three stages:

The way it works is really interesting

- In stage 1, *filtering,* the document to be indexed is opened, and a *content filter* is applied to it. The content filter, a small clone of the application used to create the document, essentially "reads" the document and passes the stream of text along in a form that Index Server can use. At this stage, the content filter might also attach tags identifying language (English, French, German) changes, and it might activate additional content filters to deal with embedded objects created by applications other than the one the filter is designed to deal with.

First it filters a document to produce a stream of text

- In stage 2, *word breaking,* Index Server divides the text stream into words. Simple as this sounds, it's a difficult job for a computer program with no eyes, so Index Server relies on programs known as *word breakers* that are designed to recognize where one word ends and another begins. Because languages differ significantly in structure, and because Index Server is designed to work with a number of languages, it uses different word breakers for English, French, German, Spanish, Italian, Dutch, and Swedish.

Next it breaks the text stream into words

● In stage 3, *normalizing,* Index Server performs the software equivalent of the work human indexers do, albeit without anywhere near the intelligence. Part of normalizing involves capitalization and punctuation, but the largest and most "intelligent" part of the process involves the removal of *noise words*—articles, prepositions, pronouns, and so on, such as *the, a, on, under, through, me,* and *you*—that are necessary to understanding a document but do not in themselves contribute to its substance. After normalizing, which cuts the number of indexed words by as much as 50 percent, Index Server places the result in a *content index* from which document references will later be pulled in response to user queries.

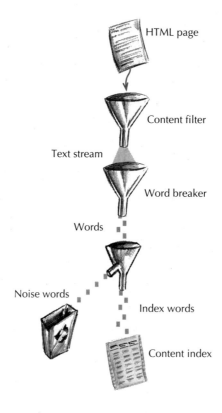

HTML page

Content filter

Text stream

Word breaker

Words

Noise words

Index words

Content index

Although it's fun to know how Index Server does its job, it's more important to know how useful it is from a business point of view. Here's a quick rundown of the high points:

- Index Server works with more than HTML, so it can be used to help people find all kinds of documents from e-mail to corporate reports and budgets. In addition, because it can index not only content but document properties such as creator, date of creation, and so on, it can be a useful tool for finding and retrieving related documents stored in multiple locations or, as happens too often, documents scattered around a hard drive by a less-than-organized individual.

Index Server works with multiple document types and can index properties, such as names and dates

- Index Server is polite. If, as can be done, document owners mark their documents as off-limits, Index Server ignores them and does not add them to its list of retrievable documents.

It leaves private documents alone

- Index Server's search capability supports simple one-word queries (such as *microsoft*) as well as those containing wildcard characters such as the asterisk (*), which takes the place of one or many unspecified characters, and Boolean operators (AND, OR, and so on). For example, a query on *micro** would apply to *microsoft, microhard, microfiche,* and *microscope,* and the query *microsoft AND stock* would limit the search to documents containing mention of both microsoft and stock.

And it lets users refine their queries

FrontPage

Microsoft FrontPage comes in two versions, client and server. The visible client portion used for creating web pages is what most people refer to as FrontPage. The far less visible portion installed on the web server is known as the *Front-Page Server Extensions* and is the part that lets the client make people happy. FrontPage architecture supports the

FrontPage is for creating web documents

open standards of the *World Wide Web Consortium,* or *W3C,* so online services created with FrontPage are accessible to all standard browsers, including Internet Explorer, Netscape Navigator, and Mosaic.

The Server Extensions are a small group of programs that are designed to do three things:

- Provide the web server with the functions needed to support the FrontPage client
- Supply the APIs needed to enable different web servers to interact and communicate
- Provide functions for end users such as searching and group discussion

These extensions essentially create the doorway through which documents and services are made available to the world.

On the client side, FrontPage is a product known as an *HTML authoring tool* or *web authoring tool* that provides even inexperienced users unfamiliar with HTML with the means of creating and publishing web documents. To help people along, the FrontPage client provides predesigned *templates* and built-in programs called *wizards* that help automate the document-creation and publishing process. With such aids, users can create web documents without knowing HTML. FrontPage also supports e-mail and the creation of interactive forms. On the administrative end, FrontPage allows for site management and automatic updates of links when documents are moved from place to place.

NetShow

Like FrontPage, NetShow is a two-part invention consisting of client and server components. Its goal: to bring sound and video to intranet users at speeds that are not (as has been in

The FrontPage Server Extensions run on the server and support the FrontPage client

The FrontPage client is an authoring tool that even novices can use

NetShow is for delivering multimedia transmissions

the past) halting and sometimes pathetically slow. In addition to the delivery mechanisms themselves, NetShow also includes the authoring tools needed by showtime producers to create multimedia presentations.

NetShow supports two ways of delivering multimedia-based transmissions over intranets and the Internet—*live* and *on-demand.* Live transmissions go out over the "airwaves" as audio, in a form known as *IP multicasting.* With multicasting, a single transmission is sent to many recipients at the same time. Its technological opposite number, the more typical distribution vehicle known as *IP unicasting,* also allows multiple recipients to receive the same information, but each receives a separate *copy* rather than the identical transmission. Because multicasting delivers information once instead of many times to many people, it eases the load on network bandwidth as significantly as you would expect. Naturally, multicasting is a great way to deliver information such as the CEO's annual speech to the troops.

It can send a transmission as it happens, or it can wait until people request it

On-demand transmissions take advantage of streaming to deliver not only audio but *synchronized illustrated audio* (supplemented with graphics, photos, slides, and so on) and video. Streaming, as already mentioned, speeds the delivery of multimedia information. It does this by "playing" the transmission as it arrives on the desktop rather than requiring the recipient to wait until the entire file has been downloaded. The difference, although obviously not in real-time speed, is much like using the telephone instead of waiting for a letter to arrive.

Streaming reduces wait times significantly

In short, whether live or on-demand, this stuff is *cool.*

Proxy Server

A proxy server, as described in the preceding chapter, is dedicated to providing all the desktops in the organization with a single, secure portal onto the Internet. Microsoft's

Proxy Server is the corporate stand-in on the Internet

entrant in this area is called, rather understandably, *Micro-soft Proxy Server.* This particular proxy server is closely integrated with Windows NT and works through a secure gateway to enable both 16-bit and 32-bit applications on Windows and other operating systems to access the Internet. Proxy Server is based on open standards and supports both TCP/IP and IPX/SPX protocols. It can handle longstanding protocols including HTTP, FTP, and Gopher, as well as new ones such as RealAudio and VDOLive (video). Proxy Server also supports the chat, mail, and news functions that add to the appeal of the Internet.

For efficiency, Proxy Server caches often-used information

To improve access times, Proxy Server *caches* frequently accessed data locally so that there's no need to make numerous connections to the same site. When a new connection becomes necessary, however, Proxy Server connects via a LAN or a dial-up connection, and then it automatically disconnects when the visitor leaves the site.

Proxy Server can also be used to enforce usage restrictions

Although (to the end user) the capability smacks of Big Brotherhood, Proxy Server is also designed to allow administrators to control the types and times that users can access the Internet. Certain sites, for example, can be placed off-limits, access itself can be restricted to certain days or times, and usage can be monitored to prevent abuse of privileges by overly freewheeling, free-spirited corporate fans of the virtual universe.

And, of course, Proxy Server keeps unwanted visitors from gaining entry to the corporate network. Not exactly a small matter, that.

Merchant Server

Merchant Server creates a virtual store on the Web

As the name implies, *Microsoft Merchant Server* takes business to the Web to create the marketplace of the Internet. Designed to help create and manage anything from a single virtual store to an entire mall, Merchant Server does the following:

- Displays goods for sale
- Supports secure financial (credit card) transactions
- Maintains inventory, working with existing, ODBC-compliant relational databases
- Enables targeted promotions and sales to selected groups as well as individual and group discounts

Typically, when potential customers connect to the Merchant Server store, they "window shop" by looking at products and product information. If they decide to make purchases, they load their items into an online *shopping cart* and, when ready to leave, they pay for their purchases with a credit card. To help ensure that credit card information remains secure, Merchant Server supports protection based on:

Because finance is involved, Merchant Server supports several security measures

- A technique known as *Secure Sockets Layer (SSL)* encryption, which is built into Web browsers, including both Internet Explorer and Netscape Navigator.
- A protocol known as *Secure Electronic Transaction,* or *SET,* which was developed by both Microsoft and the Visa credit card people.
- The VeriFone *vPOS* application, which accepts order information from the customer and uses SET to communicate the order to a bank. (To use vPOS, the organization must first establish a relationship with the bank, which provides identification information and vPOS software that enables the online seller to connect to the bank's transaction system.)

Merchant Server runs on Windows NT and is made up of three main components (not in the object sense but in the usual "parts of the whole" sense). These parts are known as the *Controller,* the *Router,* and the *Store Server.*

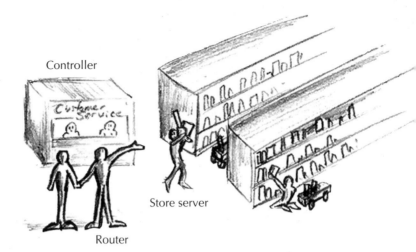

Controller

Store server

Router

Merchant Server
handles everything
from saying Hello
to figuring out the
sales tax

The Controller is the part of Merchant Server that handles the management end of online selling. The Controller takes care of all the background work that makes the store function: language, form of currency, buyer identification numbers, methods of processing orders, and so on. The Router is something like a store greeter. It receives customer requests via the Internet Information Server, sends them to the necessary handler, and returns the store's response to the customer. The Store Server is equivalent to the sales clerks, cashiers, and package handlers all in one. It takes requests from the Router, services them appropriately, and sends the response back to the Router. In performing its job, the Store Server handles everything from product availability to calculation of price, shipping, handling, taxes, and post-sale service (such as checking on order and account status).

Transaction Server

Transaction Server is
designed to help de-
velopers concentrate
on applications and
not the underlying
network

Despite its name, *Microsoft Transaction Server* does not deal overtly with finance. It does, however, provide the services that allow developers to create ActiveX and component-based applications that, in turn, do allow business transactions to take place on the Web. Basically, Transaction Server does two things:

- Shields the developer from the underlying complexities of server-based programming so that the focus can be on creating the application, not the infrastructure
- Integrates business transactions with the component model to help developers create strong applications that can preserve their integrity even when working across multiple servers, components, and databases (or, heaven forbid, when the system needs to recover from failures)

The heart of Transaction Server lies, as you would expect, in ActiveX components, and its job is to ensure that these components run correctly and cooperatively in a distributed server environment. In the process, Transaction Server handles a myriad of complex technical details, including (in nontechnical terms) overseeing components, pooling resources, and working with databases. Transaction Server also takes care of several intriguing facets of business processing that can affect the performance and accuracy of an application. These are (in their technical glory):

It ensures that database transactions are accurately recorded, even across servers

- *Atomicity,* which means that updates to a transaction must either be made permanent (committed) or aborted to an earlier state
- *Consistency,* which ensures that transactions correctly reflect the current state of the system
- *Isolation,* which is really intriguing because it keeps transactions from seeing one another in partial states of "doneness" in order to avoid inconsistencies (the transaction equivalent of human misunderstandings)
- *Durability,* which ensures that committed updates survive correctly in the event of system, application, or communication failure

How would it work? Here's an example:

1. Suppose you walk up to an ATM machine some-where and withdraw $100. As soon as you receive the cash, however, a server fails between the ATM machine and the bank, and so the withdrawal fails to be recorded in the bank's records.

2. At the same time—busy day for finances—someone in your family goes to the bank and deposits a check for $100 into the same account.

3. At this point, your $100 in cash has not been deb-ited from the account, but the $100 deposit has been added to the balance, giving you $100 more than you really have.

4. With Transaction Server, however, your improved financial situation lasts only until the server comes back on line because at that point, the first trans-action (the withdrawal) is completed, and your balance becomes correct: minus $100 from the ATM, plus $100 from the bank deposit, for a net change of zero.

Sad day for the shifty, perhaps, but you can see why the bank would be pleased.

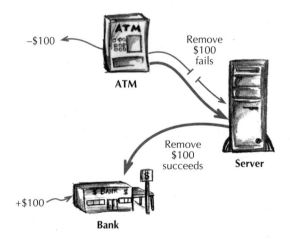

Desktop Software

Without a doubt, network/Internet infrastructure and software are far more complex than desktop PCs and the programs they run. It's also true, however, that without the desktop there'd be no use for the network. And besides, the infrastructure and its complexity fade into the background where end users are concerned. As long as everything is working, most users don't care a whit how beautifully designed, secure, or standards-based all that back-end technology happens to be. (Of course, when it *stops* working, even for short periods, those same people do become rather...vocal.) So, everybody needs desktop software to access the Internet, the intranet, and the up-and-coming *extranets,* which are simply hybrid intranets that are partly closed and partly open to the world.

A few earlier sections dealt briefly with the desktop complements of the FrontPage and NetShow servers. The following are descriptions of Microsoft's other main Internet-related offerings in the desktop derby.

All of the foregoing pieces are geared to supporting the end user

Office 97

Microsoft Office 97 is the newest release of a set of *productivity* applications tailored to work together and bundled in a single package. In this incarnation, Office includes the new Outlook *personal information manager (PIM)* described separately in the next section, as well as the expected Office suite of applications consisting of Word, Excel, PowerPoint and, in the Professional Edition, the Microsoft Access relational database.

Office 97 provides applications and information management

This is neither the place nor the time to describe the features of each of these applications. Suffice it to say that each is remarkably powerful, highly usable, and—frankly—fun to work with. This book, in fact, was written solely using Word, as you can see in the illustration on the next page (which, by the way, shows a terrific new *view* in the left "pane" known as *Online layout view*).

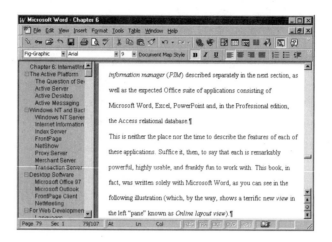

But on to Office 97 and the reason it's discussed in this book.

The applications work together and let the user concentrate on what to do rather than how to do it

One of the strongest advantages of using Office 97 or any other suite lies in the *interoperability* of the bundled applications. With interoperability, users can trust the applications to work together and thus can concentrate on what they want to do rather than on what tool they must use to do it. The user's mindset can essentially shift toward an OLE point of view and see work as *document-centric* because all the tools needed to work with various types of objects are at hand, no matter which individual application is currently running. Insert an Excel spreadsheet in a Word letter? No problem. Turn a Word outline into a PowerPoint slide show? No problem there, either. And because Office 97 also includes the Visual Basic programming language, not only interoperability but customization and automation are both real and eminently possible.

Office also supports collaborating in a number of ways

The thrust of this book, however, is not about interoperability but about collaboration over networks and the Internet. In this area, Office provides solid support as well. For example, Office users can:

- Perform group editing
- Track and annotate changes
- Insert comments and notes
- Keep track of different versions of a document as it evolves
- Store *properties* including keywords, notes, and hyperlink paths along with the document
- And, of course, use Office applications as authoring tools for intranet and Internet web pages

Outlook

Both part of Office 97 and a separate product in its own right, Microsoft Outlook is a one-stop information-and-task-management center. This is one view of Outlook (out of many):

Outlook is Exchange Client on steroids

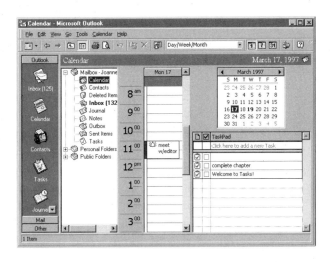

Just as the Internet is a virtual world, Outlook is a virtual desktop. On it (and in it), users can manage practically every aspect of their computer work except the creation part that requires brains. They can use Outlook to send and receive mail, maintain calendars and contact lists, schedule tasks, and even keep a daily diary in an electronic journal that can help track phone calls, mail messages, appointments, Office documents, and personal notes.

And it supports
collaboration too

In addition to these personal information-management capabilities, Outlook also includes a number of features that support its collaborative potential. It can:

- Display the properties stored with Office documents
- Group and sort documents and messages to help users filter the wheat from the (current) chaff
- Display public folders
- Show the contents of the local drive and network drives, essentially eliminating the difference between them from the user's point of view
- Recognize URLs. Clicking a URL embedded in a mail message not only opens the browser but connects to the Web and displays the document specified

Although Outlook functions so well as an e-mail client that it can be used merely for e-mail, it is really much more. Essentially, Outlook is Exchange Client on steroids and was born to roam the Web.

FrontPage Client

FrontPage client
produces HTML
without demanding
that the user
know HTML

As mentioned earlier, FrontPage client is the end-user half of FrontPage. Installed on the desktop, it is the product designed for creating web content in the form of HTML pages. Like other Microsoft products, FrontPage client includes wizards that nudge inexperienced people through the authoring and publishing process. In addition, Front-Page includes the charmingly named *WebBot* components, which help add interactivity, such as text searches and forms, without the need for programming.

And it works
with Office

FrontPage is also integrated with Office and, as you would expect from Microsoft's emphasis on OLE and objects, provides further support for content creators by responding to the intuitive drag-and-drop technique familiar to users of Windows 95 and even those accustomed to earlier versions of Office. This integration with Office also enables users to rely on such features as spell checking for proofreading and the thesaurus for inspiration.

To create a web document, users can rely on predesigned *templates*—essentially, sample documents to which they add their own content—and on a *WYSIWYG* (What You See Is What You Get) editor that does not require knowledge of HTML and that eliminates guesswork by showing on screen what the finished document will look like.

Because FrontPage is a client-server product, it responds to passwords and other methods of maintaining security yet allows individuals in separate offices or even geographic regions to work on pages stored in the same web or intranet site. Finished content can be *published* either to a server on the intranet or on the Internet—it's the user's choice.

Finished documents can go on the corporate web or the Internet

NetMeeting

A conceptual multimedia companion to NetShow, NetMeeting is the Internet version of the local water cooler and conference room. Using built-in Internet phone support, NetMeeting provides a truly collaborative real-time environment for conferencing, sharing applications and documents, and working with a virtual whiteboard.

NetMeeting provides an electronic conference room over the Internet

Based on global standards set by the telephone and modem arbiters of the International Telecommunications Union (ITU) and the Internet Engineering Taskforce, NetMeeting supports a number of standard protocols, including the ITU T.120 for *multipoint data conferencing* that enables groups of people to collaborate, and the ITU H.323 standard for audio and video conferencing. The result of such support means that NetMeeting, unlike some other conferencing

It works with other products that comply with the same conferencing standards

applications, allows people using other products to join in, as long as those products are compatible and based on the same standards. NetMeeting is currently compatible with numerous products from vendors other than Microsoft, including Intel, MCI Telecommunications, PictureTel, Vtel, and Philips Electronics. Not a bad roster of supporters for a new technology.

NetMeeting offers two distinct ways of communicating:

NetMeeting allows for two-way voice communication

- Point-to-point conferencing, which allows for two-way voice conferences over the Internet or an intranet

It also supports data conferencing among multiple users

- Multipoint data conferencing, which expands the choices to include real-time collaboration through application sharing, file sharing, and the virtual whiteboard

For connecting in the first place, NetMeeting sports a speed dial feature that makes calling faster, and it uses different compression methods to match the capabilities of the network or modem. During voice conferences, NetMeeting can, if the user wants, hang out a "Do Not Disturb sign" that prevents incoming calls from interrupting the session. If a conference is in the wind, it can listen in the background, ready to notify the user when a call comes in. And when file-sharing is involved, NetMeeting gives the recipient the right of refusal, should that be necessary.

NetMeeting's support for multipoint connections provides the following capabilities:

People don't have to install an application in order to use it during a conference

- *Multipoint Application Sharing,* which means that all participants can see and even use a Windows-based application such as Word, even if it is not installed on their computers.

- *Shared clipboard,* which moves data into a special portion of memory for temporary storage. Whereas the Windows Clipboard allows such data to be moved from one application to another on the same machine, NetMeeting's clipboard allows conferees to transfer data from storage on the local machine to a shared application.

  They can share information with one another

- *File transfer,* which allows a participant to send a file to selected individuals or to all members of the conference—all while work continues uninterrupted.

  They can exchange files

- *Whiteboard,* which is actually a drawing program that allows people to sketch, diagram, or even doodle and share the results with others in the conference.

  They can share diagrams and sketches

- *Chat,* which acts like typical chat rooms on the Internet, allowing people to send text notes to one another in a kind of instant e-mail.

  And they can "chat" via keyboard

For Web Development

Development tools, meaning programming languages and their associated development environments, are the most important and among the most technically challenging aspects of computer science. It takes a fine and logical mind to create the software that (too often, it seems) people love to hate or at least love to complain about. Nonetheless, few end users would think of denigrating developers' efforts overall, and certainly no end user who depends on the capabilities of high-performance software would consider a do-it-yourself approach either satisfactory or practical. That said, however, it's interesting to be aware of the breadth and depth of development tools available to skilled practitioners. To close this chapter, here's a quick look at some of the software-development tools available from Microsoft.

Of course, all this capability depends on programming

Languages

Programming languages are a computer's alphabet and grammar

Languages are the alphabet, the grammar, and the syntax of application development. Without them, there would be no "words" for computers to understand, process, or swap among one another. Microsoft's languages are provided as *visual* tools for developers—that is, they come in a form that makes full use of the graphical Windows interface, including drag-and-drop capability.

There are many languages; Visual Basic, Visual C++, and Java are especially important now

Over the years, Microsoft has supported numerous languages, from the low-level assembly language of the microprocessor to COBOL, Fortran, and Pascal. These days, the emphasis is on Microsoft Visual Basic, Microsoft Visual C++, and Java. Visual C++ is the primary development language for large applications, including those destined for Internet accessibility, and as you know, Java is the platform-independent language of the Internet. Both Visual Basic and Visual C++ are distributed by Microsoft in forms known as Professional and Enterprise Editions. While both are serious development packages, the latter contains tools needed by teams developing large, scalable client-server applications for the enterprise. Java is distributed by Microsoft as Visual J++ and includes support for COM and ActiveX objects.

Software Development Kits

Software Development Kits give developers the tools they need to work on particular types of programs

A number of *Software Development Kits,* or *SDK*s, are available to developers from Microsoft and other software providers. SDKs vary, depending on the type of software they're designed for. In general, however, they are collections of development tools, documentation, sample code, and code libraries packaged to help clarify and simplify application development in a particular area. For example, Microsoft offers a Win32 SDK for Windows programmers and a MAPI SDK for those involved in messaging applications. In the Internet/intranet area there are, among others, SDKs for ActiveX, Java, Active Platform, Microsoft Platform, NetMeeting, and ODBC.

Visual InterDev and Visual Studio 97

At what you might consider the top of the development pyramid are two related but independent products, Microsoft Visual InterDev and Microsoft Visual Studio 97. Both are development packages and are web-related, but they differ in focus and in the types and number of tools they offer.

Visual InterDev is designed for teams of application developers working on HTML-based Internet and intranet applications. Part of the family of visual development products, Visual InterDev works hand-in-glove with FrontPage. In this partnership, Visual InterDev provides the web-related tools needed by developers, while FrontPage provides the environment needed by content creators. Although Visual InterDev is not a programming language, it provides the foundation for incorporating components created with Visual Basic, Visual C++, Visual J++, and the Visual FoxPro development system for relational databases.

Visual InterDev is geared for development teams with an Internet/intranet focus

Visual Studio 97, while aware of the needs of Internet connectivity, is more attuned to multitier application development. What you might easily consider the whole ball of wax, the big enchilada, or the soup-to-nuts collection of development tools, Visual Studio 97 contains a suite of products needed for large-scale development. In its Enterprise Edition, Visual Studio 97 includes both Visual Basic and Visual C++, as well as a number of other products including Transaction Server, SQL Server, the Visual Source-Safe program for tracking and controlling different versions of software under development, and Visual InterDev.

Visual Studio 97 is the programmer's equivalent of "all you can eat"

Visual Studio 97 is designed to meet the needs of MIS departments and similar groups that provide scalable, enterprise-wide applications. Like the two-faced Roman god Janus, for whom the month of January is named, Visual Studio 97 looks both forward to the future and backward to the past by providing the tools that can blend the software and hardware of the past and present with the ever-widening potential of the Internet future.

It's for people working on scalable applications that satisfy the needs of large enterprises

Chapter Seven

Gazing into the Crystal Ball

Well, you've waded through a lot of stuff about network hardware, network software, protocols, groupware applications, the World Wide Web, and more. Now it's time for some fun, time to dust off the crystal ball and try to see, however darkly, what the near future holds. This chapter presents some anticipated developments that together have the potential to affect the way hardware and software are developed and deployed in the enterprise and, even more far-reaching, to change the way people see and work with computers.

What's on the immediate horizon?

Decisions about which way things will go are all guesswork, of course, because computer-related technology lives in a constantly changing environment full of moving targets, and those targets, as a friend once said, are sometimes so slippery that trying to get a grasp on them can be like trying to nail Jello to a tree. In addition, there are the occasional wildcards, like the explosion of the Internet and the development of Java, that no one can predict but that can change the thinking—and the course—of the whole darn thing.

Figuring out the future is all guesswork, really

Still, it doesn't hurt to try for a sense of direction.

Coming Attractions

Collaborative solutions are not standing still

So what about developments appearing on the immediate event horizon? There are many, but three are closely related to the collaborative, Internet/intranet–based environment: *dynamic HTML, network computers,* and the move toward differentiating between *thin* and *thick clients.* Dynamic HTML, a new technology arriving in Microsoft Internet Explorer 4 and Netscape Navigator 4, has the potential to expand intranet interactivity significantly. Network computers and thin vs. thick clients are closely allied and are actually the subject of some interesting, and sometimes heated, debates.

Dynamic HTML

Dynamic HTML is for increased interactivity

As you've seen, HTML is necessary for making web documents understandable to the browser. These documents, however, are static—they don't do much of anything. *Dynamic HTML,* or *d-HTML,* has been developed as a means of making the Web more interesting, interactive, and, hopefully, faster.

It's based on making more events scriptable

Dynamic HTML is based on the existence of *events,* a term you encounter frequently in object-oriented programming. Events are, well, things that happen—things like the movement of the mouse, a mouse click, and so on—that either can or do affect the way a program responds to the user or to other programs. What dynamic HTML does is make events such as mouse clicks *scriptable* so that the event can be used to trigger some type of response that is normally unseen but is built into the page itself. A developer can thus use dynamic HTML to build intelligence into a web page—for example, having it play sounds when the mouse pointer passes over a certain area or having it automatically display a product description, photograph, or price list.

Because these responses are not visible and are not called into action until they are started by the event they are tied to, they minimize clutter and distraction at the same time that they add considerable depth to the document. In a sense, dynamic HTML has the potential to turn an ordinary web page—say, the equivalent of a page in a book—into an adult's interactive version of a talking, pop-up, scratch-and-sniff book of the type that delights young children. In addition, because dynamic HTML is built into the page, "playable" elements need not be downloaded from a server in order to run. The net effect of this advantage is, of course, increased speed for the user.

Dynamic HTML will add depth to web pages

Both Microsoft and Netscape are working on implementations of dynamic HTML and have submitted their specifications to the W3C (World Wide Web Consortium), the arbiters and standard-bearers of the World Wide Web. Once dynamic HTML is standardized and widely available, you can expect a new and more responsive Web experience to arrive on a screen near you.

A standard is in the making

Network Computers

Ah, network computers. Championed by industry giant Oracle Corporation and supported by the equally impressive Sun, IBM, Apple, and others, the idea of a network computer is the idea of a completely server-centric computing environment in which the client is a simple receiving station that downloads software from the server and has no local storage (hard drive) of its own. Underlying the concept of the network computer are two factors crucial to the plans of any business: cost…and cost:

Network computers are seen as a way to control computing costs

- Cost in the form of initial investment
- Cost in the form of continued maintenance

Oracle's vision of a network computer, or *NC,* is essentially
one of a network node with a processor of its own and a
graphical interface but with no expansion capability or local
storage and no connectivity other than to the network. The
NC will, however, be based on open Internet standards,
such as HTTP. Likewise, Java is expected to play a large,
perhaps predominant, role because it supports small downloadable applications and was initially built for the Internet.
By creating a computer with "few moving parts," so to
speak, Oracle and the NC's supporters estimate that not only
the initial cost of the equipment ($500 U.S.) but the cost of
software updates (all server-based) and maintenance will be
much lower than the comparable costs of buying and maintaining full-fledged PCs.

Moving in a somewhat different direction, Microsoft and
Intel have defined a different type of network-based computer known as the NetPC. Expected to cost under $1000,
the NetPC will be more capable than the NC but will still
be a "stripped down" computer that is shipped in a sealed
box and cannot be modified or added to by the end user.
According to the *NetPC Reference Specification* released to
the industry by Microsoft and Intel, the NetPC will include
the following features designed to reduce costs associated
with maintenance and upgrades:

- Software-managed hardware devices that allow for
  remote (network) maintenance
- Configuration and installation of NetPCs via the
  network
- Updates scheduled for times when the system is not
  in use

Both the NC and the NetPC respond to the corporate need
to simplify network management and administration and to
control costs. Will either supplant the desktop PC? Only the
future knows, and it's not talking.

Thin vs. Thick Clients

Discussions of networking, collaboration, and the future of the industry often include mention of *thin* and *thick clients*. The NC in particular is often referred to as a thin client. The reference is not really to the heft of the machine, although the term certainly applies. Actually, "thin client" refers to the fact that the network computer is a very basic instrument that carries no software in its own head, that uses software downloaded on an as-needed basis from a network server, and that sends the data it produces to permanent storage on a server. This thin client is essentially a processing center as opposed to a complete manufacturing facility.

Thin and thick clients are closely tied to the concept of network computers

The opposite of a thin client is, obviously, a thick one. That's the PC on your desktop, equipped with its own devices, expansion slots, perhaps a modem, and, most importantly, with its own software installed permanently on its own hard drive. The distinction between thin and thick clients has gained prominence over the last year or so. Driven by the emerging vision of the network computer, the popularity of the thin client concept has been fueled by the corresponding rise of Java as a source of small, focused, platform-independent applications designed for server-based storage and distribution.

Here are some of the key features that describe each type of client. Thin clients are:

Thin and thick have their own advantages

- Inexpensive
- Easier to maintain
- Well-suited for individuals who use a limited number of applications, especially highly task-specific ones—for example, people whose primary use for a computer is e-mail, word processing, calculating, or working with network databases

Thick clients are:

- Flexible
- Customizable
- Well-suited for individuals who use a computer for a variety of tasks or who need access to a range of tools or to powerful software—for example, people whose functions involve programming, management, and administration or people who prefer to keep sensitive information on a local machine

The 100-percent pure Java initiative is related but somewhat ancillary

In some ways, the difference between thin and thick clients also corresponds to another, related issue: the current debate over Sun's "100-percent pure Java" initiative vs. developing applications optimized for a particular (read Microsoft Windows) platform. Downloadable software that is 100-percent pure Java is, of course, nicely attuned to the capabilities of network computers and so can be considered a plus in advancing the vision of a server-based network dealing the same software to clients across the board.

It is possible, however, that a 100-percent pure, 100-percent Java network represents more of an ideal than a reality, at least for the near future. Most corporations, for example, have a considerable investment in server and PC platforms and software, and their users are comfortable and productive with the software they already use. In addition, simplified machines such as the NetPC tend to make the decision of which way to go less of an either/or proposition, as does Microsoft's support for both Java in its pure form and Java and ActiveX in the "extended" forms that support Windows-specific functionality.

Open Standards

One other issue you're likely to hear about where the Internet is concerned is the question of whether, and how well, the powerhouse software providers support the open standards that have until now defined the nature of the Internet. All of those in a position to affect development of Internet/intranet accessibility (Microsoft, Netscape, and others) have espoused the cause.

Open standards are needed and are supported by the major players

Not to downplay the import of this issue, which is considerable, and not to take sides in this debate, but there are—shall we say—some kinks to be worked out among the players in terms of implementation of these open standards. Ultimately, however, software and hardware providers are responsive and responsible to the demands of the market. Given the unfettered freedom of access required for the Internet to become part of everyone's computing environment, those "kinks" should eventually be worked out in the best way to blend differing visions of the technological future with the accessibility and ease of use expected by end users.

But there are still some areas in which they diverge

Microsoft and Others

Previous chapters have not been shy about focusing on Microsoft software, but no one can reasonably say that's all there is. Microsoft itself is fully aware of its competitors, and there are some keen ones who are not shy about focusing on Microsoft—for example, Netscape, IBM/Lotus, Sun, and Oracle. This is not the place for either an in-depth or a superficial look at their strategies, products, or visions of the future. Suffice it to say that these and many other companies are actively pursuing their own development plans, some of which parallel Microsoft's, some of which do not.

Microsoft is not the center of the computing universe (but it *is* close)

This book has provided you with a basic understanding of the groupware environment and of Microsoft's approach to client-server networking, the Internet, and intranets. By now, you should be comfortable wandering off in whatever direction you care to go. If you have Web access, here are some starting points to consider:

www.microsoft.com

www.netscape.com

www.javasoft.com

www.ibm.com

www.lotus.com

www.sun.com

www.oracle.com

The Future

The Internet poses some interesting and important questions

The rise of the Internet has meant the rise of many, many issues focused on the future of computing. Some, such as questions related to encryption, software export, privacy, copyrights, and the pros and cons of censorship, affect policy at very high levels. Others, such as improving the infrastructure, increasing modem speeds, and finding new ways of transmitting information, belong to engineering and communications experts. Still others, such as ways of connecting poor or remote communities to the Internet and somehow ensuring that societies—even entire countries—don't become information haves and have-nots, must be left on the one hand to dedicated individuals and on the other to social experts with the knowledge to judge wisely and to formulate appropriate policies. None of these are questions that a book like this can or should attempt to address, but all should concern everyone from schoolchildren to government officials. At any rate, what you've read here describes the state of the art in the here and soon-to-be now. Where are things likely to go in the somewhat more distant future?

Java will almost certainly grow and thrive. Modems perhaps will become faster. New ways of moving information at greater speeds are under development, including some ambitious projects that rely on satellite transmission. More people will discover the Internet.

Beyond these are dreams of the more distant future—dreams that Bill Gates speaks of when he talks about computers that can think and do far more than simply(!) process information. These same dreams occupy the thoughts of researchers such as those you read about in the newspaper and those active in the Advanced Technology research and development group at Microsoft. Their concerns are truly visionary, although in many cases you're likely to see the results in little bits and pieces rather than in monumental shifts in direction.

Technology will march onward to even greater visions…

Research into an area called *natural language recognition,* for instance, is ultimately aimed at enabling computers to respond to human speech. It's a difficult job, for sure. How, for example, do you teach a computer what "cough up the dough" means? Microsoft, IBM, and other organizations are working on software that provides just this capability, and if you have Microsoft Office 97 on your desktop, you can see a little of the future right now in the Office Assistant, the cartoon character that pops up and asks you to type a question—in your own words—when you need help in performing some task. The feature works, but even its creators would admit they have a ways to go until you can ask, "What *is* that thing?" and the computer responds, "Sorry, Captain, insufficient data at this time."

…such as language recognition

Here's hoping you're part of the parade

So where will it end? Who knows? It's said that the Chinese sometimes wish an ambiguous future on people by saying, "May you live in interesting times." Where computer technology is concerned, you *do* live in interesting times indeed. But these times, while perhaps ambiguous, are neither fearsome nor hostile. They are full of promise, there are some bright days ahead, and the dreams are alive and thriving. May you walk with a surer step into these new tomorrows.

Glossary

acoustic coupler Cuplike device used in the 1970s era of computing to hold a telephone handset for remote data transmission.

Active Platform The Microsoft software-development technology that blends component software and Web technologies with the client-server environment to make Internet-style accessibility and distributed computing part of the desktop. Active Platform includes a server-based portion called Active Server and a client-based portion called Active Desktop. It gives developers the option of creating either cross-platform or platform-specific (Windows-based) applications.

ActiveX Software technology developed by Microsoft that allows, among other things, components known as controls to be created. Controls are commonly embedded in web documents. ActiveX controls add action and interactivity to the page and can be written in any of several languages, including Java. To some extent an extension of Microsoft's older OLE technology for creating compound documents, ActiveX is supported by Microsoft Internet Explorer. ActiveX controls are equivalent in purpose to Netscape's downloadable plug-ins. The ActiveX technology is expected to be turned over to an independent standards organization.

ADSL Short for Asymmetric Digital Subscriber Line. ADSL is a developing technology for enabling high-speed communication over regular telephone lines. It is a possible successor or adjunct to ISDN, the current speed leader in readily available communication technology.

analog Information stored or transmitted by a continuously variable signal. Telephones, seismographs, dimmer switches, and radios are analog devices. *See also* digital.

API Abbreviation for Application Programming Interface, a set of routines that provide programs with a well-defined means of communicating with the operating system when it needs to request services.

architecture In computing, the way in which hardware or software is designed. To some extent, use of the word is comparable to its use in building design and construction. *Architecture* can refer either to the structure of an actual product or to a more generalized concept. So, for example, you can refer both to the architecture of Microsoft Windows NT and to the architecture of a network.

asynchronous Describes events in which timing is not a controlling factor. Asynchronous events happen when they happen, as opposed to synchronous events, which adhere to strict timing requirements. In the real world, conversations are asynchronous; political debates are (or should be) synchronous.

backbone The main transmission line on which a network depends. Often a fiber-optic cable in large networks, the backbone serves the same purpose that the vertebral column does in people—it holds everything together.

bandwidth In computing and communications, the amount of information that can be transmitted via a particular type of carrier signal or technology. Bandwidth essentially translates into speed—the broader, or wider, the bandwidth, the greater the speed. (In the trivia category: Computer people whose ability to absorb and process information is exceptional are sometimes described as having "broad bandwidth.")

baseband A form of digital transmission in which the full bandwidth is dedicated to a single channel used for both sending and receiving. Baseband transmission is currently the rule on networks, but it does not have the potential speed and carrying capacity of broadband transmission. *See also* broadband.

bit The smallest unit used by computers to represent information. The word *bit* is a shortened form of *binary digit;* a *bit* is always represented as one of two values, 0 or 1, which are the only possible digits in the binary (base-2) numbering system.

bps Abbreviation for bits per second. Bps is a measure of transmission speed, as on modems and networks. Until recently, modem speeds in particular were often given as *baud*. The correct measure is bps, however, because *baud* does not account for some of the extremely sophisticated ways that present-day modems load information onto a carrier signal.

bridge A hardware element used for routing messages from one network to another. Bridges monitor all network traffic but are "intelligent" in the sense that they pass along only messages destined for a different network.

broadband A form of analog transmission in which a given range of frequencies is divided into multiple channels. To guard against interference, each channel is separated from the next by a "blank" zone of frequencies known as a *guard band*. Broadband networks are not yet in common use, but they do offer potentially greater speed and carrying capacity than baseband networks, in part because separate broadband channels can be dedicated to different types of information, including voice, data, and video. This ability to transmit multiple data types is particularly valuable for the growing emphasis on Internet and multimedia transmissions.

brouter A hardware device on a network that functions as either a router or a bridge. A router both transmits and determines the routing for messages; a bridge, the lesser of the two devices, transmits but does not route messages.

byte The smallest collection of bits (binary digits) handled by computers. Bytes are collections of eight bits. Programmers commonly refer to bytes, but because they are so small, most people refer to larger units such as megabyte (roughly 1 million bytes) and gigabyte (roughly 1 billion bytes). *See also* bit.

bytecode An "intermediate" form of executable program code that has not yet been refined into the native code specific to a particular computer chip. Bytecode is produced by Java programs and runs in a special software environment known as a Java virtual machine. Because bytecode is not specific to any microprocessor, it can be run on any computer and is therefore platform independent.

C2/E3 security A set of guidelines that specify the type and level of security that must be met by qualifying computer software. C2 security was set by the United States Department of Defense. The corresponding E3 assurance level was designed by the Information Technology Security Evaluation Criteria (ITSEC) organization of the United Kingdom and Germany.

cable modem A developing form of communications hardware designed to enable computers to use cable television facilities to connect to networks and the Internet. Cable modems rely on an Ethernet connection and are expected to provide broader bandwidth and greater transmission speeds than are available through standard modems. However, because cable television is a broadcasting technology rather than a receiving technology, "upstream" transmission (from the desktop) is slower than "downstream" transmission (to the desktop).

class In object-oriented programming, a "blueprint" that defines a particular object. All objects belong to classes. When a particular object is called into action by a program, it is said to be *instantiated*—that is, it becomes a functional instance (a "real" object) representing the class blueprint from which it is created. (If you find this confusing, don't worry; it is.)

class library A collection of objects—program code—designed to perform certain routine tasks. Because class libraries provide groups of usable (and reusable) objects, developers do not have to create the code themselves. The net result is that developers save time and effort, they can concentrate on what they want their applications to do, and they usually benefit from the skills of specialists in creating the types of objects included in the library.

client The user, or recipient, of resources or services handed out by a network server. The term refers to either the computer or the software used for making requests of the server. A network node (computer), for example, is a client machine; the Microsoft Outlook e-mail application that runs on the node is client software.

client-server network A type of network in which resources located on powerful computers known as servers are shared out with desktop machines, the clients.

COM Acronym for Component Object Model, a programming standard designed by Microsoft and intended to provide task-specific software objects with a means of communicating among themselves. COM enables objects to request and provide services among themselves, regardless of the program they belong to. In this sense, COM can be considered the equivalent of a universal "language" that anyone any-where can use to communicate with anyone else.

conferencing The use of communications hardware, such as Internet phones, and group software, such as Microsoft NetMeeting, to enable two or more people to speak and share information in real time via computer.

DCOM A variation of the COM standard that extends the con-cept of communication between objects and processes to the network. DCOM is short for Distributed Common Object Model. *See also* COM.

digital Describes information that is stored or transmitted in discrete electronic units as opposed to the "connected" and continuously variable changes in a single (analog) signal. Digital information in computers is always represented by strings of the two binary digits 1 and 0. *See also* analog.

DNS Short for Domain Name System (or Domain Name Service), a hierarchical naming and classification scheme used to give each site on the Internet a unique name. DNS names are stored in multiple, distributed databases. *See also* IP address.

domain An organizational unit on the Internet that serves to identify a site or a related group of sites. Large domains can be divided into multiple subdomains that reflect different areas of interest or responsibility. A typical domain name looks like this: *www.microsoft.com*

dynamic HTML A developing technology that will allow devel-opers to include more interactivity and depth in web pages by making making specific elements on the page responsive to events such as a mouse click. The dynamic HTML specifi-cation has been submitted to the World Wide Web Consor-tium for approval as a standard.

e-mail Software that enables network and Internet users to send electronic mail messages to one another. E-mail is supported on the desktop by an e-mail client and on the server by an e-mail server. The term *e-mail* is also applied to the messages transmitted.

encryption A means of ensuring privacy in transmissions by encoded messages based on the use of *keys,* which are binary strings that perform much the same function as cereal-box decoder rings but on a vastly more sophisticated scale. An encrypted message normally can be decoded only by the intended recipient, who must use the key to make sense of the message.

extranet The marriage of intranet and Internet accessibility, extranets are designed to allow authorized "outside" individuals access to selected, quasi-public sections of a corporate web. Extranets are viewed as a valuable, up-and-coming extension of corporate networking and Internet technologies.

firewall A protective mechanism, usually a combination of hardware and software, designed to form a barrier forbidding access to an internal network by anyone other than authorized individuals.

gateway An intelligent, dedicated server designed to transfer information between differing environments—for example, between a PC-based network and a mainframe computer. Gateways mediate between the two environments by transforming information from the format used by one to the format used by the other, so that each environment receives information in the form it expects to "see." On the Internet, the term *gateway* is used to refer to similar servers that route information between one network and another.

gigabyte Roughly 1 billion bytes. The precise value depends on whether a megabyte (1,048,576 bytes) is multiplied by 1000 or by 1024, which is the power of 2 closest to 1 million. In the former case, a gigabyte equals 1,048,576,000 bytes; in the latter, a gigabyte equals 1,073,741,824 bytes. Most people don't need to worry about which is "correct."

groupware A relatively nebulous term used to describe software designed to promote or enhance collaboration via a computer network. Applications that generally fall into the groupware category include those that support e-mail, scheduling, conferencing, and group editing. To a lesser extent, application features such as document annotation, routing, and file sharing can also be considered groupware of sorts.

HTML Abbreviation for HyperText Markup Language, a system of codes, or tags, that are used in web publishing to describe the way the elements on a web page should look on screen. HTML tags are embedded in the document itself and are read by the browser software, which uses the tags to display the page in the appropriate fonts, colors, and layout.

HTTP Abbreviation for HyperText Transfer Protocol, the transport protocol used for document access on the World Wide Web. HTTP carries all the requests for documents that take place on the Web. In this sense, it is comparable to the tracks on which freight moves through the railway system.

hyperlink A "live" element on a web page that, when clicked with the mouse, transports the user to a new location, either in the same document or a different document—even a different document on a different web site. Hyperlinks are embedded in web pages by their publishers and are the navigational aids that enable Web users to wander randomly through web sites, following any direction that strikes their fancy. Without hyperlinks, people would have to plow sequentially through sets of pages to reach the information they want.

hypermedia Document elements such as sound, graphics, animation, or video, which are used in addition to text. Hypermedia flash and dazzle is one of the distinguishing features of World Wide Web documents.

Internet The global network of computers (servers) supported by the TCP/IP protocol; the parent of the graphical World Wide Web. *See also* TCP/IP.

intranet A private web site maintained by a corporation. An intranet extends the TCP/IP-based technologies of the Internet to private networks. A growing influence in the corporate world, intranets combine the standardization and ease of access characteristic of the Internet with the need for controlled access to corporate information.

IP address The numeric identification that corresponds to the "friendly" domain name used by people accessing Internet sites. IP addresses are used by computers when they contact one another on the Internet. The DNS database, in addition to listing sites, matches domain names to their corresponding IP addresses. *See also* DNS.

ISDN Abbreviation for Integrated Services Digital Network, a digital communications technology gaining in popularity as a means of speeding up Internet access. Although ISDN is phone-related, it relies on a dedicated ISDN line and a special modem for access. ISDN is supplied in two forms: BRI (Basic Rate Interface), which operates at 128 Kbps, and PRI (Primary Rate Interface), which runs at either 1.544 Mbps or 2.048 Mbps. Both are significantly faster than standard modem speeds, which are currently at a maximum of 56 Kbps.

ISO/OSI model A seven-layer networking model devised by the ISO (International Standards Organization). Known as the Open Systems Interconnect (OSI) model, the ISO/OSI model provides a blueprint for the ways computers communicate over a network. Each layer of the ISO/OSI model deals with a separate aspect of networking, from hardware (the bottom layer) on up through application software (the top layer). The complete model defines everything from the types of cabling to the way networking sessions are started, conducted, and ended to the way applications access the network. In the ISO/OSI model, each layer builds upon and uses the services provided by the layer(s) below it.

Java A platform-independent, object-oriented programming language developed by Sun Microsystems. Java is designed for creating distributed network applications and has been widely adopted for use in creating small applications, called applets, that add action and interactivity to web pages. Unlike other commonly used programming languages, Java compiles to an intermediate form of executable instructions known as bytecode. Because bytecode is not refined to the point of relying on processor-specific instructions, Java applications can run on any system, regardless of processor or operating system. Java programs use an interpreter, which executes the program instructions in a software environment known as the Java virtual machine. *See also* bytecode *and* Java virtual machine.

Java virtual machine The environment in which Java programs run. The Java virtual machine, or JVM, gives Java programs a "computer" with which to interact. Because the JVM exists in software rather than in hardware, Java programs can run on any platform provided with an interpreter (to execute the instructions) and a JVM (on which they can run).

Just-In-Time compiler Software that translates (compiles) Java bytecode into machine-specific native code, which runs faster than bytecode. Unlike typical language compilers, the Just-In-Time compiler, or JIT, compiles a Java program on the fly and begins running the program while it is still compiling the remainder. The upshot for users is a shorter waiting period before the program begins running.

LAN Acronym for local area network, a computer network that typically covers a limited geographic area, such as a single floor or building. LANs are larger than workgroups, which generally consist of a dozen or so computers, but are smaller than wide area networks, or WANs. *See also* WAN.

leased line A private communications line leased from a service provider and dedicated to the use of the company or organization that leases it.

legacy system An organization's existing computer facilities, especially mainframes.

mainframe A very powerful computer used for high-level, intensive computing chores. Mainframes are often accessed by multiple users through terminals that have no processing power of their own.

MAPI Acronym for Messaging Application Programming Interface, a set of routines designed to enable any MAPI-based messaging program to exchange information with any other MAPI-based program.

megabyte Roughly 1 million bytes. In actuality, a megabyte is 2^{20}, or 1,048,576 bytes. (Computers, being binary, are very comfortable with powers of 2.)

megahertz 1 million hertz, or 1 million cycles per second. Megahertz is a measure of frequency commonly applied to sound and to the speed at which microprocessors work (based on oscillations of an internal timer). Abbreviated as MHz.

modem An internal or external computer device that sends and receives transmissions over telephone lines. The term *modem* is short for modulator/demodulator and refers to the way the device works: by converting (modulating) the computer's digital signals into analog form for transmission and reconverting (demodulating) received signals from analog back to digital. Although ISDN devices are also known as modems, ISDN is digital from beginning to end and transmission requires no modulation or demodulation. ISDN modems do, however, plug into a computer's serial port, just as "normal" modems do.

multimedia A term used to describe documents or devices that present more than one type of data. Typically, multimedia refers to a combination of text, sound, and graphics. Animation and video are also increasingly included in the definition. On the World Wide Web and on CD-ROM products, both of which are multimedia-based, hyperlinks are also a characteristic, indeed defining, feature.

multiplexing A means of transmitting multiple signals over a single line. In multiplexing, the transmission channel is divided by time, space, or frequency into discrete segments known as time slices. Packets of data from each of the multiple signals are then interleaved onto these time slices for transmission.

multipoint data conferencing Technology governed by the ITU T.120 standard that enables groups of people to collaborate by holding conferences via computer and telephone connections.

multiprocessing The distribution of a computer's workload among multiple processors. Multiprocessing can be either symmetric, with the work balanced across all processors, or asymmetric, with some processors dedicated to system functions and others dedicated to application functions.

multitasking A means of making a computer appear to be performing more than one task at the same time by devoting segments of the processor's time to different tasks. Multitasking is effective because the computer works at speeds far greater than humans can attain. Some device-intensive tasks, however, such as downloading or copying large files, can visibly affect other operations. In preemptive multitasking, the operating system can interrupt one task to allow a higher priority task to run; in nonpreemptive, or cooperative, multitasking, applications must be designed to voluntarily work together.

multithreading A technology in which a process (roughly, an application) is separated into multiple tasks, known as threads, each of which is sent to and executed by the processor separately. Multithreading is a means of optimizing a computer's performance by allowing tasks to be prioritized, scheduled, and handled individually to use the processor's time as efficiently as possible.

multitier application development A form of application development in which logic is separated into three rather than the traditional two (client and server) functional tiers, or layers. In multitier application development, work is divided among the client, the application server, and a database that handles information storage. Applications of this type are scalable, secure, and lend themselves to the intranets within large, multiserver environments.

NetPC The Microsoft-Intel vision of a thin network-client computer. As defined in the companies' jointly released *NetPC Reference Specification,* the NetPC is essentially a stripped-down, closed, Windows-compatible computer with local storage (a hard drive) but without expansion capability. The NetPC provides Windows-based client computing while lowering the total cost of ownership (TCO) in a number of ways, including remote (network) configuration, management, and software installation.

network A group of computers linked by cabling or communications that enable individual machines to exchange information and share resources among themselves. Networks are grouped into numerous categories defined by size, configuration (topology), method of transmission (for example, packet switching), and so on. All networks, however, connect computers in one way or another.

network computer The network client envisioned by Oracle Corporation. Usually called the NC, the network computer is a thin client that is based on Internet standards and has its own processor and a network connection but has no local storage or expansion capability. The NC, like the NetPC, is designed to lower the cost of purchasing and maintaining network machines. In part, savings are expected to come from the NC's use of downloadable software stored on network servers.

node A computer or terminal on a network. Every node on a network is assigned its own unique network address, which is similar in function to a person's street address and which identifies the node for communications purposes to other machines on the network.

NOS Short for network operating system, which is complex software designed for managing the numerous, complex, day-to-day "housekeeping" and support functions that keep a network up and running.

OLE Originally an acronym for Object Linking and Embedding, which was a means of enabling applications to create compound documents containing objects, such as graphics, created by other applications. Now no longer known by its original definition, OLE has been extended to refer to any object that can be manipulated by other software. It is now part of the Internet-aware, ActiveX specification.

OOP Acronym for object-oriented programming, a form of programming based on the key concept of creating reusable, self-contained objects that perform specific tasks and that can be called upon by other objects needing their services. The foundation object in OOP is known as a class.

packet Any unit of information transmitted over a network or over communication lines. Packets vary in size, depending on the protocol used, but all are tightly structured bundles of bytes that include addressing information in addition to the data itself.

packet switching A form of transmission in which packets travel from origin to destination over variable routes, which are determined by the sending and receiving computers and are chosen on the basis of factors such as availability and amount of traffic. Because routes in packet switching are determined totally by computers, diagrams of packet-switched networks simply show transmissions entering a cloud at one end and exiting from the same cloud at the other.

page On the World Wide Web, a document viewable with a browser program and identified by its own URL. Web pages are the content of the World Wide Web. Typically, they are multimedia documents containing text, graphics, and perhaps sound, video, or animation. Such pages contain hyperlinks to other web documents or locations and commonly contain embedded ActiveX controls or Java applets that add interest to the contents.

parallel A form of transmission in which all the bits in a byte are transferred "side by side." Information moves around inside computers and, usually, to printers, in parallel. *See also* serial.

peer-to-peer network A type of network in which each computer is the equal, or peer, of every other computer. Each computer on such a network can be a server or a client, depending on whether it needs to share or to use network resources.

platform The foundation on which a computer is built and operates. Depending on the context, *platform* can refer to the hardware, especially the type of processor, or it can refer to both the hardware and the operating system that runs on it.

platform-independence A term referring to software that runs on more than one hardware–operating system platform. The hallmark of a platform-independent program is that it does not need to be recompiled in order to run on different computers.

polymorphism A characteristic of object-oriented programs in which a group of related objects can respond to the same message but in different ways, depending on what each is designed to do. In everyday life, polymorphism would be equivalent to the different behaviors of pedestrians and drivers at a stoplight. The single message "yellow light," for instance, might cause one "object" to step on the brake, another to stop walking, and yet another to step on the gas. Polymorphism in programming simplifies the development process yet increases software flexibility. The concept is difficult to understand.

programming language The "grammar" and "vocabulary" used to produce a set of instructions that can be used to make a computer perform some type of activity. The instructions written in a programming language are known as source code. Before this source code can actually be executed by the computer, it must be either interpreted (translated line by line) or compiled (translated all at once) and turned into far less readable machine code.

protocol A set of rules that computers and programs follow in order to exchange information. Numerous different protocols have been defined that govern all aspects of communication and transmission, from the hardware level to the application level. All protocols, however, are similar in enabling communication to take place according to agreed-upon rules.

proxy server A computer, or the software it runs, that forms a barrier between a private network and the Internet. A proxy server insulates the network by representing the organization on the Internet. Its primary responsibility is to forward requests from network clients to Internet sites and to return the desired information to the client.

pull model The technology through which clients seek out information on the Internet. In this model, the client plays an active role in finding and gathering information. *See also* push model.

push model The technology through which a site on the Internet can send information, such as news reports and stock quotes, to clients. In this model, the client plays a passive role by receiving rather than searching out information. Push technology is gaining in importance on the Internet and is seen by some as one potential way to make the Internet lucrative for businesses. *See also* pull model.

real time Time, and the passage thereof, as humans (rather than computers) perceive it.

relational database A type of database in which information is organized into multiple tables rather than into a single large file. Relational databases take their name from their support for the creation of relations—links—between related entries in different tables. These relations allow database designers to make a wide variety of information available while still maintaining closely related data in individual tables.

remote access The ability to access a network via telephone. Remote access is valuable in enabling off-site individuals to use network resources.

repeater A simple type of network device that boosts and retransmits signals so that they can travel farther than they would without such assistance. Repeaters are comparable to the transformers that strengthen electrical signals as they travel along power lines.

replication The process of duplicating databases on multiple servers. Replication improves access to information, but in order to be truly useful it must ensure that databases are updated and synchronized regularly so that all copies present the same information.

resource sharing The ability of a network server to make files, printers, and other shared resources available to clients.

router A network device that both transmits information packets and determines the best routes for them to take from origin to destination. A router can, if necessary, send packets through separate networks for delivery.

RPC Short for remote procedure call, a programming method that enables an application to communicate with another application, either on the same computer or over a network.

scheduling Time management with the help of computer software. To most people, scheduling is synonymous with using a computer to make and notify the user of appointments. Scheduling can, however, also refer to other calendar-based activities, such as task management. Within the computer, scheduling refers to the operating system's task of handling program requests for resources and processor time.

scripting language A type of programming language used to create special-purpose files containing commands that enhance the abilities of some type of software. Scripting languages have been available for many years and have often been used to automate or customize frequently used or repetitive activities, such as logging on to a remote computer. With the rise of the Internet, scripting languages have become part of mainstream web development. Programs written in scripting languages are often used to add interactivity to web documents.

serial A form of transmission in which all the bits in a byte are transferred one at a time over some type of pathway, such as a cable. Serial transmission is characteristic of mice and modems. *See also* parallel.

server A computer, or computer software, on a network that administers and provides access to shared resources.

SNA Abbreviation for Systems Network Architecture, a multi-layered networking model designed by IBM to enable its computers to communicate and interact with one another. SNA is similar to the seven-layer ISO/OSI networking and communications model. *See also* ISO/OSI model.

software development kit A collection of software tools, documentation, code, and code libraries that help developers create a particular type of software. Software development kits, or SDKs, are available for a wide variety of programming efforts ranging from the design of low-level, device-oriented software to Windows, Java, and database programming. SDKs give developers all the tools they need in a single package.

SQL Acronym for Structured Query Language, a collection of commands designed for use with relational databases. SQL is similar to a programming language but is not used for creating executable applications. The sole focus of SQL is in managing, updating, and retrieving database information. It is a standard recognized by many relational databases, especially those designed for large networks.

T1 A very fast digital transmission line used in environments that rely on high-speed, high-volume transmissions. T1 is available in North America, Japan, and Australia and transmits data, voice, and graphics or video at a rate of 1.544 Mbps. A comparable technology known as E1 is available in Europe, Mexico, and South America. To produce even faster transmissions, T1 lines can be multiplexed to produce the carriers known as T2 (6.312 Mbps), T3 (44.736 Mbps), and T4 (274.176 Mbps).

TAPI Acronym for Telephony Application Programming Interface, a set of programming routines used to enable computer software to answer, dial, and otherwise use telephones.

TCP/IP Abbreviation for Transmission Control Protocol/Internet Protocol, the suite of protocols developed for and now a defining feature of the Internet. TCP/IP is the standard that enables information to travel so freely on the Internet and the World Wide Web. It is also a cornerstone in the rapidly growing extension of Internet technology to corporate intranets.

terminal emulation The use of software to make a computer appear to be the type of terminal expected by a mainframe computer.

thick client Essentially, a desktop computer—a stand-alone machine with a hard drive and expansion capability. *See also* thin client.

thin client Essentially, a network computer—a machine without expansion capability that is designed specifically for use with a network and that relies heavily on network servers for software and, perhaps, data storage. *See also* thick client.

topology The overall shape or configuration of a network. Bus, ring, and star formations are standard topologies used in local area networks.

transaction processing A type of computer-based activity in which events known as transactions are handled by software elements distributed on a network. Transaction processing is a complex form of programming that requires coordination and agreement among multiple programs in order to be successful (accurate). Databases are at the heart of transaction processing. Applications are diverse, ranging from order-entry systems to financial tracking.

URL Short for Universal Resource Locator, a technical-sounding term for the string of names that precisely defines the location of a document on the Internet. URLs begin with the protocol used (for example, http) and commonly include domain, subdomain, and server names. The last element in a URL is the name of the document itself. Individual parts of the URL are separated by forward slashes.

WAN Acronym for wide area network, a large, often geographically dispersed computer network that uses communications facilities to link computers at different locations within the network. A WAN can span multiple buildings or even cross national boundaries. Widely dispersed networks that are linked together are sometimes called internetworks rather than WANs. *See also* LAN.

workgroup In terms of hardware, a small group of computers that can communicate with one another. In terms of people, a group of individuals, usually with a common interest, who share resources and information via computer.

World Wide Web The portion of the Internet characterized by documents that include sound, graphics, animation, and video in addition to text. The World Wide Web, also referred to as WWW or W3, is defined by its HTML pages and hyperlinks and is becoming an increasingly sophisticated, interactive environment fueled by enormous interest and explosive growth. Web technology forms the basis for the corporate networking offshoots known as intranets.

Index

Page numbers in italics refer to figures and illustrations.

A

AAL (ATM Adaptation Layer), 76
abstraction, 184
acoustic couplers, 6
Active Client. *See* Active Desktop
Active Desktop, 207–8
Active Directory, 178–79
Active Messaging, 208–9
Active Platform. *See* Microsoft Active
    Platform
Active Server, 205–7
Active Server Pages. *See* ASPs (Active Server
    Pages)
active topology, 31
ActiveX, 187–88, 192–93
    Active Desktop, 207–8
    Active Messaging, 208–9
    Active Server, 205–7
    security, 204–5
adapters, 24–26
    ISDN, 71
ADC (Advanced Data Connector), 127
addresses, 22. *See also* IP (Internet Protocol)
    addresses; URLs (universal resource
    locators)
    assigning, 44
    web site, 148–49

ADSL (Asymmetric Digital Subscriber Line),
    67, 72–74
Advanced Data Connector (ADC), 127
Advanced Program to Program Communica-
    tions. *See* APPC (Advanced Program to
    Program Communications)
algorithms, 180
analog signals, 38. *See also* signals
    converting from digital, 53–54
Andreessen, Marc, 143
APIs (application programming interfaces), 96
APPC (Advanced Program to Program
    Communications), 129–30
applets, 194, 195–96, 204
application development
    Exchange Server and, 114–15
    MAD, 202–3
    Transaction Server and, 220–22
    two-tier client-server, 202, *203*
application program interfaces. *See* APIs
    (application programming interfaces)
application protocols, 42
applications, creating with Exchange, 114–16
Archie search service, 170
architecture
    Exchange Server, 107–9
    network, 39–41
ARCnet, 46
ARPANET, 140
articles, 122
ASCII, converting mail files to, 103
ASMP (asymmetric multiprocessing), 92
ASPs (Active Server Pages), 206–7
Assisted Telephony, 100
Asymmetric Digital Subscriber Line. *See*
    ADSL (Asymmetric Digital Subscriber
    Line)
asymmetric multiprocessing (ASMP), 92
asynchronous collaboration, 2–3
asynchronous communication, 12
Asynchronous Transfer Mode. *See* ATM
    (Asynchronous Transfer Mode)

ATM Adaptation Layer (AAL), 76
ATM (Asynchronous Transfer Mode), 75–76
Attached Resource Computer network. *See* ARCnet
audio, intranet, 216–17
audio/telephony technology, 13
authenticated connections, 126–27
Authenticode, 205
Automatic Desktop, 134
automatic synchronization, 125

B

backbone cable, 29
backbone networks, *141*
back-end processing, 29
BackOffice. *See* specific servers and applications
bandwidth
    baseband, 37–38
    broadband, 37, 38–39
    defining, 34
        electronically, 35–37
        traditionally, 34–35
    network, 37
    size of, 36
    and World Wide Web popularity, 67–68
baseband networks, 37–38
Basic Rate Interface (BRI) transmissions, 72
Basic Telephony, 101
B channels, 72
bearer channels, 72
Bell specifications, 54
bis, 54–55
BISDN (Broadband ISDN), 75
bits, 25
    measuring bandwidth with, 36
BNC (British Naval Connector), 23
BRI (Basic Rate Interface) transmissions, 72
bridges, 58–59, 65
    ISDN, 71

British Naval Connector. *See* BNC (British Naval Connector)
Broadband ISDN (BISDN), 75
broadband networks, 37, 38–39
broadcasts, 30
browsers, 146–47
    Mosaic, 143–44
    Netscape Navigator *vs.* Internet Explorer, 144–45
bulletin boards, 115
buses, 24
bus networks, 29–30, *30*
bytecode, 195, 207
bytes, 24–25

C

cable modems, 68–70
cables, 22–23
    and bus networks, 30
    and information transmission, 25
    and star networks, 33
    transferring signals between types of, 57–58
    trunk, 29
cable television service, 69–70
carrier-sense multiple access [with] collision detection (CSMA/CD), 46–47
CCITT (Consultive Committee for International Telegraphy and Telephony), 55
C2/E3 security, 97
CGI (Common Gateway Interface), 172–73
channels, 36, 38–39
    bearer, 72
    capacity of, 37
    data, 72
Chat, 229
child objects, 185
CISC (complex instruction set) chips, 86
cladding, 23
classes, 183–84

DCOM, 191
　　Active Server and, 206
DDS (digital data service), 65–66
DEC (Digital Equipment Corporation), 158
demodulating, 54
desktop information manager, 110–11
DHCP (Dynamic Host Configuration Proto-
　　col), 44, 171–72
DHCP servers, 171
d-HTML. *See* dynamic HTML
Digital Equipment Corporation (DEC), 158
digital phone connections, 65–66
digital signals, 37–38. *See also* signals
　　converting to analog, 53–54
Directory Access Protocol. *See* DAP (Direc-
　　tory Access Protocol)
directory services, 177
　　protocols, 177–79
Directory System Agents (DSAs), 178
Directory User Agents (DUAs), 178
Distributed COM. *See* DCOM
distributed computing, 188, 191, 206
distribution
　　of computer intelligence, 10–11
　　of information sharing, 9
distribution server, 122–23, *123*
DLC, 130
DNS databases, 154–56
DNS (domain name system), *149,* 149–53,
　　153
　　classifications, *150*
DNS name servers, 154–55
documents
　　collaboration on, 15–16
　　compound, 187
　　indexing, 213–14
　　Lotus Notes, 15
domain names, 148–49
domain name service. *See* DNS (domain
　　name system)
domain name system. *See* DNS (domain
　　name system)

Donne, John, 1
downstream data flow, 70
　　ADSL and, 72–73
DSAs (Directory System Agents), 178
DSU/CSU (data service unit/channel service
　　unit), 65–66
　　SMDS, 77
DTE (data terminal equipment), 63
DUAs (Directory User Agents), 178
dumb terminals, 6
　　PCs emulating, 128–29
Dynamic Host Configuration Protocol. *See*
　　DHCP
dynamic HTML, 234–35

E

EFD (Exchange Forms Designer), 114–16
Electronic Forms Designer. *See* Microsoft
　　Electronic Forms Designer
e-mail, 12, 101–2
　　Microsoft Exchange Server handling,
　　　103–4
　　protocols, 45, 175–76
　　standards, 103–4
encapsulation, 184–85
encryption, 105–6
enterprise networks, 128–32
Ethernet network, 29, 46–48
Exchange. *See* Microsoft Exchange Client;
　　Microsoft Exchange Server
Extended Telephony, 101

F

fault tolerance, 92
FDDI (Fiber Distributed Data Interface), 76–77
Fiber Distributed Data Interface. *See* FDDI (Fiber Distributed Data Interface)
fiber-optic cable, 23
    and bandwidth, 37
    frame relay and, 74
    SONET and, 78
fields, 117
files, transferring, 44, 229
file sharing, 98–99
File transfer, 229
file transfer protocol. *See* FTP (file transfer protocol)
firewalls, 147, 164–66, *165*
flat-file database, 117–18
folder-based applications, 115
forwarder, 155
fractional T1 digital line, 66
frame relay, 74–75
frequency, 35–36
front-end processing, 29
FrontPage, 160, 215–16
FrontPage client, 226–27
FTP (file transfer protocol), 44, 170–71
full-duplex mode, 54
full-duplex transmissions, 72–74
Full Telephony, 100–101

G

Gates, Bill
    on intranets, 18
    on Zero Administration initiative, 134
gateways, 60–62. *See also* CGI (Common Gateway Interface)
    SNA Server similarity to, 130–32
geographical domains, sample, *151*

Gopher, 171
group computing
    defined, 1–2
    enabling, 3–5
    evolution of, *9*
    history of, 6–13
    paradigm for, 18–20
    reasons for, 13–18
GTE telephone company, 73
guard bands, 38

H

half-duplex mode, 54
hardware. *See also* specific items
    connecting LANs, 57–62
    evolution of, 8
    for networks, 22–26
    for real-time collaboration, 13
Hayes compatibility, 54
HDSL (High Digital Subscriber Line), 73
hertz (Hz), 35
High Digital Subscriber Line (HDSL), 73
home pages, 148. *See also* web sites
host-based systems. *See* mainframe-based networks
hosts. *See* servers
HTML authoring tools, 216
HTML (hypertext markup language), 159–62. *See also* dynamic HTML
HTML Rendering Object Library, 209
HTTP (hypertext transfer protocol), 45, 156–57
hubs, 33
    for Token Ring network, 48–49
hyperlinks, 156–62
hypermedia, 141–42
hypertext, 141
hypertext transfer protocol. *See* HTTP (hypertext transfer protocol)

I

IANA (Internet Assigned Numbers Authority), 150
IBM PC, 7. *See also* personal computers
IBM Token Ring network. *See* Token Ring network
IDC (Internet Database Connector), 173
IEEE 802 specifications, 39–40
IETF (Internet Engineering Task Force), 160
IIS. *See* Internet Information Server (IIS)
IMAP (Internet Mail Access Protocol), 176–77
indexes, 158
    creating, 213–15
Index Server, 211, 212–15
    indexing process, *214*
        information. *See also* data; databases; messages; packets; signals
    breaking down/rebuilding, 25–26
    converting, 24
        network formats, 61
    directories, 177
    filtering excess, 166
    finding, 14–15
    sharing, 14–15
        distribution of, 9
    storing in databases, 117
    transmission of, 24–25, *25*
        bandwidth and, 36
information revolution, 7
inheritance, 185
instantiation, 184
integrated security, 126–27. *See also* security
Integrated Services Digital Network. *See* ISDN (Integrated Services Digital Network)
intelligence. *See* computers, distribution of intelligence
Intel ProShare Conferencing Video System, 13
interfaces, 189
International Organization for Standardization/Open Systems Interconnect networking model. *See* ISO/OSI networking model

International Telecommunications Union. *See* ITU specifications
Internet. *See also* FTP (file transfer protocol); Gopher; World Wide Web
    future of technology for, 240–42
    history of, 140
    names, 148–49
    open standards, 239
    overview, 137–39
    protocols for, 43
        early problems with, 140
    publishing on, 16–18
    technological growth of, 9
    traffic and modem speed, 69
Internet Assigned Numbers Authority (IANA), 150
Internet Database Connector (IDC), 173
Internet Engineering Task Force (IETF), 160
Internet Explorer. *See* Microsoft Internet Explorer
Internet Information Server (IIS), 211
    Active Server and, 206–7
Internet Mail Access Protocol. *See* IMAP (Internet Mail Access Protocol)
Internet Network Information Center (InterNIC), 152
Internet sites. *See* web sites
Internetwork Packet Exchange/Sequenced Packet Exchange. *See* IPX/SPX protocols
InterNIC (Internet Network Information Center), 152
interoperability, 43
    of Exchange Server, 104–6
    of Office 97, 224
interpreters, 196
intranets
    overview, 162–64
    publishing on, 16–18
    security on, 164–66
IP (Internet Protocol) addresses, 153–54
    assigning on the fly, 171–72
    converting, 154
    examining, 166

IP multicasting, 217
IP unicasting, 217
IPX/SPX protocols, 43
ISAPI (Internet Server Applications Program-
    ming Interface), 173
ISDN (Integrated Services Digital Network),
    66, 67, 70, 71–72
ISO/OSA networking model, *129*
ISO/OSI networking model, 40
    layers, *41*
iterative query, 155
ITU specifications, 54–55

J

Java, 193–95
    creating program, 195–96
    future of, 241
    and network computers, 236
    security, 204–5
Java virtual machine (JVM), 196
Just-In-Time (JIT) compilers, 196–97
JVM. *See* Java virtual machine (JVM)

K

kernel mode, 96

L

LANs, 26
    common, 45–49
    connecting, 56–62
    functionality of, 27–28
    limitations of, 51
    linking, 51, 75–76, 77
    remote access and, 52–56
LDAP (Lightweight Directory Access Proto-
    col), 178
LED (light-emitting diode), 23

legacy systems. *See* mainframe-based
    networks
Lightweight Directory Access Protocol
    (LDAP), 178
links, 15, 142. *See also* hyperlinks
load balancing, 92
local area networks (LANs). *See* LANs
logical rings, 31
logical units (LUs), 129–30
log readers, 124
Lotus Notes, 15
low-impedance ArcNet, 33

M

Macintosh OS/2, 86
MAD. *See* multitier application development
    (MAD)
mainframe-based networks, 9
    intelligence of, 10
mainframe computers, 6–7
    connecting to, 128–32
    linking client-server networks to, 29
    SNA, *131*
MANs (Metropolitan Area Networks), 77
MAPI, 112–13
MAU (Multistation Access Unit), 48
message queues, 207
messages, broadcasting, 30
Messaging Object Library, 209
Metropolitan Area Networks (MANs), 77
MFC (Microsoft Foundation Class) library,
    182
Microsoft Active Platform, 134, 200–209
Microsoft Corporation, ADSL testing and, 73
Microsoft Electronic Forms Designer, 111–12,
    114–16
Microsoft Exchange Client, 103, 111–13
Microsoft Exchange Server, 12, 102
    application development, 114–15
    architecture of, 107–9
    core components of, *108,* 108–9

network adapter, 22
network adapter card, 24
Network Basic Input/Output System. *See*
    NetBIOS protocols
network computers, 10–11, 85, 235–36
network foundation, 11–13
networking services, 74–78
network interface card (NIC), 24
Network OLE. *See* DCOM
network operating system (NOS), 28. *See also*
    operating systems
networks. *See also* client-server networks;
    Internet; LANs; mainframe-based
    networks; WANs
  accessing, 21
  advanced, 74–78, *79*
  architecture, 39–41
  authenticated connections, 126–27
  bandwidth, 34–39
  defining, 26
  early, 8
  hardware for, 22–26
  mainframe connectivity and, 128–32
  managing, 88
  protocols, 39, 41–45, 42
  remote access, 51, *52*, 52–56, 68–74
  resource sharing on, 98–99
  security on, 97
  shape of, 29–33
  size, 26–27
  trusted connections, 126
network software, 52–53
network support, 11
NIC (network interface card), 24
nodes, 22. *See also* personal computers
  hardware linking, 57–59
nonportable platforms, *86*
nonpreemptive multitasking, 91
normalizing, 214
NOS. *See* network operating system (NOS)
Novell Networks, 43
numbers, in IP addresses, 153–54

O

object linking and embedding. *See* OLE
    Automation
object-oriented programming (OOP), 180,
    181–83
  core concepts of, 183–85
  simplified, 185–86
objects, 181, 183–85
  client-provider interaction, 188–91
ODBC (Open Database Connectivity), 120,
    179
  IDC and, 173
ODSI (Open Directory Services Interface), 179
OLE Automation, 115, 187–88
OLE controls, 192
100BaseX, 47
OOP. *See* object-oriented programming
    (OOP)
Open Database Connectivity. *See* ODBC
    (Open Database Connectivity)
Open Directory Services Interface (ODSI),
    179
operating systems, 83–84
  adding networking capabilities to, 84–86
  client, 85
  network, 28
    history of, 86–87
    improving efficiency of, 89–92
  server, 85, 88
Oracle Corporation, 235–36
organizational domains, *151*

P

packet filtering, 166, *167*
packets, 25–26. *See also* packet switching;
    transmissions
  advantages of, 62–63
  ring networks and, 31–32
  routing, 63–64
  transmitting, 173–75

trough, 34
trunk cable, 29
trusted connections, 126
trusted networks, 165
tunneling, 175
twisted-pair wiring, 23
two-tier client-server application development, 202, *203*

U

Uniplexed Information and Computing
  System. *See* UNIX
United States Department of Defense, 16
UNIX, 86–87
untrusted computers, 165
upstream data flow, 70
  ADSL and, 72–73
URLs (universal resource locators), 156–57
  finding, 157–58
U.S. Robotics, 69
user mode, 96
users, managing, 88
UUDECODE, 103
UUENCODE, 103

V

VDSL (Very Digital Subscriber Line), 74
VeriFone vPos application, 218
Very Digital Subscriber Line (VDSL), 74
video, intranet, 216–17
video technology, 13
virtual circuit, 75
virtual private network (VPN), 174
Visual Basic, 230
Visual C++, 230
Visual J++, 230
VPN (virtual private network), 174

W

W3. *See* World Wide Web
WANs, 26, 56
  advanced networking services for, 74–78
  breaking down/rebuilding information on,
    62–65
  building, 56–62
  connecting, 60
  remote access, 68–74
wavelength, *34,* 34–35
waves, 34–35
web authoring tools, 216
Web crawlers, 158
web pages. *See* web sites
web sites, *161. See also* hyperlinks
  authoring, 162
  building intelligence into, 234
  companies offering groupware products,
    240
  connecting to, 154–56
  creating, 211, 215–16
  defined, 147–48
  displaying elements of, 159–62
  DNS and, 149–53
  enhancing powers of, 208–9
  IP addresses, 153–54
  names of, 148–49
  registration of, 152
  static, 194
Whiteboard, 229
wide area networks (WANs). *See* WANs
wideband networks. *See* broadband networks
Windows NT Server, 86, 92–94, 210
  Active Server and, 206
  components, *96*
  connecting workstations to mainframes,
    130
  executive components, 95
  Exchange Server relation to, 102, 104–6
  modes, 96
  and multithreading, 89–90

Windows NT Server, *continued*
    protected subsystems, 95–96
    redirector, 95
    resource sharing capabilities, 98–99
    security and, 97
    SQL Server integration with, 120
    structure, *94*, 94–96
        modularity of, 97–98
Windows Open Services Architecture
        (WOSA), 179
Windows socket. *See* Winsock
Win32 Reference Implementation, 196
Winsock, 172
wizards, FrontPage, 216
word breakers, 213
World Wide Web, 45, 67–68. *See also*
        Internet
    browsers, 146–47
    hosts, 146–47
    Mosaic and, 143–44
    overview, 138–40, 141–42
    providing interactivity on, 208–9
WOSA (Windows Open Services Architec-
        ture), 179

X–Z

X.25 standard, 65
zones, 152

About the Author

JoAnne Woodcock is the author of several popular computer books, including *The Ultimate Microsoft Windows 95 Book* and *The Ultimate MS-DOS Book,* both published by Microsoft Press. She is also a contributor to the *Microsoft Press Computer Dictionary.*

The manuscript for this book was prepared and submitted to Microsoft Press in electronic form. Text files were prepared using Microsoft Word 97. Pages were composed by Frog Mountain Productions using Adobe PageMaker 6.01 for Windows, with text in Optima and display type in Optima Bold. Composed pages were delivered to the printer as electronic prepress files.

Cover Graphic Designer
Becker Design

Cover Illustrator
Becker Design

Interior Graphic Designer
Kim Eggleston

Interior Illustrator
Travis Beaven

Interior Graphic Artist
David Holter

Compositor
Frog Mountain Productions

Principal Proofreader/Copy Editor
Teri Kieffer

Indexer
Leslie Leland Frank

You work with Microsoft® **Office.**

Now you want to build a great **intranet.**

Congratulations, you're **nearly done.**

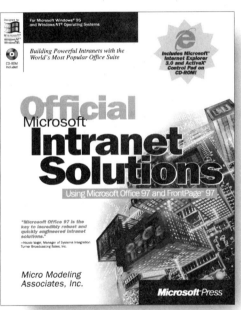

For Microsoft Windows® 95 and Windows NT® Operating Systems

Building Powerful Intranets with the World's Most Popular Office Suite

Includes Microsoft® Internet Explorer 3.0 and ActiveX™ Control Pad on CD-ROM!

Official
Microsoft
Intranet Solutions

Using Microsoft Office 97 and FrontPage™ 97

"Microsoft Office 97 is the key to incredibly robust and quickly engineered intranet solutions."

—Nicole Vogel, Manager of Systems Integration, Turner Broadcasting Sales, Inc.

Micro Modeling Associates, Inc.

Microsoft Press

You don't need to start from scratch. In fact, once you upgrade to Microsoft Office 97, all you add is Microsoft FrontPage™ 97, Microsoft Internet Explorer, and this book. Here technical managers and developers can discover how to use these popular programs to quickly create awesome, full-featured intranets that are easy for everyone to use—administrators and users alike. So build on the foundation you've already put in place. To find out how, get OFFICIAL MICROSOFT INTRANET SOLUTIONS.

U.S.A.	**$39.99**
U.K.	£52.99 [V.A.T. included]
Canada	$54.99
ISBN	1-57231-509-1

Microsoft Press® products are available worldwide wherever quality computer books are sold. For more information, contact your book retailer, computer reseller, or local Microsoft Sales Office.

To locate your nearest source for Microsoft Press products, reach us at mspress.microsoft.com, or call 1-800-MSPRESS in the U.S. (in Canada: 1-800-667-1115 or 416-293-8464).

To order Microsoft Press products, call 1-800-MSPRESS in the U.S. (in Canada: 1-800-667-1115 or 416-293-8464).

Prices and availability dates are subject to change.

Microsoft ®Press

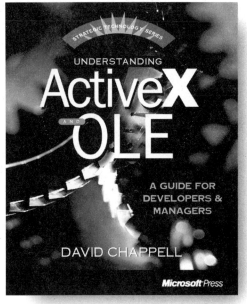

To understand the *future of* information **flow,** you have to understand the *pipeline.*

If you work with and plan for the Internet, video conferencing, or business communications, you need UNDERSTANDING BANDWIDTH. Here you'll find clear, comprehensive explanations from well-known technology observer and analyst Cary Lu. And in short order, you'll understand the issues and technologies surrounding bandwidth, as well as their strategic importance. Get UNDERSTANDING BANDWIDTH and open up your company's information pipeline.

The *Strategic Technology* series is for executives, business planners, software designers, and technical managers who need a quick, comprehensive introduction to important technologies and their implications for business.

U.S.A.	**$19.99**
U.K.	£18.49
Canada	$26.99
ISBN	1-57231-513-X

Microsoft®*Press*